M. M

J. H C.
June 1956

D1351510

STREET-NAMES
OF THE
CITY OF LONDON

STREET-NAMES
OF THE
CITY OF LONDON

BY

EILERT EKWALL

OXFORD
AT THE CLARENDON PRESS
1954

Oxford University Press, Amen House, London E.C. 4

GLASGOW NEW YORK TORONTO MELBOURNE WELLINGTON
BOMBAY CALCUTTA MADRAS KARACHI CAPE TOWN IBADAN

Geoffrey Cumberlege, Publisher to the University

———

PRINTED IN GREAT BRITAIN

PREFACE

THE writer has for some years past devoted a good deal of attention to early London personal names, as well as to early London history, and some results have been given in *Early London Personal Names* (1947) and *Two Early London Subsidy Rolls* (1951) and in other publications. These studies aroused an interest in London street-names. Many among these are simple and straightforward, but for a good many the etymology is by no means self-evident. For such names little help was to be got from the works of earlier investigators, and I began to collect material so as to be able to form an independent opinion on them. At the outset I contemplated at most a paper dealing with a number of particularly obscure names, but by degrees I came to feel that a book dealing with the etymologies of City street-names was needed and worth writing. This made me enlarge my original plan and include practically all street-names found before 1500 and some recorded even later.

But the study is restricted to the street-names of the City of London. Those of other parts of London were mostly formed at a comparatively late date and under circumstances different from those obtaining when the majority of City street-names arose. Many were given deliberately. Besides, sufficient information on these names is generally to be found in the recently published Middlesex volume of the English Place-name Society survey. The names that interest students of place-names are chiefly the ancient ones of medieval London.

I take this opportunity of tendering my grateful thanks to the authorities of the Public Record Office for supplying photostats of the important Hundred Roll for London of 1279, and to the Librarian and Staff of Lund University Library for arranging loans of valuable books not available in Sweden from English libraries. Last and not least I thank my wife for efficient help in the proof-reading.

E. E.

LUND, SWEDEN

March, 1954

NOTE ON THE MAP

THE map accompanying the volume is identical with that appended to Kingsford's edition of Stow. It thus really represents the London of *c*. 1600, but will on the whole give a good idea of the system of streets also of medieval London.

CONTENTS

SELECT LIST OF
WORKS CONSULTED

BARDSLEY, C. W. *A Dictionary of English and Welsh Surnames*. London, 1901.

BEAVEN, A. B. *The Aldermen of the City of London*. London, 1908–13.

BESANT, W. *Early London*. London, 1908.

BOHMAN, HJÖRDIS. *Studies in the ME Dialects of Devon and London*. Göteborg, 1944.

BONNER, A. 'Some London Street-names', *LMAS*, N.S. ii. 185–216, 287–320 (1917).

BOSWORTH, J., and TOLLER, T. N. *Anglo-Saxon Dictionary*. Oxford, 1882–1921.

CLUNN, HAROLD P. *The Face of London*. Revised ed. London, 1951.

CURTIS, MARGARET. 'The London Lay Subsidy of 1332.' In Unwin, G., *Finance and Trade under Edward III*. Manchester, 1918.

EJDER, BERTIL. *Marknamn och Kulturhistoria*. Lund, 1951.

EKWALL, E. *English River-names*. Oxford, 1928.

——*Two Early London Subsidy Rolls*. Lund, 1951.

English Historical Documents, 1042–1189. Ed. D. C. Douglas and G. W. Greenaway. London, 1953.

Essays in Medieval History presented to Thomas Frederick Tout. Ed. by A. G. Little and F. M. Powicke. Manchester, 1925.

FRANSSON, G. *Middle English Surnames of Occupation, 1100–1350*. Lund, 1935.

GODEFROY, F. *Dictionnaire de l'ancienne langue française*. Paris, 1881–1902.

GOVER, J. E. B. *The Place Names of Middlesex*. London, 1922.

GROSS, C. *The Sources and Literature of English History*. London, 1915.

HARBEN, H. A. *A Dictionary of London*. London, 1918.

HARMER, F. E. *Anglo-Saxon Writs*. Manchester, 1952.

——*Select English Historical Documents*. Cambridge, 1914.

HEUSER, W. *Alt-London*. Strassburg, 1914.

HOLTHAUSEN, F. *Altenglisches etymologisches Wörterbuch*. Heidelberg, 1934.

KARLSTRÖM, S. *Old English Compound Place-names in* -ing. Uppsala, 1927.

KENT, W. *An Encyclopaedia of London.* London, 1937.

KNUDSEN, G., and KRISTENSEN, M. *Danmarks gamle Personnavne.* Copenhagen, 1936 ff.

LIEBERMANN, F. *Die Gesetze der Angelsachsen.* Halle, 1903–16.

LOFTIE, W. J. *A History of London.* London, 1883.

MACKENZIE, B. A. *The Early London Dialect.* Oxford, 1928.

MAITLAND, F. W. *Domesday Book and Beyond.* Cambridge, 1907.

MATTHIESSEN, HUGO. *Gamle Gader.* Copenhagen, 1917.

PAGE, W. *London. Its Origin and Early Development.* London, 1929.

RAWLINGS, GERTRUDE B. *The Streets of London.* London, 1926.

RILEY, H. TH. *Memorials of London and London Life in the XIIIth, XIVth, and XVth Centuries.* London, 1868.

ROUND, J. H. *The Commune of London and other Studies.* Westminster, 1899.

SALTER, H. E. *The Historic Names of the Streets & Lanes of Oxford.* Oxford, 1921.

SALZMAN, L. F. *English Life in the Middle Ages.* Oxford, 1926 (1945).

SCHÖNFELD, M. *Veldnamen in Nederland.* Amsterdam, 1949.

STENTON, DORIS MARY. *English Society in the Early Middle Ages.* Harmondsworth, 1951.

STENTON, F. M. *Anglo-Saxon England.* Oxford, 1943.

—— *Norman London.* Historical Association Leaflets, Nos. 93, 94. London, 1934.

STIMMING, A. *Der anglonormannische Boeve de Haumtone.* Halle, 1899.

STUBBS, W. *The Constitutional History of England.* 5th ed. Oxford, 1891 (1926).

SUGDEN, E. H. *A Topographical Dictionary to the Works of Shakespeare and his Fellow Dramatists.* Manchester, 1925.

TENGVIK, G. *Old English Bynames.* Uppsala, 1938.

The Victoria History of London. Ed. W. Page. London, 1909.

WALLENBERG, J. K. *Kentish Place-names.* Uppsala, 1931.

—— *The Place-names of Kent.* Uppsala, 1934.

WEIBULL, L. *Kartor över staden Lund och dess jordar.* Lund, 1919.

WEINBAUM, M. *London unter Eduard I. und II.* Stuttgart, 1933.

WHEELER, R. E. M. *London and the Saxons.* London Museum Catalogues: no. 6. London, 1935.

WIJK, A. *The Orthography and Pronunciation of Henry Machyn, the London Diarist.* Uppsala, 1937.

ZETTERSTEN, L. *City Street Names.* London, 1917, 2nd ed. 1924.

ABBREVIATIONS

The list is at the same time a list of sources
of early forms of street-names

a	ante (before).
Abbr	*Placitorum abbreviatio.* Record Com. London, 1811.
Acts Privy Council	*Acts of the Privy Council of England.* Ed. J. R. Dasent. London, 1890 ff.
ADA, ADB, &c.	*A Descriptive Catalogue of Ancient Deeds in the Public Record Office.* London, 1890–1906. ADA = Series A, &c.
AF	Anglo-French.
Aldersg	Aldersgate ward.
Aldg	Aldgate ward.
AnnLond	*Chronicles of the Reigns of Edward I and Edward II.* Vol. I. Ed. William Stubbs. Rolls Ser. London, 1882.
AntLeg	*De Antiquis Legibus Liber.* Ed. Thomas Stapleton. Camden Soc. London, 1846.
Arber	*A Transcript of the Registers of the Company of Stationers of London, 1554–1640 A.D.* Vol. V. Index. Ed. Edward Arber. Birmingham, 1894.
ASC	*Two of the Saxon Chronicles Parallel.* Ed. Earle and Plummer. Oxford, 1892.
ASCh	*Anglo-Saxon Charters.* Ed. A. J. Robertson. Cambridge, 1939.
ASWills	*Anglo-Saxon Wills.* Ed. Dorothy Whitelock. Cambridge, 1930.
ASWrits	*Anglo-Saxon Writs.* Ed. F. E. Harmer. Manchester, 1952.
BarthR	*The Records of St. Bartholomew's Priory.* Ed. E. A. Webb. Oxford, 1921.
Bas	Bassishaw ward.
BCS	*Cartularium saxonicum.* Ed. W. de Gray Birch. London, 1885–93.
Bill	Billingsgate ward.
Bish	Bishopsgate ward. BishE, BishI = Bishopsgate Without, Within.

BM	*Index to the Charters and Rolls in the British Museum.* London, 1900, 1912.
Bodl	*Calendar of Charters and Rolls in the Bodleian Library.* Oxford, 1878.
Book of Seals	*Sir Christopher Hatton's Book of Seals.* Ed. Lewis C. Loyd and Doris M. Stenton. Oxford, 1950.
BreadSt	Bread Street ward.
Bridge	Bridge ward.
BroadSt	Broad Street ward.
Bury Charters	*Feudal Documents from the Abbey of Bury St. Edmunds.* Ed. D. C. Douglas. London, 1932.
Cand	Candlewick ward.
CastleB	Castle Baynard ward.
Cely Papers	*The Cely Papers, 1475–88.* Ed. H. E. Malden. Camden Soc. 3rd Ser. London, 1900.
Ch	Charter Rolls.
Character Books	*A Bibliography of English Character-Books, 1608–1700.* By Gwendolen Murphy. Oxford, 1925.
Cheap	Cheap ward.
ChronEve	*Chronicon Abbatiæ de Evesham.* Chr. & Mem. 29 (1863).
Cl	Close Rolls.
Clerkenwell	*Cartulary of St. Mary Clerkenwell.* Ed. W. O. Hassall. Camden Soc. 3rd Ser. London, 1949.
Colchester Cart	*Cartularium Monasterii Sancti Johannis Baptiste de Colecestria.* Ed. S. A. Moore. Roxburghe Club. London, 1897.
ColemSt	Coleman Street ward.
Cor	*Calendar of Coroners Rolls of the City of London.* Ed. R. R. Sharpe. London, 1913.
Cordw	Cordwainer ward.
Cornh	Cornhill ward.
Crip	Cripplegate ward. CripE, CripI = Cripplegate Without, Within.
Cur	*Curia Regis Rolls of the Reigns of Richard I and John.* London, 1922 &c.
CW	*Calendar of Wills proved and enrolled in the Court of Husting, London.* Ed. R. R. Sharpe. London, 1889, 1890.
DB	*Domesday Book.* London, 1783–1816.
DEPN	Ekwall, E. *The Concise Oxford Dictionary of English Place-names.* Oxford, 1936 ff.

Dowg	Dowgate ward.
Du	Dutch.
Earle	Earle, J. *A Hand-Book to the Land-Charters, and other Saxonic Documents.* Oxford, 1888.
EDD	Wright, J. *The English Dialect Dictionary.* Oxford, 1898 ff.
EHR	*The English Historical Review.*
ELPN	Ekwall, E. *Early London Personal Names.* Lund, 1947.
ELSR	Ekwall, E. *Two Early London Subsidy Rolls.* Lund, 1951.
Ep	Episcopal Registers. EpCant, EpHeref, EpLo &c. Episcopal registers of Canterbury, Hereford, London &c. In Canterbury and York Soc. and Hampshire Record Soc. (EpWint).
ERN	Ekwall, E. *English River-names.* Oxford, 1928.
ExchJews	*Select Pleas, Starrs, and other Records from the Rolls of the Exchequer of the Jews, 1220–84.* Ed. J. M. Rigg. Selden Soc. London, 1902.
F	French.
FacsCh	*Facsimiles of Royal & other Charters in the British Museum.* Vol. I. Ed. G. F. Warner and H. J. Ellis. London, 1903.
Farr	Farringdon ward. FarrE, FarrI = Farringdon Without, Within.
fem.	feminine.
FF	Feet of Fines.
Fine	*Calendar of the Fine Rolls.* Rolls Ser. 1911 ff.
Fr	*Calendar of Documents preserved in France.* Ed. J. H. Round. Rolls Ser. 1899.
Fridesw	*Cartulary of the Monastery of St. Frideswide.* Oxford Historical Soc. Oxford, 1894–6.
G	German.
gen.	genitive.
GloucesterCart	*Historia et Cartularium monasterii S. Petri Gloucestriæ.* Chr. & Mem. 33.
Grey Friars	The Grey Friars Chronicle. *Monumenta Franciscana II*, 143–260. Chr. & Mem. 1882.
GtChron	*The Great Chronicle of London.* Ed. A. H. Thomas and I. D. Thornley. London, 1938.
Hansisches Urkundenbuch	*Hansisches Urkundenbuch.* Ed. K. Höhlbaum. Halle, 1876 ff.

HMC	The Historical Manuscripts Commission.
Ipm	*Calendar of Inquisitions Post Mortem*. Rolls Ser. 1898 ff.
KCD	*Codex diplomaticus ævi Saxonici*. Ed. J. M. Kemble. London, 1839–48.
Kingsford	Stow's Survey of London. Vol. II. Notes by C. L. Kingsford.
Langb	Langbourn ward.
Lappenberg	Lappenberg, J. M. *Urkundliche Geschichte des hansischen Stahlhofes zu London*. London, 1851.
Lat	Latin.
Laws	Liebermann, F. *Die Gesetze der Angelsachsen*. Halle, 1903 ff.
LBA, LBB, &c.	*Calendar of Letter-Books of the City of London*. Ed. R. R. Sharpe. London, 1899 ff. LBA = Letter-Book A, &c.
Lewes	*Chartulary of the Priory of . . . Lewes*. Sussex Record Soc. 1932 ff.
LibAlb, LibCust	*Munimenta gildhallæ Londoniensis: Liber albus, Liber custumarum et Liber Horn*. Ed. H. T. Riley. Chr. & Mem. 1859–62.
LibWint	*Liber Winton'*. Domesday Book IV, 529–62. London, 1816.
LimeSt	Lime Street ward.
LIpm	*Abstracts of Inquisitiones Post Mortem relating to the City of London*. Ed. G. S. Fry. London, 1896 ff. Transactions of London and Middlesex Arch. Soc. Appendix.
lit.	literally.
LMAS	*Transactions of the London and Middlesex Archæological Society*. London, 1860 ff. New Ser. 1892 ff.
Lo	London.
LoEngl	*A Book of London English, 1384–1425*. Ed. R. W. Chambers and Marjorie Daunt. Oxford, 1931.
LP	*Letters and Papers, Foreign and Domestic, Henry VIII*. London, 1864 ff.
Machyn	*The Diary of Henry Machyn, 1550–1563*. Ed. J. G. Nichols. Camden Soc. London, 1848. (Forms corrected after Wijk; see Works Consulted.)
Mayors	*Calendar of Early Mayor's Court Rolls A.D.*

	1298–1307. Ed. A. H. Thomas. Cambridge, 1924.
ME	Middle English.
MemStEdm	*Memorials of St. Edmund's Abbey*. Ed. Th. Arnold. Chr. & Mem. 1890–6.
Misc	*Calendar of Inquisitions Miscellaneous*. Rolls Ser. 1916 ff.
MLG	Middle Low German.
Mon	Dugdale, W. *Monasticon Anglicanum*. London, 1846.
MonFranc	*Monumenta Franciscana*. Ed. J. S. Brewer. Chr. & Mem. 1858–82.
MxFF	*A Calendar to the Feet of Fines for London & Middlesex*. Ed. W. J. Hardy and W. Page. London, 1892 f.
n.d.	no date, undated.
NicolasChron	*A Chronicle of London, from 1089 to 1483, written in the Fifteenth Century*. London, 1827.
ODan	Old Danish.
OE	Old English.
OED	*A New English Dictionary*. Oxford, 1884–1933.
OF	Old French.
OG	Old German.
OHG	Old High German.
ON	Old Norse.
Oriel Records	*Oriel College Records*. By C. L. Shadwell and H. E. Salter. Oxford Historical Soc. Oxford, 1926.
Orig	*Rotulorum originalium . . . abbreviatio*. Record Com. 1805–10.
OScand	Old Scandinavian.
Oseney	*Cartulary of Oseney Abbey*. By H. E. Salter. Oxford Historical Soc. Oxford, 1929 ff.
OSwed	Old Swedish.
Oxf	*Facsimiles of Early Charters in Oxford Muniment Rooms*. Oxford, 1929.
P	Pipe Rolls.
(p)	personal name.
Paston	*The Paston Letters, 1422–1509*. Ed. J. Gairdner. London, 1900 ff.
Pat	Patent Rolls.
PaulsCh	*Early Charters of the Cathedral Church of St. Paul, London*. Ed. Marion Gibbs. Camden Soc. 3rd Ser. 1939.

PaulsMSS	Unprinted charters of St. Paul's, quoted by Harben.
PaulsMSS	'Report on the MSS. of the Dean and Chapter of St. Paul's', by H. C. Maxwell-Lyte. *Historical MSS. Commission*, Ninth Report, 1883. Forms from a survey of the lands of St. Paul's on p. 66 are quoted from the edition by H. W. C. Davis in *Essays . . . presented to T. F. Tout*, pp. 55 ff.
Pepys	S. Pepys, *Diary*. London, 1893 f.
Plea	*Calendar of Plea and Memoranda Rolls . . . at the Guildhall*. Ed. A. H. Thomas. Cambridge, 1926 ff.
PNCa	*The Place-names of Cambridgeshire*. Cambridge, 1943.
PND	*The Place-names of Devon*. Cambridge, 1931–2.
PNER	*The Place-names of the East Riding of Yorkshire and York*. Cambridge, 1937.
PNEss	*The Place-names of Essex*. Cambridge, 1935.
PNMx	*The Place-names of Middlesex*. Cambridge, 1942.
PNSr	*The Place-names of Surrey*. Cambridge, 1934.
PNW	*The Place-names of Wiltshire*. Cambridge, 1939.
Ports	Portsoken ward.
PRO	The Public Record Office.
Qu or Queenh	Queenhithe ward.
QW	*Placita de quo Warranto*. Record Com. 1818.
Ramsey Chron	*Chronicon Abbatiæ Rameseiensis*. Ed. W. D. Macray. Chr. & Mem. 1886.
RH	*Rotuli hundredorum I*. Record Com. 1812.
RHT	Hundred Roll for London of 7 Edward I (1279), Tower Series I (PRO). Quoted from photostats. Printed in part by Weinbaum, *London unter Eduard I. und II.*, pp. 142 ff.
Riley, *Mem*	Riley, H. Th. *Memorials of London and London Life in the XIIIth, XIVth and XVth Centuries*. London, 1868.
SalisburyCh	*Charters and Documents illustrating the History of the Cathedral, City, and Diocese of Salisbury*. Ed. W. D. Macray. Chr. & Mem. 1891.
Selborne	*Charters . . . relating to Selborne*. Hampshire Record Soc. 1891 ff.

Selden	The Publications of the Selden Society.
StAug	*The Register of St. Augustine's Abbey, Canterbury.* Ed. G. J. Turner and H. E. Salter. London, 1915, 1924.
St. Benet of Holme	*The Eleventh and Twelfth Century Sections of Cott. MS. Galba E ii. The Register of the Abbey of St. Benet of Holme.* Transcribed by J. R. West. Norfolk Record Soc. 1932.
StJohn	*A Cartulary of the Hospital of St. John the Baptist.* Ed. H. E. Salter. Oxford Historical Soc. Oxford, 1914 ff.
StMary	*The Medieval Records of a London City Church (St. Mary at Hill), A.D. 1420–1559.* Ed. H. Littlehales. E.E.T.S. London, 1904 f.
Stonor	*The Stonor Letters and Papers, 1290–1483.* Camden Soc. 3rd Ser. London, 1919.
Stow	Stow, J. *A Survey of London* (1598, 1603). Ed. C. L. Kingsford. Oxford, 1908. References, unless otherwise stated, are to the edition of 1603.
Subs	Subsidy Roll. For 1319 Subs see Ekwall; for 1332 Subs see Curtis in Works Consulted.
t.	*tempore*, t. Hy 2 = in the time (reign) of Henry II, &c.
Templars	*Records of the Templars in England in the Twelfth Century.* Ed. Beatrice A. Lees. London, 1935.
Thorpe	*Diplomatarium Anglicum ævi Saxonici.* Ed. B. Thorpe. London, 1865.
Vi or Vintry	Vintry ward.
Walbr	Walbrook ward.
Wardon	*Cartulary of the Abbey of Old Wardon.* Ed. G. H. Fowler. Beds Hist. Record Soc. 1930.
Will	Will enrolled in the Court of Husting; cf. CW supra.

Note. Where two dates are given, e.g. '734 (*c.* 840)', the first is the date of the document, the second that of the extant copy (or, in the case of wills, the date of enrolment). A date such as '1068 (copy)' indicates that the document is preserved in a later copy.

INTRODUCTION

I. STREETS AND LANES

THE majority of London street-names are compounds with the words *street* and *lane* as second members. Other elements (*row*, *alley*, *hill*) are of small importance, and enough information will be found concerning these in the respective chapters devoted to them in the body of the book.

OE *stræt* (*strēt*), from Latin *strata*, meant 'a road' and 'a street in a town'. It was used especially to denote a paved road, a highway, particularly an old Roman road. Also combinations such as *herestræt*, *heahstræt*, *cyninges stræt* occur and, of course, proper names such as *Wæclingastræt* 'Watling Street'. It is not clear if *stræt*, when used of a road in a town, was restricted to more important thoroughfares. OE *lane* is chiefly found in charters, generally referring to country lanes, where it probably has its modern meaning of a narrow way between hedges or banks and the like. But as pointed out in Bosworth-Toller, there are a few examples of the word in the *Blickling Homilies* (xix, St. Andreas), pp. 237 ff., where it refers to roads in a town, viz. the City of Marmadonia. The people of the town, we are told, dragged St. Andrew through the lanes of the City (*þisse ceastre lanan, þære ceastre lanan*). The editor renders *lanan* by 'streets', but the meaning may be more general, streets and lanes being included. There is also a compound *stræt-lanu*, which appears to refer to a street.

A *stræt* (or *heahstræt*, *strata regia*, *cyninges stræt* or the like), according to the laws of Henry I, was to be sufficiently broad for two loaded carts to meet and for sixteen armed knights to ride abreast.[1] A main road in the country is doubtless meant,

[1] Liebermann, *Gesetze der Angelsachsen*. Rechts- und Sachglossar (*Strasse*). Lady Stenton, *English Society in the Early Middle Ages*, p. 254.

but it is probable that a street in a town as a rule fulfilled these requirements. No information, so far as I know, is available as to the width of early London streets. On lanes some items have come down to us. Fye Foot Lane was only 5 feet broad at the west end (Stow ii. 1). The lane called *Desebournelane* in St. Mary Somerset is stated in 1348 to have been 215 feet long and 7 feet wide, except at the southern end, where it was one royal ell wide. Crocker Lane by Whitefriars was 12 feet wide, 660 feet long in 1349, according to a Patent Roll.

Important information is found in the Hundred Roll of 1279 (*RHT*). Thus a lane running between the Priory of Holy Trinity and the city wall, presumably the later Duke Street with its continuations, is stated to have been 16 feet wide (m. 7). Another lane, which had been shut up by the nuns of St. Helen's and used to run from St. Mary Axe to Bishopsgate Street, had a width of 18 feet (m. 7). The lane is referred to as *Seint Eleyne Lane* 1249 Pat (Harben), *Seint Eleine Lane* 1275 RH 426. Adam Bruning, while alderman of Castle Baynard, had obstructed (*obstruxit*) a lane 4 feet wide (*venellam latitudinis quatuor pedum*) between the house of the Prior of Okeburne and that belonging to Hillarius le Porter, along which people used to go to the Thames to fetch water in tubs (*cum tinis*) (m. 19). The lane was in Castle Baynard, where the Prior of Ogbourne had a house situated in Castle Lane (Stow ii. 13). If the lane was only 4 feet wide it would not be quite easy to carry a tub of water along it, and possibly the meaning is that the lane had been narrowed by 4 feet. This is evidently the meaning in a passage found on m. 22, where it is stated that Benedict de Hakeneye had narrowed (*artauit*) the King's way (*regiam viam*) outside Aldgate (Aldgate High Street) by 4 feet (*latitudinis quatuor pedum*). But here a different verb is used.

In the same source (m. 1) is found the statement that a lane (*venella*) in Queenhithe called *Kinggesgate* ought to be wide enough for a cask of wine to be rolled along it transversely (*ex transuerso*) with one man on each side, but was narrower (*strictior*) than it should be in the lower part.

Many lanes were doubtless available for wheeled traffic, even if some may not have been wide enough for carts to meet, while some could only be used by foot-passengers or people on horseback. On Rose Street, the earlier Cecile Lane and Dicer Lane, we are told in a document of 1320–1 (PaulsMSS 49 a) that formerly men went by it with horses and carts from Paternoster Row to *Cornechepinge* (the corn-market by St. Michael le Querne). St. Swithin's Lane, according to *RHT* (m. 24), had been obstructed before 1279 by two large buttresses so that carts could hardly get through there. In the same document (m. 2) is recorded a complaint that the common way (*via communis*) for foot-passengers (*hominibus pede euntibus*) leading from Gutter Lane to Huggin Lane had been shut up.

In medieval London records a distinction between *street* and *lane* is fairly well kept up in street-names. But the difference between a comparatively narrow street and a comparatively wide lane might be slight, and there are cases of vacillation between *street* and *lane* in street-names. Seething Lane is *Sivethenestrate* and the like between 1257 and *c.* 1300, *Syvidlane* and the like from 1259 on. The present Old Jewry was formerly Colechurch Lane or Colechurch Street, the former 1280–93, the latter 1278 ff. The two variants seem to have been about equally common. Grub Street is *Grubbestrate* and the like from the early 13th century on, but sometimes *Grub(be)lane* in the 14th century. Moor Lane appears as *Morstrate* 1310–1502, as *Morelane* from 1331 on. Paternoster Row was *Paternosterstrete* 1307 ff., *Paternosterlane* 1321–35, finally Paternoster Row from 1334 on. Addle Street (CripI) was generally *Addelane* in the 14th century, but *Adlyngstrete* 1399–1400 Pat, *Adelstrete* in the 16th century and later. Occasionally normal *-street* is replaced by -*lane* or vice versa. Basing Lane is exceptionally *Basinge-strete* in 1303. One Carter Lane (so 1349 ff.) is *Carterestrate* 1295. Ironmonger Lane is *Ismongerstrete* in 1267. Beech Street is generally *Bechelane* (1279 &c.), but *Bechestrete* 1285. Billiter Street is exceptionally *Belleʒeterestret* in 1349, otherwise a name in -*lane* till the 19th century.

Cordwainer Street (1216 &c.) is replaced by Hosier Lane in the second half of the 14th century, and the latter by Bow Lane. New Street (1185 ff.) was superseded by *Converslane* (1278 ff.) and by Chancery Lane. Another New Street (*nouus vicus* a 1218) was replaced by Soper Lane (*c.* 1246 &c.).

It will be seen that several of the occasional variants with -*street* instead of normal -*lane* are found in relatively early records. It looks as if -*street* was more extensively used in the 13th century than later.

A good deal of variation is seen in the use of the words *street* and *lane* or their Latin equivalents in references to streets and lanes. Most of the texts from which we get information on street-names are in Latin. A street in Middle Latin texts is generally called *vicus*, a lane *venella* or rarely *viculus*.[1] Latin *vicus* is as a rule rendered by 'street' in translations of early deeds, *venella* by 'lane'. *Viculus* is probably rendered by 'little street', sometimes perhaps by 'little lane'.

It is very common, however, to find the word *vicus* used in reference to lanes, and this appears to hold good particularly as regards comparatively early sources. Very likely, therefore, *vicus* in the 13th century and earlier was not used only in the sense '(main) street', but also in the sense 'lane'. A few examples may be given by way of illustration. Honey Lane is *vicus de Hunilane c.* 1212–13 PaulsCh 263; Cecile Lane, *vicus Cecilie de Turri* 13th; Convers Lane, *Vicus Conversorum* 1253 Cl;

---

[1] Stinking Lane, the later King Edward Street, is called *viculus* 1282 MonFranc i. 500.

Clement's Lane (Cand), *vicus sancti Clementis* 1241; Gutter
Lane, *vicus de Goderunlan'* 1251; Ironmonger Lane, *vicus de
Ismongerelane* 1278 ExchJews, 'the little street' (*viculus*?)
1213–16. The 'street' often found in English translations in
reference to lanes is no doubt as a rule a rendering of *vicus*,
as when Mark Lane, Seacoal Lane, and Woodroffe Lane are
called streets in 1272, 1279–80, 1285 respectively (ADA 2655,
CW i. 44, Ch).

There are also cases where a street is referred to as a lane,
probably Latin *venella*, and also some where there seems to have
been real uncertainty as regards the terms 'street' and 'lane'.
Silver Street (*Silverstrete*) is called a lane in 1357 (ADA 2457)
and Wood Street in 1324. Cordwainer Street is called a lane in
1321–2, a high street in 1358 (Cl). Watling Street (*Atheling-
streta*) is a lane 1303 Lewes ii. 87. Old Change is a lane t.
Edw I (PaulsMSS 24 b), a street in 1297–8, a King's road in
1377 (CW ii. 201).

There are in early records various other designations for
'street', in Latin texts especially combinations of words for
'road' with *regius*, *regalis* or *regis*. These doubtless generally
refer to main streets, important thoroughfares, but some of the
roads so termed cannot have been of real importance, and the
word *regius* (*regalis*, *regis*) sometimes very likely means 'common, public'. Thus the road running between the Priory of
Holy Trinity and the city wall, which had been stopped up, is
referred to in *RHT* (1279) as *via regia* (m. 6 &c.), *via domini
Regis* (m. 10), and *venella* (m. 7), and in the same text a lane
leading from St. Helen's to St. Mary Axe is called *vicus regius*
(m. 8), *via Regia* (m. 10), *venella* (m. 7). *Venella regia* is rare;
Fosterlane in Vintry (not Foster Lane) is so called in 1275
(RH). *Viculus regius* 1252 Ch apparently refers to the later
Bearbinder Lane. On *Iter reale* see infra.

A few notes may be added on designations for 'street'.

Strata has been noticed 1275 RH (St. Mary Axe), 1548 Pat, referring to Bishopsgate Street. *Strata regia* has been found applied to Fleet Street and Newgate Street (1279 *RHT* m. 3), and to Thames Street (1321 LibCust), *regia strata* to lost streets between Ludgate and Newgate and between New-gate and Aldersgate (1279 *RHT* m. 3) and to Lambeth Hill (1400 EpHeref). *Communis strata* refers to a road in Tower ward 1275 RH 406, and Cheap is called *Stratum nobilem* in 1377.

Vicus regius is frequent. It refers to Dowgate (1244 &c.), Hog Street (1275 RH), Milk Street and Wood Street (1282 ExchJews), Fleet Street (1279 *RHT* m. 2). Not rarely a street is referred to simply as *vicus regius*; in such cases it is sometimes erroneously rendered 'King Street'. Old Jewry is so called in 1265 (ADA 1673), Thames Street in 1270 (ib. 1776), Basinghall Street in 1277 (ib. 1857).

Magnus vicus t. John EHR xvii. 483 must be Thames Street. *Magnus vicus de Aldredesgate* is found 1266 Cl. Newgate Street is *Altus vicus in macellis* in a Patent Roll of 1394, and *Altus vicus vulgariter dictus Chepe* occurs 1419 EpCant.

Via regia and *regia via* are not very common, *via regia* referring to St. Mary Axe and other roads in 1275 RH, to Aldermanbury 1279 *RHT* (m. 31), *regia via* 1548 ff. Pat in reference to High Timber Street, Tower Street, and others. *Via domini Regis* occurs occasionally 1279 *RHT*.

Regalis via 1275 RH 413 is Aldgate Street.

Communis via is found 1275 RH 420 referring to a road along the city wall from Aldgate to the Tower; the same road is called *via regia* ib. p. 426. *Via communis* is the epithet of Desborne Lane 1275 RH and 1279 *RHT* (m. 1) and of Water Lane 1275 RH. Aldermanbury is referred to 1275 RH variously as *via regia communis* (p. 410), *vicus publicus* (p. 415), *vicus Regis* (p. 430). *Venella communis* is found twice 1279 *RHT* m. 1.

Iter reale has only been noticed in *RHT* (1279), m. 2, referring to the later Pye Corner and the lost roads along the city wall from Ludgate to Newgate and from Newgate to Aldersgate, also to a lane from the Fleet to Shoe Lane. *Iter* alone is used in the same text, m. 7: *Iter quo itur uersus Bissopesgate. Realis* is a Normanized form of *regalis*.

Original English texts from the Middle English period in which street-names occur are very few. The chief sources available are the texts in *London English*, especially those from Plea Rolls of 1422 f. A main street is here variously referred to as *the hye wey* (apparently Fleet Street), *the hie strete* (the Old Bailey), *þe kynges hye (hie) way* (Bread Street), *þe kyngys heywey* (probably Lime Street), *þe kynges way* (apparently Thames Street). *þe commune waye* corresponds to Latin *via communis*.

In translations of Latin texts into modern English expressions such as *highway, high road, high street* are frequent, but without access to the originals it is impossible to judge what is the Latin equivalent. As a rule the Latin probably has *vicus*, sometimes perhaps *via* or *strata*, possibly *altus vicus* or *alta via*.

The common expressions *the King's highway* (or *way*) and the like doubtless render *via regia, vicus regius*, and the like. In the Patent Rolls for 1548 ff. *regia via* is rendered by 'the king's highway'. I have found 'the king's highway' applied to Finch Lane in BroadSt (1293), Fleet Street (1285 Cl), Tower Street (1276 LBB 258), 'the king's road' to Old Change (1377 CW ii. 201), 'the king's high road' to Cheap (1286). These are only a few examples of early usage.

II. THE FORM OF THE FIRST ELEMENT IN COMPOUND NAMES

The first element of street-names appears variously in the genitive and in the uninflected form. This is sometimes of value as a criterion of the nature of the element and thus for the etymology. The genitive is chiefly found if the first element is a personal designation (or name) or the name of an animal, but occurs occasionally also in other cases. The *s* of the common Old English genitive ending -(*e*)*s* would be merged in the initial *s*- of a following *street*, and it is impossible to decide if the original first element in such names was in the genitive or not. Names in -*street* are therefore generally omitted in this chapter.

A distinction must be made between names with the first element in the singular and those with that element in the plural. It is still more important to distinguish street-names with a personal designation as first member from names with other first elements.

i. The first element is a personal designation or name

A. The first element is in the singular

In a few cases there may be some doubt as to whether the first element is in the singular or in the plural. Examples will be discussed below.

The usual Old English genitival ending of masculine and neuter words was -(*e*)*s*, but words with so-called weak inflexion (*n*-stems) had the ending -*an* (thus OE *cempa* 'warrior', gen. *cempan*), whence ME -*en* and -*e*. Words with the latter inflexion are very rarely found in street-names, and they began early to form an analogical genitive with the ending -*s*. Feminine words only rarely had an Old English genitive in -*s*, at least in southern dialects, but in Middle English the ending -*s* began fairly early to be transferred to them. There are in street-names hardly any certain traces of a genitive in OE -*an* (ME -*e*) in masculine words, but not a few safe instances of early *s*-less genitives of feminine words.

In early examples the genitival -*s* of masculine words or names is mostly preserved in street-names, but in the course of the 14th century it begins to be dropped and is generally absent in the late 15th century and later. Dropping of -*s*, however, occasionally occurs already in the late 13th century. Feminine words rarely have the *s*-genitive in street-names.

1. *The first element is a font-name*

All the men's names found in London street-names are such as formed their genitive with -*s* in Old English or else names of French origin. Some names exclusively found in early records show *s*-forms only, as Alsies Lane (3 exx.), Craddock Lane (4 exx.), *Germayneslane* (1 ex.), *Wancelineslane* (2 exx.). Philip Lane is *Philippeslane* and the like from the 12th till the 15th century. Stephen Lane has *s*-forms exclusively from 1329 till 1455. Wolsy Lane is *Wolsi(e)slane* from 1307 till 1421, *Wolsylane* from 1379 on. Pentecost Lane is normally *Pentecost(e)lane* from 1280 on, *Pentecosteslane* having been noted twice only (1290 and 1294). The abnormal loss of *s* is doubtless due to the *s* in the preceding syllable. Lambeth Hill is normally *Lamberdeshelle* and the like from 1281 on; *Lamberhull* 1305 Mayors is exceptional, possibly an abbreviated spelling. *Folkemares lane* (13th) shows the ending -*es*, but there are *s*-less forms of the name of 1280 and 1285. The first element may be a surname rather than a font-name, but in either case the early loss of the *s* is remarkable.

Women's names generally appear without a genitival *s*, especially in early records, but often also in later ones. Thus only *s*-less forms are recorded for Desborne Lane, Golden Lane, Mark Lane. Gutter Lane and the two Kiron Lanes only occasionally appear with *s*-forms (*Godruneslane* c. 1206–7, but in a transcript of c. 1250, *Goddereslane* 1279 *RHT* m. 20, *Goderoneslane* 1300; *Ky-*, *Kironeslane* 1275). Cecile Lane has a few early s-forms (*c.* 1200, 13th cent.). Noteworthy is *Sabelinesbury* 1258–9. The two names *Cecile* and *Sabeline* are French.

2. *The first element is a surname*

A distinction should be made between surnames that were originally by-names or nicknames or the like, inclusive of original font-names, and local surnames. The latter names were originally preceded by a preposition, in Latin sources usually *de*, corresponding to English *of*, sometimes *in* or *at*. This preposition began to be dropped in the 14th century, occasionally earlier. The former, of course, never had a preposition before them. An *s*-genitive would be more readily formed from a name of the former type than from local surnames, at least so long as the preposition was preserved. In reality there is little real difference between usage in the two groups, but local surnames generally appear somewhat later in street-names than surnames of the other type.

If the first element ended in -*s*, no genitival -*s* is added, thus only *Wendegos(e)lane* and the like, *Armenterslane*. A sibilant may have had the same effect in *Fresshfisshlane*.

(*a*) In the first group *s* regularly appears, except in late examples, in *Batteslane* (1311–1508), *Dibleslane* (1301–1422, but *Debillane* 1459), *Fatteslane* (1279–1343), *Fynamoureslane* (1316), Finch Lane, BroadSt (*c.* 1240–1376), Finch Lane, Bill (1333–1449), *Hardeleslane* (1431), *Palmereslane* (1343 &c.), *Pikardeslane* (1279 ff.), Pope Lane (*Popes lane* 13th, 1334), *Pourteslane* (1368–1408), Sermon Lane (t. Hy 3 &c.), Trig Lane (1422). Cousin Lane is normally *Cosyneslane* 1305–1430, occasionally *Cosynlane* 1379 and later. Philpot Lane and *Pyellane*, both late names, only have *s*-less forms.

Some names show a somewhat different distribution of forms.

Gayspur Lane (1332–*c.* 1450) has *s*-less forms only. Gofair Lane is *Gofairelane* 1313 &c., *Govereslane* 1348–1456. Sevehod Lane is *Seuehodeslane* 1354 &c., *Sefhodlane* and the like 1377 &c., once *Sevehodenelane* (1412). Popkirtle Lane mostly has *s*-less forms (1275–1505), but occasional *s*-forms of 1275 and 1324. *Sevehodenelane* looks like a form with an analogical genitive plural ending in *-ene* (OE *-ena*), and if that is right the first element would seem to have been in the plural and to mean 'of the people with the surname *Sevehod*'. The lane would then have been named from two or more inhabitants with this surname. A similar explanation is possible for the other three. In any case it is unlikely that the *s*-less form of *Gayspur* in Gayspur Lane is a relic of an Old English genitive singular in *-an*, though the name contains OE *spura* 'spur', an old *n*-stem, whose genitive was *spuran*, or that *Gofaire*, which contains the adverb *faire* 'fairly', in early Middle English came to form an analogical genitive in *-en* (*-e*).

Two names which might be supposed to have surnames as first element may be mentioned here. Do Little Lane never shows *s*-forms, though there are numerous early instances of the name. Its first element is probably not a surname. Woodroffe Lane is frequently *Woderovelane* 1260–91, no *s*-form being recorded. This renders it doubtful if *Woderove* is here the common surname. It is true the surname is the Old English plant-name *wudurofe* (fem.), whose genitive was *wudurofan*, but it is unlikely that the word as a by-name and surname preserved its old inflexion.

Several late names in *-alley* show the genitive form in the late 14th and the 15th century, as *Langhornesaley*, *Leggesaleye*, *Trestremesaley*, but *Fastolf Aley* appears in 1417.

Bucklersbury always has the *s*-form (1270 &c.). Lothbury shows no *s*-form. Its first element would have been an Old English *Hlopan-* or *Lopan-*, whence ME *Lothe-*, whose meaning would not be understood in the 12th century. The name is no doubt of Old English date.

(*b*) Though the names in this group are on the whole later than those in the first group, yet we find Basing Lane recorded as early as 1275, Greenwich Lane 1279–80, *Hadestokeslane* 1297–8. A name-form such as *Grenewichislane* (1279–80) must indicate that *Grenewich* without a preceding *of* had already become a surname from which a genitive could be formed with the ending *-s*. It follows that colloquially the preposition (*of* &c.) had begun to be dropped already in the second half of the 13th century, though it was generally retained in the written language.

Some names first recorded in the 15th century show only *s*-less forms, as *Arundellane, Cressynghamlane, Wirehalelane. Southamlane* (1383) may be placed here.

Some street-names have been found only with the *s*-form, as *Hadestokeslane* (found once in 1297–8), *Coventreslane, Dorkynggeslane, Reygateslane* (all found once in 1343), *Weylandeslane* (found once in 1421), and Stodies Lane (1394 ff.). Grantham Lane is *Granthameslane* 1343, *Granthamlane* 1382, 1421; Weston Lane, *Westoneslane* 1357 &c., *Westonlane* 1377 &c. Greenwich Lane is *Grenewichislane* 1279–80, *Grenewichlane* already in 1283. The sibilant *ch* may account for the early loss of *s*.

Basing Lane shows remarkable variation between *s*-forms and *s*-less forms. The earlier examples generally show forms like *Basingelane* (1275 &c.); later appear *Basingeslane* and the like (1307 &c.). The place-name *Basing*, from which the surname was taken, was originally plural in form, OE *Basingas*, really a folk-name. Both the place-name and the surname *Basing* varied between the forms *Basing*(*e*) and *Basinges*. This may sufficiently account for the variation in the street-name. It is possible, however, that the street-name was felt to mean 'the street of the Basings' (that is the people of Basing), so that early *Basinge-* in *Basingelane* was a normal genitive plural, which was later changed to *Basinges* in the same way as *Ismongere(lane)* became *Ismongeres(lane)*. In any case Basing Lane holds a position of its own in the group. A similar interchange of *Basinge-* and *Basinges-* is seen in Basinghall (Bassishaw).

3. *The first element is a personal designation of some other kind*

These form a small group.

Chancery Lane, originally Chancellor Lane, is recorded from 1338, in the earliest instances *Chauncellereslane* or the like (1338 &c.), but without *s* already in 1340 and later (e.g. 1366, 1380 Pat).

Old Dean's Lane is *Eldedeneslane* and the like 1257 &c., only rarely *Eldene Lane* (1392 PaulsMSS 10 b), *Eldenelane* (1434, 1442 CW ii. 470, 497), *Eldenlane* (1411–12 ib. 392, 1424 LoEngl). The name became obsolete in the late 15th century.

Aldermanbury, which was not originally a street-name, is frequently recorded. The earliest forms have a genitival *s*, as *Aldresmanesberi c.* 1130 &c. But *Aldermanneberi* and similar forms turn up about 1190, and the *s*-less form after some vacillation becomes regular in the course of the 13th century. The name, which originally meant 'the alderman's manor', may have come to be understood to mean 'the aldermen's manor', and the early genitival form *aldermanne-* (plur.) was introduced. *Aldermanneberi* was not later changed to *Aldermannesberi*, as might have been expected in view of the common *s*-form in the street-names with an occupational word as first element. The genitive plural -*manne* is preserved also in the isolated *Baremanelane* (1285).

Bereward's Lane (two), one recorded 1285 &c., the other 1279 &c., generally shows *s*-forms, but the ending is absent in the earliest example. The name in both cases went out of use early. *Bereward* probably means 'the bearward'.

Bearbinder Lane is a doubtful instance. The first element regularly has the *s*-form in the 14th century, the *s*-less form from *c.* 1500.

B. *The first element is in the plural*

The genitive plural in Old English generally had the ending *-a*, in some cases *-(e)na*, and in early Middle English the normal ending would be *-e* (or *-ene*). The originally weak ending *-ene* has left some traces in London street-names, which will be discussed under iv. In the course of the Middle English period the early genitive plural *-e* was gradually changed to *-es*, an ending which turns up in London street-names early. The *s*-form was probably in the majority in street-names in the 14th century and common in the 15th, but gradually the *s* began again to be dropped and from the 16th century on it is as a rule absent. Some names are frequently recorded and show a good deal of variation. Others are found only rarely, some only once or twice.

Here belong a good many street-names with an occupational word as first element. It has generally been taken for granted that the first element in such names was in the plural, but it is possible that in some cases it was in the singular, even an occupational term used as a surname. A possible case is Roper Lane in Bill, which is *Ropereslane* in 1313, *Roperelane* 1455.

Ironmonger Lane generally has *s*-forms in the earliest instances, as 1213–16, 1220–1 (ADA 2022), 1275 (RH), 1280, and sometimes in later ones. The *s*-less form appears *c.* 1190, *c.* 1250, 1272 &c.

Soper (or Soper's) Lane. Forms like *Sopereslane* appear to be in the majority in early records, e.g. *c.* 1246, 1257, 1278

(CW), and often occur later also, e.g. 1311 (LBD), 1331 (Cl), 1421 (Plea) &c. *Soper(e)lane* is frequent also, examples having been noted from 1279, 1282, 1285 (CW), 1290 (ib.), 1315 (Pat), 1328–9, and of course later. It is difficult to be quite sure about the relative frequency of the forms. The name is now lost. Harben usually has the spelling Soper's Lane.

Dicer Lane is *Dicereslane* and the like 1275–1394, while *Diserlane* and the like turn up 1279, 1412, and 1417. The first element is here possibly in the singular.

Billiter Lane (or Street) has *s*-forms 1298–1468, only one early *s*-less form having been noted (1421).

Birchin Lane appears with an *s*-less form in the late 12th century, but usually with *s*-forms in the period 1260–*c.* 1400. The meaning of the first element was obscured early and the name was radically altered.

Carter Lane (CastleB) has *s*-forms 1349–1413, *s*-less forms from 1397 on.

Crocker Lane appears as *Cro(c)kerelane* 1277, 1283, with *s*-forms 1291–1349.

Only *s*-forms are recorded in medieval sources for Limeburners' Lane (1308–1415), Needlers Lane (1400–72), Spurrier Lane (1295–1459).

Huettawiereslane (a 1200) is the earliest *s*-form noted.

Bowyer Row has *s*-forms 1359–1405,[1] *s*-less forms 1378 &c. Stockfishmonger Row (1373 &c.) and Paternoster Row (1321 &c.) have no *s*-forms. *Paternoster-* very likely came fairly early to be supposed to mean 'paternoster' instead of 'maker of rosaries'.

Street-names with other personal designations as first element are few.

Fetter Lane has *s*-forms from 1292 to 1447, *s*-less forms 1329, 1340, and later. Ing Lane is *Engleslane* exceptionally in

---

[1] *Bowyerysrowe* 1405 (1408) CW ii. 377.

1331. Staining Lane is normally *Staningelane* and the like from the late 12th century, *Stanigeslane* exceptionally in 1278. Bassishaw (Basinghall) shows much variation between *s*-forms and *s*-less forms.

Mincing Lane is usually *Mengenelane* and the like from the late 12th century on, but *Mengeoneslane* 1324, 1332 CW i. 309, 378, *Maioneslane* 1325 ib. 317. Maiden Lane is late except for an isolated *Maden lane* t. Hy 3.

ii. The first element is the name of an animal

The probability is that the first element is here generally in the plural.

In this group *s*-forms are comparatively rare, apart from Cock Lane, which is regularly *Cockeslane* and the like from about 1200 on. Chicken Lane (FarrE) is *Chikennelane* and the like from 1197 on, but *Chikeneslane* sometimes in the late 12th century. Chicken Lane (Tower) is regularly *Chikenelane* from 1235 on. Variation is seen in *Ratoneslane* (1327 &c.), *Raton Lane* (1367). Huggin Lane (CripI) is *Hoggeslane* in 1234–5. Duck Lane, Cow Lane, Hog Lane are late.

Rother Lane is derived from *Retheresgate* (*Rederesgate*), the name of a watergate. The latter appears with the genitival *s* regularly from the early 12th century on. This form is kept when the name is used as a street-name and in the new-formation *Rethereslane*, but *Retherlane* has been found 1372–3 CW ii. 153. Also the variant form of the street-name in which *lane* is added to the full name *Retheresgate* preserves the *s* of *Retheres-*, thus *Retheresgatelane*. But it is possible that *Rether* in the name is a collective singular, and a similar explanation may apply to the first element of Cock Lane. The Canterbury name *Riðerescæp* 'cattle market', found in a late copy of a charter of 605 (BCS 5), seems to be an early example of such a collective use of OE *hrȳðer* 'cattle'.

iii. The first element is the name of an object or a place-name

In street-names of this kind the first element is generally un-inflected, but exceptions occur.

Coneyhope Lane is *Conyhopeslane* in 1422. The full form of Rother Lane just mentioned, *Retheresgate(s)lane*, is *Retheresgateslane* and the like 1322 &c., but *Retheresgatelane* is found 1321 (1322–3), *Rederesgatelane* 1333–4 CW i. 301, 393. Spittle Lane is *Spiteleslane* 1343, *Spitellane* 1344, 1421 f. Turnbase Lane is *Tornebastoneslane* in 1329, *Tornebastonlane* and the like 1328 &c. *Dystaves lane* (1298) and the like will have an analogical genitive plural in -*es*.

A special group is formed by names derived from those of churches, such as Clement's Lane. The church was named from its patron saint, and *Seintclementeslane* probably really meant 'the lane by St. Clement's church', though it may alternatively have been taken to mean 'the lane of St. Clement' (the saint). In early records the saint's name is generally in the genitive, as *Seyntbotulfeslane*, *Dunstoneslane*, *Seint Uastes* (*Fastes*) *lane* &c. Later the genitival -*s*- generally disappeared, and the modern forms appear as Botolph Lane, Foster Lane &c. Foster Lane appears as *Fasterlane* 1422 ff., Bartholomew Lane as *Seint Bartilmew lane* already in the time of Edward III, if the form is reliable. No genitival *s* is found if the saint's name ended in -*s*, as Nicholas Lane. Laurence Lane appears variously as *Seint Laurencelane* and *Seint Laurenceslane* (1320, 1348). Bride Lane and Sise Lane were named ultimately from women saints. The former is *Bridelane* 1349, *Brideslane* 1374, *Seintebrideslane* 1379, while the latter is *Seint Sytheslane* and the like regularly and has kept the *s*-form till the present day. Some other street-names retain the genitive form, as Clement's Lane, Martin's Lane, Miles's Lane. In the last the genitival *s* has even been duplicated.

C

iv. Street-names containing genitive plural forms in -ene

There are not a few such names, and it is evident that the genitive plural in -ene (OE -(e)na) was quite common in London in late Old English and early Middle English times. The ending was in many cases analogical, being added to nouns that originally had a genitive plural ending in -a. An early example, not in a street-name, is the name of the old London Knights' Guild. The name appears as (on) *Ænglisce cnihte gilde* 1042–4 Hunterian MS (Harmer, *Anglo-Saxon Writs*, p. 234), as *Knyttegilda* n.d. LBC 217, but as *Cnihtenegilda* t. W 1 &c. ib. 218 f., *Cnithtengilda* t. Hy 1 ib. 220, *Engliscecnithtengilda* 1140–4 ib. 222, *Anglica Cnithenegild, -geld* 1321 QW.[1]

Ing Lane is *Englenelane* 1282, *Inggelenelane, Inggenelane* 1310 ff., which forms go back to OE *Englena lane*. *Ingelane* 1320 &c. is very likely a reduced form of *Ingenelane*, but might represent a side-form *Engla lane*.

Haggen(e)lane 1260 ff. (*Hoggenelane* 1257) very likely has as first element a genitive plural in -ena of an OE *hæcge* 'hag'. *Haggelane* 1202–4 may be miswritten or it may contain a side-form with a genitive plural *hagge*.

Wyvenelane 1328 ff. has as first element an analogical genitive plural in -ene of OE *wif*, a neuter noun with the genitive plural *wifa*.

On *Sevehodenelane* see p. 11.

An interesting example is *Ismongernelane* (1326), which shows an analogical genitive plural *ismongerne* instead of *ismongere*. Analogical formations of this kind from agent-nouns in -ere are sometimes evidenced in the street-names of

---

[1] Here may also be mentioned the lost name of a garden in St. Giles (CripE), which is *le Juesgardyn* 1341, *Jewesgardin* 1349 CW i. 452, 620, but *le Jewengardyn* 1405–6, *Jewengardyn* 1422 (1426), *le Jewen gardyn* 1429 (1433–4) CW ii. 365, 440, 468. From the name, which means 'the Jews' garden', was formed the late street-name Jewin Street.

other southern towns. Thus Holloway Street in Exeter was *Carterne strete* in 1291, but *Carterestrete* in 1314 (PND), and Catharine Street in Salisbury was *Carterestrete* in 1339, *Carternestret* in 1393 (PNW). Both names mean 'the street of the carters'. It might be suggested that *Selvernestrate*, *Silvernestret*, early forms of Silver Street in London, indicate that the first element was an OE *silfrere* 'silversmith', but such a word is unrecorded. *Silverer* 1598 ff. is evidently a late formation.

Some names of animals have a genitive plural in *-ene* in street-names.

Cattonlane, a variant of Cateaton Street, and *Cattenelane* (Bill) contain the genitive plural of OE *catt*.

Huggin Lane CripI (*Hoggenelane* 1256 ff.) and Qu (*Hoggenelane* 1329–30) both contain a genitive plural of OE *hogg* 'hog'.

On *Downgate* by the side of Dowgate see this name.

Possible instances of a genitive plural in *-ene* in names with a first element denoting an object are Seething Lane (olim *Sivethenelane* &c.) and some forms of Beech Lane (*Bechenelane* 1396 &c.).

III. ENGLISH AND FRENCH ELEMENTS IN STREET-NAMES[1]

Names containing French elements need not be later than many purely English names, but they will at any rate have been formed after, and as a rule not until some time after, the Norman Conquest, when French had begun to influence the English vocabulary. Practically all London street-names are purely English formations which presuppose an English-speaking community. No doubt many people of French extraction settled in London at different periods after the Conquest, and they would continue for some time to speak their native

[1] Late names such as College Street or Noble Street are disregarded here.

tongue. Also many London citizens of English birth were probably able to speak French, but this only influenced the vocabulary. Name-forms such as *rue de Thamise* were only used in
documents written in French. The definite article *le*, *la*, so
common instead of English *the* in Latin texts, is not due to
French influence on English, but to French influence on Anglo-
Latin.

Two names, however, may hold a separate position. One is
the old name of College Hill in Vintry, *the Riole* (*la Riole*).
This is the French *la Réole*, the name of a town near Bordeaux,
from which vintners came to London on business. It is possible that these vintners called a house they used as a hostel so,
and that this name was then generally adopted. The other is
Babeloyne, an old name of part of London Wall. It is evidently
from the French form of the name *Babylon*, but there is no
reason to suppose that the street-name was given by French
people in London. The French name was adopted by English
people, who for some reason applied it to a London street.

We begin with names in *-street*. Here French influence is
very slight indeed.

If we follow the division into groups adopted in the main
part of the book, we find that no French influence is to be seen
in groups A and B (names with a first element denoting a
characteristic of the street or a commodity or article produced
there). In the remaining groups there are a few partly French
names. They are Cordwainer Street, a fairly early name, which
has as first element a word that was introduced early and for
which there was no Old English equivalent; Paternoster Street,
a lost name containing a French occupational word; Little
Britain (earlier *Brettonestrete*), whose first element is the surname of an early owner; and Tower Street. The word *tower*
was adopted by the English very early, being recorded (as *tur*)
in the Anglo-Saxon Chronicle, MS E, under the year 1097.

Lombard Street replaced a somewhat similar English name (Langbourn Street) in the early 14th century. The word *Lombard* may be Italian just as well as French.

Names in -*lane* show stronger French influence, but the purely English names far outnumber those partly French, and the latter generally belong to a fairly late period.

In group A we find over a dozen English names (inclusive of names possibly containing an Old Scandinavian element). All names with an adjective as first element belong here. Partly French are Turnagain Lane, which is a late modification of normal early Wendagain Lane, a purely English name, and *Raton(es)lane*, whose first element is French *raton* 'rat' and which is first recorded in 1327.

In group B are fifteen names of purely English origin and possibly one partly French, namely the lost *Viterilane* (1294 ff.).

In group C (streets named from persons) some subgroups must be distinguished.

Among names containing occupational words (as Soper Lane) we find some twenty names of purely English origin. Partly French are the lost Sporon Lane (1268 &c.) and perhaps Dicer Lane (1275 &c.).

In the subgroup formed by other names containing personal designations the percentage of partly French names is larger. To some seven or eight English names correspond five partly French: *Converslane* and its successor Chancery Lane, Old Dean's Lane (lost), Fetter Lane, and *Sakfrerelane*, all except Chancery Lane found fairly early.

Names with an English font-name and those with a French font-name as first element are about equal in number, see further p. 23. This is really remarkable since French font-names began to be adopted by English people very early and Old English font-names, with few exceptions, were soon discarded. The English font-names found in street-names are all such as were lost early (*Alsi, Craddoc, Deneburg, Godrun, Golde, Kiron (Cynerun), Wolsi*). There are 12 or 13 street-names containing English surnames that were originally nick-names or the like, 9 or 10 containing French surnames of the same type, while among street-names with a local surname as first element only one is partly French (*Armenterslane*, found first in 1343) as against 18 purely English names. *Gayspur* in Gayspur Lane is a hybrid (F *gai* and English *spur*).

In group D (streets named from their situation) the dis-tinction between purely English and partly French names is not so easy to draw. Street-names derived from names of churches had better be placed by themselves. It is not always clear if a saint's name should be looked upon as Old English or French. Some continental saints' names were of course familiar to the Anglo-Saxons, and churches were sometimes dedicated to such saints even in the Anglo-Saxon period. St. Andrew Holborn is a typical case (cf. p. 36). On the other hand, the *Saint* is French in form. If such names are excluded, there are among early street-names some fifteen purely English names. French are partly Bretask Lane, Pillory Lane, Spittle Lane, Turnbase Lane, while *Coneyhope* in Coneyhope Lane is a hybrid. As regards names derived from those of churches Abchurch Lane and Bow Lane are purely English, while Paternoster Lane is partly French. Some of the churches were named from English (or at least British) saints, viz. Botolph Lane, Bride Lane, St. Dunstan's Lane, St. Swithin's Lane, the remaining ten from continental saints, as Bartholomew Lane, Foster Lane, Martin's Lane, Pancras Lane, the saint's name being generally French in form. Sise Lane may commemorate an Italian saint.

In group E (Do Little Lane, Love Lane &c.) there are hardly any French names.

Names in -*row* are comparatively late, and it is no matter

for surprise that three have a French first element, Budge Row, Curriers' Row, Paternoster Row.

Names in -*alley* and -*hill* are late and offer no interest here.

Several street-names not formed with a word for 'street' consist of or contain French words, as Barbican, (Old) Bailey, Bucklersbury, (Old) Change, Jewry (and Old Jewry), Petty Wales, Poultry, the old names of College Hill (*Riole*), and London Wall (*Babeloyne*). Most of these names are fairly late. Purely English names are in the majority.

IV. THE DISTRIBUTION OF NAMES WITH A PERSONAL NAME AS FIRST ELEMENT

It is a curious fact, and one not easily to be accounted for, that the greatest number of street-names with a font-name as first element are found in Farringdon Within: Alsies Lane, Cecile Lane, Gutter Lane, Kiron Lane (Carey Lane, partly in Aldersgate), Pentecost Lane, perhaps Friday Street (partly in Bread Street), *Folkemares lane*. All are found in early records and will date from the 12th or early 13th century, some farther back.

There are further in Farringdon Without Golden Lane, in Cripplegate Within Philip Lane, in Queenhithe Desborne Lane, in Vintry Kiron Lane, in Dowgate *Germayneslane*, *Wancelineslane*, and Wolsy Lane, in Bridge the late Stephen Lane, in Tower Craddock Lane and Mark Lane, perhaps *Sygrymeslane*. The majority are recorded early or fairly early. If Coleman Street was named from an early inhabitant, one more name is to be added to the list.

The distribution of street-names with a surname as first element is quite different and rather significant. The majority are found in the wards along the Thames.

In Castle Baynard there is Sermon Lane (t. Hy 3).

In Queenhithe are found: *Dibleslane*, Finamour Lane,

Fresshfisshlane (somewhat doubtful), *Hadestokeslane*, *Parkerislane*, *Pyellane*, Townsend Lane, Trig Lane. Only *Hadestokeslane* is recorded before 1300 (1297–8).

In Vintry the number of such names is considerable: Brickhill Lane, *Coventreslane*, *Cressynghamlane*, earlier *Palmerslane*,
Dorkynggeslane, *Fatteslane* (1259), *Hardeleslane*, later Stodies
Lane, *Pikardeslane* (1279), *Reygateslane*. Those for which a
date is not given appear first after 1300.

In Dowgate the number is much the same as in Vintry:
Armenterslane, later Weston Lane, *Arundellane*, *Batteslane*,
later Campion Lane, Cousin Lane (1305), Gofair Lane (1313),
Grantham Lane, Greenwich Street (1279–80, partly in Vintry),
Southam Lane, Suffolk Lane (late), Windgoose Lane (1279).

Billingsgate: Finch Lane, Philpot Lane, *Wirehalelane*.

Tower: *Pourteslane*, perhaps *Sygrymeslane*, Woodroffe Lane
(1260).

In the remaining wards examples are few.

Farringdon Within: Warwick Lane (doubtful). Aldersgate:
Pope Lane (t. Edw I), Little Britain (olim *Brettonestrete*;
partly Farringdon Without). Cripplegate Within: Gayspur
Lane. Cripplegate Without: ?Grub Street (early 13th). Bread
Street: Basing Lane (1275; also Cordwainer). Cheap: Popkirtle Lane (1275), Sevehod Lane. Broad Street: Finch Lane
(1231–45; also Cornhill). Portsoken: Weyland Lane (first
mentioned 1421, but evidently a good deal older).

The persons from whom the lanes were named will have
been local owners of property. Some lanes may have been
named after a family, several members of which were residents
there. Basing Lane is probably an example in point. It is not
necessary to assume that the whole of a lane named from a person was owned by him or her. The most prominent inhabitant
or one who had a house at the head of the lane may have had
his name attached to it. An illustrative instance is that quoted

under *Parkerislane*, which is referred to as the lane by the house formerly belonging to John Parker. But no doubt many lanes were the property of one particular person. Simon Frank, probably a copper-beater, by his will of 1332 left to his daughter his whole lane, containing about twenty shops on either side, in tail (CW i. 374). The testator was a taxpayer in Coleman Street ward in 1319 (Subs). It is surprising that his tax was only 40*d*. There is nothing to indicate that the lane was ever called *Frankeslane*, but whatever its name he was the owner. Most of the lanes with names derived from that of a person in Queenhithe, Vintry, and Dowgate were short lanes leading from Thames Street to the Thames, which would in many cases be owned by a wealthy merchant, a fishmonger, draper, corder, vintner, or the like. Such lanes would be apt to change their names with a fresh owner. The lanes in other wards are generally longer and would not so often be the property of one person, and we have to reckon with the probability that they were named from some prominent owner of land there. Names such as Gutter Lane, Finch Lane, Pentecost Lane may be cases in point.

V. THE DEFINITE ARTICLE IN STREET-NAMES

In early Latin records the definite article is practically always French *le, la*.

Names in -*street* only rarely have the article. It is then curious that names in -*street* found in Cripplegate Without, apart from the unique example of *Bechestrete* (a variant of Beech Lane), have the article, at least occasionally. Fore Street and Moor Street have the article regularly in the 14th century. Red Cross Street appears sometimes with the article, e.g. 1318, 1329, 1331. Only one example each of the article before White Cross Street and Grub Street has been found (*la White-crouchestret* 1359 CW ii. 73, *le Grubbestrete* 1331 CW i. 376).

Moor Street, Red Cross Street, and White Cross Street are derived from names that had the article themselves, the Moor, the Red and the White Cross. The only other name in *-street* that frequently has the article is Tower Street, named from the Tower. Examples are numerous from 1287 till about 1350. Thames Street has not been found with the article, but river-names in Middle English did not as a rule have the article.

An isolated instance of *le olde fysshe strete* has been found in 1486 (BM i. 479). Some occasional formations with *-street* added show the article, as *la Barbycanstret* 1377, *le Crouched-frerestrete* 1405 (from *the Barbican, the Crouchedfreres*).

Names in *-lane* somewhat more often show the article. While names in *-street* with an adjective as first element, as Broad Street, *Neustrate*, an old name of Chancery Lane, never have the article, names in *-lane* containing an adjective often have it, thus *le Brodelane* 1335–75, Crooked Lane (*la Crokedelane* 1278 &c.), *le Derkelane* 1355, *la Newe lane* 1304 LBC 194 (in St. Martin Vintry). But *Fulelane* 1265 &c., Stinking Lane 1228 &c. without the article.

Occasional instances of the article have been found before Cousin Lane (once 1305–6), Love Lane (once 1357), Mede Lane (once 1317–18), *le Trinite lane* 1332.

The article is sometimes found before street-names derived from the name of a place or the like which had the article itself. Bow Lane (Vi) was originally *le* (*la*) *Bowe* (really meaning 'the arched bridge'), found 1307 &c. From this was formed Bow Lane, often *la Bowelane* 1317–54. Bush Lane, *Le Bussh(e)lane* 1445 f., is derived from a tavern called *le Busshe*. The alternative Moor Lane (used by the side of Moor Street) has the article in 1331 f. *Le Pillorye lane* is found in 1542. Beech Lane, though derived from a locality called *la Beche* in 1257, has only once been found with the article (1279 *RHT*).

Names in *-alley* often have the article, especially those

derived from inns or taverns, as *the Cok Alley* 1524–5 LP, *ye Panyer Ale* 1442, but also others, as *le Chirch Aley* (Cornh) 1455 (1458) CW ii. 536, *le Churchealey* (FarrI) 1486 Pat, *le Kyngesaleye* 1393, *þe Skaldynge aley* 1424.

Many street-names are derived from names of fortifications, districts, or the like which had the article in their original sense. Such names frequently have the article, sometimes quite late, as Barbican (1307 ff., though often not referring to the street), Old Bailey (article often quite late), Old Change (article still 17th century), Old Jewry (1328 &c.), Poor Jewry (1366), Poultry (1424 &c.), *la Rydye*, Tower Royal (often *la Ryole*), The Crouched Friars, The Minories.

Cheap is usually *Chepe*, for instance in Chaucer, Langland, Usk, but *the Chepe* in Lydgate, *le Chepe de Londoniis* 1377 LibCust 476. Cheapside often has the article, as *the Chepe Side* (*Syde*) 1479, 1511, *le Chepsyde* 1545 LP. Eastcheap is generally *Estchep*, but *le Estcheape* 1544 LP.

VI. CHANGES AND VARIATION OF NAMES

In early records occasional appellations are frequently found instead of the normal street-name. Sometimes an occasional name is derived from that of a church or other structure in the street. Thus Maiden Lane or Noble Street seems to be referred to as *vicus Sancti Johannis Zakariæ* 1241 LibAlb 102, Broad Street as St. Christopher's Street 1301 Mayors, Wood Street as *vicus de Crupelgate* 1281 Pat, while Bread Street is the street of All Hallows de *Bredestrete* 1407 CW ii. 378. Some names contain a shorter or longer description, as when Red Cross Street is referred to as a street leading to the Red Cross 1279 CW i. 41, or Bishopsgate Street as the high street leading to *Bisopesgate* early 13th HMC, Wells MSS i. 16, or Tower Street as the highway leading to the Tower 1278 LBB 275, or Watling Street as the street leading from Walbrook to St. Paul's 1332 ADC 413. Poultry is called *vicus regis inter le Stockes et conduct'* (the Conduit in Cheap) 1345 LBF 123. *Vicus qui extendit se ab ecclesia sancti Michaelis in foro ad bladum uersus occidentem* 1236–41 PaulsCh 271 will be Paternoster Row. Miles's Lane is called alternatively the lane of St. Michael and the lane (*venella*) of Gilbert de Mordone 1325 Cor 115. Gilbert de Mordone, a stockfish-monger, is mentioned as a tenant here in the document.

In not a few cases the street or lane is referred to simply as 'the street', 'the highway', or the like, the identity of the street being indicated, often not very clearly, by the context. Examples need not be given. Some will be found on pp. 5 f.

In the case of long streets separate sections are not rarely referred to by special names or occasional appellations. It was not really an advantage, in a time when numbering of houses was unknown, if a long street was called by the same name for the whole of its length. Some names for special sections of streets seem to have been customary for a long period.

Thames Street was London's longest street, extending from Tower to Castle Baynard wards. It is referred to as 'the high-way from Castle Baynard as far as the Tower' 1277–8 LBA 218. The name Thames Street was applied to the whole length of the street, but there were several alternative names for sections of it. The part in Billingsgate ward is often called *Vicus de Billingesgate* or the like, for instance 1229 LibAlb 89, 1275 RH 430, 1292 CW i. 107, *Billingsgate Strete* 1539 LP, *Byllyngesgate Strete* 1549 Pat, the street called *Billingsgate* 1588 LIpm. A section in Bridge ward was known as Stockfish-monger Row (q.v.). Two sections in Dowgate ward are called respectively *Alhalwenestrete the litel under the lofte* 1379 Pat (in All Hallows the Less) and Roper Street (q.v.). The street called *la Vinetrie* 1344–5 Cl, *the Vyntre* 1550 LIpm and else-where has been identified with Thames Street or with College

Hill, but Thames Street must be meant, since *vicus regius . . .
le Vynetrie* is stated, 1409–10 Hansisches Urkundenbuch v, to
be the southern boundary of a piece of land. The highway
called *Quenehith* (*Queenhith*) 1546–7, 1585 LIpm must be
Thames Street in Queenhithe ward, since it was the northern
boundary of a piece of land in St. Michael (Qu). Harben's suggestion that it is identical with the present street called Queenhithe, which runs from Upper Thames Street to Queenhithe
Dock, cannot well be correct.

The northern part of Cordwainer Street was known as
Hosier Lane *c.* 1350–*c.* 1530, later as Bow Lane.

Part of Ludgate Street was called Bowyer Row.

The eastern part of Watling Street came to be called Budge
Row about 1350.

Newgate Street is recorded under its present name from
1617. Before that year various names or appellations are found,
but no definite English name can be proved to have been used
in medieval times. Harben says that at least the western part
was St. Nicholas Shambles Lane, but that is probably not correct. *Via regia . . . a porta de Newgate . . . per murum civitatis
usque ad vicum Sancti Nicholai* 1275 RH 404 (429) must have
been a road from Newgate along the city wall; it had been
obstructed by the Friars Minors and does not exist now. *Vicus
Sancti Nicholai* must be a lane running south from the wall to
St. Nicholas Shambles. The same lane is no doubt referred to
as the street leading from St. Nicholas' church to the city wall
1196 ADA 2507. Newgate Street would have been called the
street leading to Newgate. The lane of St. Nicholas Shambles,
venella sancti Nicholai de Macellis (or *juxta Macellum*) is
mentioned also 1275, 1306 CW i. 25, 178, 1285 f. MonFranc i.
501 f. To judge by the map in Stow, St. Nicholas Shambles
church was not in Newgate Street, but some way north of it.

Probable or possible early names of Newgate Street are the

following: *vicus regius versus Newgate* (*ubi carnifices vendunt carnes suos*) 1275 RH 404, *vicus regius juxta Newgate* 1317 MonFranc i. 506, the road on the north of St. Michael at Corn 1305 Mayors 220, the High Street opposite the church of St. Michael *atte Corne* 1337 Cor, *Vicus Carnificum Occidentalium in Parochia Sancti Nicholai* 1324 LibCust 276, the West Street of the butchers in St. Nicholas 1324 Pat, the *Bocherie* in the parish of St. Nicholas 1349 CW i. 576, *le Bocherye* in St. Nicholas Flesshammes 1409 LBI 82, *altus vicus in macellis* 1394 Pat, (the Ball) *yn þe Shameles* 1425–6 LoEngl 190, street called *le Fleshambles* 1530 LP. See also pp. 91 f. It is somewhat difficult to believe that Newgate Street, or at least its western portion, was really known for centuries as the Shambles or the Fleshshambles, but no other name has sufficient authority. The examples of 1321 ff. may indicate that a name meaning 'Butcher Street' was used, but the exact form of the name is unknown.

In the light of what has just been said it is easy to understand that changes of names would be apt to take place. Some examples of partial changes of street-names have already been given, cases like Bow Lane for the north part of Cordwainer Street &c. In the following survey we mainly consider early changes, that is such as took place before 1500. The rise of names in -*hill*, which have to a great extent replaced earlier names, will not be gone into here. Only a selection of examples will be discussed.

A complicated early case is Old Fish Street. The original Old Fish Street was apparently part of Cheap and is referred to from *c.* 1130 till 1286. But in the 12th century the fish-market appears to have been moved farther south to Knight-rider Street, the middle part of which was for some time called Fish Street or New (or West) Fish Street, but later the name Old Fish Street was transferred to it. Eventually the name

Knightrider Street was restored to the middle part of the street.

Bridge Street was so called from London Bridge, and it is really remarkable that this name was given up. It is found used from *c.* 1200 till the 16th century. The new name Fish Street, later supplanted by Fish Street Hill, is recorded from the early 14th century, and it may have arisen in the 13th century. The new name was of course due to there being a fish-market in Bridge Street. The two names were used side by side, and it looks as if Fish Street was the colloquial name, which is found used by Chaucer and Shakespeare, while Bridge Street was a traditional official name preferred by lawyers and scriveners. The fact that St. Margaret Fish Street Hill retained its early name St. Margaret Bridge Street till the 16th century may have helped to preserve the old name.

Watling Street till about the year 1300 was called *Athelinge-strete* (*c.* 1213–1303). The change is probably due to a mistaken identification of the old name of the street with that of the famous Roman road called Watling Street. The change may be looked upon as a case of popular etymology.

The present College Hill is referred to as *vicus de Pater-nosterchirch* or *Paternosterstret(e)* 1232–1334. Since there was another street called Paternoster Street, the later Paternoster Row, it is easy to understand why a new name came to be preferred. This new name was taken from a tenement in the street (*la Ryole*) and is found from 1331.

The Old Jewry, known by this name from about 1325, was earlier called Colechurch Street or Lane (1246 ff.) from the church of St. Mary Colechurch, sometimes *Sakfrerelane* (1310) from a settlement of Friars of the Sack in the street. It is not clear why the name Old Jewry, which denoted a large district, came to be restricted to the street.

The change of Langbourn (or earlier Langbord) Street to

Lombard Street is explained by Lombards having settled in the street, but the new name may possibly to some extent be looked upon as a modification of the old.

The cases so far noticed are mostly names in *-street*. These are comparatively seldom subjected to change. Far more often names of smaller roads, lanes, show changes. Often a whole series of successive names is evidenced.

Names derived from personal names are particularly liable to change; on this point see also pp. 23 ff. First a few names containing font-names.

Alsies Lane (12th) is replaced by *Folkemares lane* (t. Hy 3, 1285) and this by Ivy Lane (t. Hy 3 &c.); Cecile Lane (*c.* 1200 ff.) by Dicer Lane (1275–1424), varying with *la Rydye*, and eventually by Rose Street. *Wancelineslane* (1235–41) is superseded by *Germayneslane* (1313) and this by *Batteslane* (1311 ff.), later by Haywharf Lane (1328 ff.) and eventually by Campion Lane.

Next follow a few names with a surname as first element.

Armenterslane (1343 &c.) is replaced by Weston Lane (1357 ff.) and the latter by Coldharbour Lane (1461 ff.). *Hardeleslane* (1352 ff.) superseded earlier Spittle Lane and was itself replaced by Stodies Lane (1394 ff.) and Little Cheapside. *Palmereslane* (1343 ff.) was replaced by *Cressynghamlane* (1432 ff.); Weyland Lane (1421) by Pillory Lane (1421).

Some further instances may be added.

Baremanelane (1285) appears to denote the lane later called Bearbinder Lane (1338 ff.). Roper Lane (1313 ff.) is replaced by Love Lane (1394 ff.). *Haggenelane* (1202–79) is the later St. Benet's Lane (1341 Cl &c.). New Street (*nouus vicus*) in FarrE (1185 ff.) is later *Converslane* (1253–1338), still later Chancellor Lane (1338 ff.) and finally Chancery Lane (1454). In this case the reasons for the changes are evident. Old Dean's Lane (1257–1513) is replaced by Warwick Lane (1475).

Many more examples might be added, and the number would be considerably increased if still later changes were included. Some changes were no doubt called forth by the Great Fire of 1666, but on the whole old street-names survived that catastrophe surprisingly well. Prince's Street and Queen Street are examples of newly built streets with names dating from the period of reconstruction.

There are many cases of two different names being used side by side in the same period. It is true this variation is to some extent only apparent. Stow, who was intimately familiar with the old names of London streets, sometimes refers to obsolete old street-names as if they had been current in his time. In wills old names sometimes live on, at least as aliases, long after they had ceased to be generally used. Now and then an alternative name is stated to be obsolete, as when Love Lane (Bill) is stated to have been formerly *Ropereslane* in 1394 and 1455, or *Sporyerslane* is given as the old name of Water Lane in 1459. In some other cases where two alternative names are given in the same document, as *Batteslane* and *Heywharfe Lane* in 1508-9, *Pylorylane* and *Weylandeslane* in 1421, it is probable that one of the alternative names was really obsolete, though it was remembered because found in some early will or other document familiar to the clerk who drew up the deed.

The use of two different names for a short period must have been common. If a street changed its name it is improbable that as a rule the old name was disused and the new one arose simultaneously. In general the two names will have been used side by side for a shorter or longer period, till the new one definitely carried the day. Very likely the older generation often preferred the old name that younger people had abandoned.

But there are cases where two names must actually have been used alternatively for some considerable time. On Bridge Street and its variant (New) Fish Street see p. 31. These two names were used side by side for at least a couple of centuries. College Street was at first *Bowe* (1275–1318), later Bow Lane (1327–*c.* 1550) or Elbow Lane (1343–19th cent.). By the side of this series of names appears the name Paternoster Lane, found from 1300 till *c.* 1600. *Bowe* was originally the name of a bridge over the Walbrook, which was near the middle of the lane. The other name was taken from St. Michael Paternoster Royal at its western end. One would have supposed that the name Bow Lane was restricted to the eastern half of the lane, the other name to its western part, but this is not the case. There are instances of Bow Lane referring to all the sections of the lane, and the same is true of Paternoster Lane. The only difference seems to be that Bow Lane is more frequently evidenced. The two names were kept alive by their association with the arched bridge and the church of St. Michael.

There is a good deal of competition between the names Rother Lane (and its variants) and Pudding Lane. The first name-type, derived from a water-gate called *Retheresgate*, is the older, being recorded from *c.* 1280 till about 1500 or later. Pudding Lane is first found in 1360 and is still in use. The two names are not rarely given as equivalents in documents, for instance 1372–3 CW ii. 153, 1477 BM. They must have been used side by side for a couple of centuries. The old name was kept from oblivion by its association with the water-gate.

The earliest known name of Little Cheapside was *Spiteleslane* (1343–1422); this name is used in Plea Rolls of 1421 f., a trustworthy source. Another name, taken from an early owner, was *Hardeleslane*, found 1352, 1431. The two names must have been in contemporary use from *c.* 1350 till *c.* 1430.

Batteslane, a name taken from an early owner, is recorded from 1311 till *c.* 1500. The lane is also called Haywharf Lane, a name derived from a wharf and found from 1328 till the late

17th century and the usual name from about 1350. *Batteslane* was apparently a rare variant.

The present Rose Street in Farringdon Within, originally Cecile Lane, is usually *Dicereslane* and the like from about 1275 till about 1425 or later. But in two instances, one of the time of Richard II or later, one of 1423, the lane is stated to be otherwise called *la Rydye* or *le Redye*. An earlier instance of the latter name is very likely the surname *atte Rydye* of 1319. The lane is quite short. The later name is from OE *ripig* 'a stream' and would seem to indicate that there was a stream (or a ditch?) by the lane, whence the alternative name, which seems to have been in use for a considerable time.

VII. CHRONOLOGY OF STREET-NAMES

It is to be regretted that so few Old English sources for London are extant. The main system of streets in the City will have developed in pre-Conquest times,[1] but no London street-name now in use is recorded in Old English sources, and no London street-name in its English form is found so early. Very few London place-names of any description are recorded before the Norman Conquest. A list and a brief discussion of these early names will be useful.

London Bridge is *Lundene brigc* 10th (*c.* 1200) BCS 1131.

London port is *portus Lundoniæ* 734 (*c.* 840) BCS 152, *lundentunes hyð* 743–5 (11th) ib. 171. It is possible that Queenhithe is meant, but the term may be used more generally and refer to various quays and wharves.

Queenhithe is *Æðeredes hyd* 898 (13th) BCS 577. According to Page, *London*, pp. 130 f., the harbour was named from

[1] Cf. Page, *London*, p. 269: The growth of the London streets and lanes was gradual, but the general plan, with the exception of a few well-known alterations, had, there can be little doubt, acquired its present form before the Conquest.

Ethelred, Alderman of Mercia. This is very likely, but the suggestion that Ethelred built the harbour is open to doubt.

Five city gates are mentioned, three with their later names, two with earlier, now obsolete names. There is first (from) *Uuestgetum* 857 BCS 492, generally supposed to be Newgate. The plural form possibly indicates that the two western gates of Newgate and Ludgate are meant, but may also be explained from the fact that Newgate consisted of a double gateway between two flanking towers (Page, op. cit., p. 13). *Æst geat* 'Eastern gate' (Aldgate) is mentioned 1052 (*c.* 1120) ASC MS E. Billingsgate, Cripplegate, and Aldersgate appear as *Billingesgate, Cripelesgate, Ealdredesgate* 991–1002 (*c.* 1114) Laws, Cripplegate as *Cripelesgata, Crepelesgate* 1068 (copy) EHR xi. 740 ff.

Several churches are mentioned. St. Paul's, St. Andrew Holborn, All Hallows Lombard Street, Gracechurch, one church of St. Peter, and St. Martin le Grand are recorded with their English names, while a few others are referred to with latinized names.

St. Paul's is often referred to, in a Latin form as early as 678–81 BCS 55 ('Monasterium . . . quod dedicatum est in nomine Sancti Pauli Apostoli'), and *c.* 730 in Bede's Historia Ecclesiastica ii. 3 (*ecclesia sancti Pauli apostoli*). The English form varies a good deal, as *Sancte Paules kirke c.* 950 (14th), *Paules mynster, Paulusbyrig c.* 975 (11th) ASWills, *sanctus Paulus mynster* 1012 (*c.* 1120) ASC MS E.

St. Andrew Holborn is (ðære) *ealde stoccene sancte andreas cyriecan* 959 BCS 1048. The church is outside the city wall. The old church was built of wood.

St. Peter is mentioned in a will: (into) *sancte Petre binnon Lunden c.* 1035 (early 14th) ASWills (the will of Bishop Ælfric). There is some reason to suppose that St. Peter Cornhill is meant.

All Hallows Lombard Street is *alre haleȝene cheriche* and

Gracechurch, probably St. Benet Gracechurch, (æt) *Gerschereche* 1054 (14th) ASCh.

St. Martin le Grand: *Sancte Martines mynster* 1068 (copy) EHR xi. 742.

Some messuages (houses) or pieces of land in London are further mentioned.

The earliest is a town house (*haga*) called *Ceolmundingchaga* 857 (11th) BCS 492, described as 'gazifer agellulus in vico Lundonie'. An earlier owner is stated to have been Ceolmund præfectus, whence no doubt the name.[1] The place was near the western gate (Newgate).

Another name in *haga* is *Stæningahaga* 1053–65 ASWrits 98, on which see Staining Lane.

Hwætmundes stan is mentioned 889 (11th) BCS 561 in the following context: 'curtem que verbotenus adad antiquum petrosum ædificium id est æt Hwætmundes stane a civibus appellatur'. The Latin translation indicates that the 'court' was called *Hwætmundes stan* and that this name meant 'Hwætmund's stone house'. On such a meaning of *stān* see my *Dictionary of English Place-names* under Boston (Add. 1). *Hwætmund* is an otherwise unrecorded personal name. This Hwætmund is probably the first English London citizen known by name; *Ceolmund* in *Ceolmundingchaga* may have been a Mercian. Since profane stone houses built by Anglo-Saxons were probably rare in this early period, the stone house may well have been the ruin of an old Roman house. The property was of considerable extent, measuring 26 perches in length and 13 perches 7 feet in breadth at the upper end and 11 perches 6 feet at the lower, that is nearly 2 acres. It was given by King Alfred and Æthelred the Alderman to Werfrið, bishop, and the church of Worcester. It was situated between the public

---

[1] Cf. Karlström, *Old English Compound Place-Names in -ing*, p. 110.

street and the city wall, and the reference to 'ripa emtoralis' in connexion with the mercantile privileges mentioned in the sequel seems to indicate that it was near the Thames. It may have been near the property at Queenhithe given in 898 by King Alfred and Æthelred to the same Werfrið. One wonders if possibly the same land is referred to in the charters of 889 and 898. It is at any rate remarkable that the area involved seems to have been of the same extent in both charters. See further infra.

Wermanecher was the name of a property given by Edward the Confessor to the church of St. Peter of Ghent in 1044 (Thorpe 358). It may be that the property was included in the grant made by King Alfred to the church (see Page, *London*, pp. 132 ff.), but this must remain a guess. The name appears as *Waremanni-Acra* 1081, as *Wermanacra* 1103–9 Fr, as (soca de) *Waremanshaker* 1235 Mon vi. 624. Page thinks the soke of Warmansacre embraced the later Tower ward, but this can hardly be considered as proved, and the original place called Warman(s)acre was doubtless far smaller in extent, as indicated by the name, which must mean 'Wærmann's acre'. The place was doubtless near the Thames, since the original grant mentions a wharf as connected with it. The Old English personal name *Wærmann* is not well evidenced, but it is a regular formation. The meaning of *æcer* is probably 'field, arable land' rather than 'acre'.

Some London streets and lanes are actually referred to in Old English charters.

In the charter of 889 (the *Hwætmundes stan* charter) is mentioned *strata publica*, parallel to the city wall and probably to the Thames. Knightrider Street might be meant.

The charter of 898 referred to supra[1] (BCS 577) records

---

[1] The charter of 898, which occurs in two forms, both in MS Lambeth 1212 (at pp. 406 and 321), is held to be genuine by Page,

grants by King Alfred and Æthelred the Alderman of land in London to Archbishop Plegmund and Bishop Werfrið. The land is described as being near Queenhithe and containing two 'jugera' ('agri' BCS 578) situated between the lane running to the east (*semita tendente ad orientem*) and the city wall with stations of ships outside the wall. The two jugera were divided by 'via publica a flumine Tamis', the archbishop's land lying to the west, Bishop Werfrið's to the east. The western boundary of the two jugera was 'arta semita', the eastern being 'via arta'. Page thinks the land was of the width of the parish of St. Mary Somerset and in length from Knightrider Street to the river. A Roman jugerum is stated to have measured 240 by 120 feet, but in Anglo-Latin the word was often used as a synonym of *acre*. The land represented by the two 'jugera' was very likely about 2 acres.

Here four streets or lanes are mentioned. The northern boundary of the land (*semita tendens ad orientem*) might be, as suggested by Page, the later Knightrider Street, but a lane south of it might be meant. *Via publica a flumine Tamis* may have been on the line of the present Old Fish Street Hill. *Arta semita* and *via arta* mean 'the narrow lane (street)' and might represent real Old English street-names *Nearwelane* and *Nearwestræt*, but they may be simply descriptive. *Arta semita* will have been near the western end of Queenhithe ward (for instance Lambeth Hill). *Via arta* will have been near the present Bread Street Hill. In the often-quoted document giving a list of the lands of St. Paul's *c.* 1130 (PaulsMSS 66) occurs a street-name *strictus uicus*, which is synonymous with *via arta*. The street was probably in Bread Street ward and

but rejected as spurious by B. W. Kissan, LMAS, N.S. viii. 227. If the charter is not authentic, it is probable that it is an old fabrication founded on some genuine document(s). It is difficult to believe that the detailed boundaries are inventions by a late forger, but they may conceivably be of a somewhat later date than 898.

ran south from Cheap. The only streets to be thought of, so far as known, are Bread Street and Friday Street. Bread Street is nowadays remarkably narrow for a street. Bread Street Hill was doubtless called Bread Street in medieval times. It would be very interesting if we could trace Bread Street (or Friday Street) back through *strictus uicus* of *c.* 1130 to *via arta* of 898.

A charter purporting to have been issued in 1067, but generally held to be a forgery of the time of Henry I (1100–35), is preserved in various transcripts, one printed in full in the original Latin in a Charter Roll of 1335. Here are mentioned several contemporary Londoners and also a few London places, among them *Westceap*, *Baermannecyrce*, and *Duuegate*. The name-forms may well be trustworthy.

Few street-names are recorded in Old English charters referring to other cities than London, but some streets and lanes in Canterbury, Rochester, and Winchester are referred to, and a number of street-names in these cities are mentioned in Old English records.

Canterbury charters mentioning streets or even street-names are BCS 4 f., 192, 373, 426, 519.

BCS 4, dated 605, but preserved in a copy of about 1400, mentions *via of* (var. *oþ*) *Burhgate* and *Drutingstræt* (var. *Drutingestræte, Drutinge*), both in connexion with a grant of land by King Æthelbert to the Abbey of St. Peter and St. Paul. BCS 5, preserved in the same MS, is really a variant of no. 4. Here *Drutingstræt* is also mentioned. *Via of Burhgate* is the present Burgate Street, and *Drutingstræt* probably Ruttington Lane (Wallenberg, *Kentish Place-names*, p. 4). There is no reason, so far as I know, to doubt the genuineness of the early charters in a general way, but it is not self-evident that the boundaries formed part of the original text. The lateness of the transcript at any rate renders it very doubtful if the street-names can be trusted to appear in their original form. If the street-names were in the original charters they are the oldest English street-names on record. But it would be rather remarkable if these names had really become customary so early as 605.

BCS 192 (A.D. 762, MS. *c.* 1400) only has *forum* (*in foro*).

BCS 373 (A.D. 823) has *publica strato* (sic), BCS 426 (A.D. 839) *publica strata*.

BCS 519 (A.D. 868) mentions *wistræt* (*an ðara wistræte*), which means 'the street leading to Wye' (Wallenberg, op. cit., p. 221). The name is not evidenced elsewhere.

Vicus qui dicitur curringtun (on the north side of the market) 786 BCS 248 is probably not a case in point. *Vicus* will mean 'messuage' not 'street' here.

In Rochester charters (BCS 3, 502) there are only general terms such as *norðlane, stræt* 604 (12th) BCS 3, *sio ealdæ stret* 860 ib. 502.

Important and interesting information on early street-names in Winchester is found in Old English charters.

BCS 605[1] (A.D. 901–4, MS *c.* 1150) records a grant of land in Winchester towards the foundation of New Minster. The boundaries of the land are roughly: south to St. Gregory's church, west to *ðære strete*, north to *ðære norðstræte*, east to *ðære east strete*, south to *ðære suðstrete*, west along *ðære suðstrete*, then north. Miss Harmer suggests that *norðstræt* is the main street, which runs east and west, while *eaststræt* may possibly be Colebrook Street. To me it looks more probable that *stræt* is the main street, the later *Magnus Vicus* (1148 LibWint). It is doubtful if *norðstræt* &c. were really street-names; they may have been descriptive.

BCS 630 (A.D. 909) gives the boundaries of a town house (*haga*). It was situated on *þa ceap stræt* (*þære ceap stræte*). The same street is called *cypstræt* 996 (*c.* 1150) Earle, p. 364. The name means 'the market street' and will be the main street just referred to. This need not have been a full-fledged street-name.

Two real street-names are mentioned in the document of 996 just quoted: *flæs[c]mangere* (*flæscmangara*) *stræt* and *scyld-wyrhtana stræt*. The two joined each other, and *flæscmangara*

---

[1] Also in *Select English Historical Documents of the Ninth and Tenth Centuries*, ed. F. E. Harmer (Cambridge, 1914), pp. 27 f.

stræt ran out of *cypstræt*, which itself ran east and west. Both
streets are recorded later. The first is *Flesmangerestret* early 12th
LibWint, *vicus Carnificum* 1322 EpWint. The latter is *Sild-
wortenestret* 1148 LibWint, *Shuldewrtenestret* 1258, *Showl-
worthstrete* 1556 Selborne ii. 78, 96. The two names mean
respectively 'the butchers' street' and 'the shield-makers' street'.

There is good reason to suppose that other street-names of a
similar type that are found in the Liber Wintoniensis are of the
same date as the two recorded in 996, namely *Scow(e)rtenestret*
'the shoemakers street' and *Tannerestrete* 'the tanners' street'.

At least two Winchester street-names lived on from the 10th
century till the 14th century or later.

For the identification of the streets see *Victoria History of
Hampshire*, i. 537.

It is clear that street-names can generally not be proved
definitely to be older than the date of the earliest reference to
them in trustworthy sources. But it is as a rule unlikely that a
new name of a street happened to be recorded immediately
after it arose, apart, of course, from late names given deliberately. Exceptions will not be numerous, and they will
hardly belong to an early period. A name recorded very
shortly after it came into being is Chancery Lane, or more correctly its earlier form Chancellor Lane, if the suggestion is correct that the name did not arise till the year 1337, when the
Bishop of Chichester became Chancellor and settled in his
hostel in the lane then called *Converslane*. The new name is
found as *Chauncelereslane* in 1338 and is commonly recorded in
1339 and the following years. It will hardly be possible to find
other examples of a new name being recorded so soon after it
first came to be used. In the present case we have to do with a
district often referred to in contemporary sources and a period
from which ample material is available.

Some street-names derived from persons can be dated fairly
exactly. Cecile Lane is often mentioned *c.* 1200 and later, and

Cecile de Turri, who gave the lane its name, must have been living about the same time, but all we can say is that the street-name came into being about 1200, say between *c.* 1190 and 1210. That is, of course, very satisfactory. Grantham Lane commemorates John de Grantham, who died in 1344. It is called *Granthameslane* in 1343, thus before John's death. The new name can hardly have arisen more than a couple of decades before 1343. A very similar case is Southam Lane, first mentioned in 1383, named from John Southam, whose will, dated 1382, was enrolled in 1394–5. *Palmerslane* in Vintry, first recorded in 1343, was doubtless so called from Henry le Palmer, who flourished *c.* 1319–52. Since he lived in Cheap ward in 1319, but had removed to Vintry by 1332, the name cannot well have arisen till some time after 1319.

Cases like those discussed are exceptional. There are many names for which the probable date can be determined with a fair amount of accuracy, but as a rule the earliest instance is a good deal later. In these cases we have chiefly to do with street-names derived from persons. A few examples will suffice.

Pentecost Lane, first recorded in 1280, will commemorate a Pentecost who held land in the district about 1210. The new name can hardly have arisen long after 1210. *Armenterslane*, first recorded in 1343, got its name from John de Armenters, whose will was enrolled in 1306, but who is first mentioned already in 1275. The name can hardly be later than about 1306, but may well be older. Weyland Lane, first found in 1421, must have been named from Thomas de Weyland, a judge, who was banished in 1290, his estates being seized. The name cannot well have arisen later than about 1290. *Germayneslane* (recorded in 1313) was named from German le Cordier, mentioned in 1241 as an earlier tenant in the lane. A still earlier name of the lane was *Wancelineslane*, recorded in

1235. German will have flourished almost a century before the first mention of the name *Germayneslane*.

Some street-names containing a surname cannot be dated very accurately, because persons with the same surname belonging to different generations may have been resident in the street or lane. Thus Finch Lane, first recorded 1231–45, may have been named from Ailwin Fink, who flourished between *c.* 1165 and 1190, or from James Finke, who is mentioned as an earlier tenant in 1231–45. Basing Lane, first recorded in 1275, took its name from the Basing family, but this was an old London family, successive members of which may have been resident there. Cousin Lane (1305–6 &c.) commemorates the Cousin family, but it is not clear when members of it took up their residence there. Gofair Lane (1313 &c.) may have been named from Roger Gofayre, mentioned in 1275, or from Elias Gofaire, whose will was enrolled in 1309–10; Trig Lane (1422 &c.) from William Trig, who flourished *c.* 1319–45, or from John or Andrew Tryg, mentioned in the late 14th century.

For names not derived from a person whose lifetime can be to some extent dated we often have only the first appearance in sources to go on. But we have just seen that many names must have been in existence for a century or more at the time of their first appearance, as *Armenterslane*, *Germayneslane*, *Weylandeslane*. We must always reckon with the probability that street-names are a good deal older than the earliest reference indicates.

As regards the *terminus post quem* for street-names there are some criteria, which may be touched upon here. A name that contains a French element must be later than the Norman Conquest, as Cordwainer Street (1216–17), Paternoster Street (1232), Tower Street (1259), Old Dean's Lane (1257), Coney-hope Lane (1292). See further chapter III. In some cases other historical facts afford a clue. Thus Old Change (1293–4) cannot have come into use till after the Exchange had been removed from the street, which no doubt took place in the 13th century. Old Jewry (1327) must be later than the expulsion of the Jews in 1290, since *Old* in this name as in Old Change means 'former, late'. *Converslane* (1253) is later than 1231, the year in which the House of Converts was founded. *Sakfrere-lane* (1310) postdates the advent of the Friars of the Sack (second half of the 13th century).

Some streets, to judge by their names, must have been built at a comparatively late date, as those called New Street (or *novus vicus*) in early records. See under Chancery Lane, Needlers Lane, Soper Lane.

Of particular interest are names found at a comparatively early date, say before about 1275 or 1280. Names such as Cheap or Cornhill, which did not originally denote streets, are disregarded here. The number of street-names recorded in the period indicated is considerable. Out of about 45 early names in *-street* 35 are found before 1280, 16 before 1200 or *c.* 1200, 10 between *c.* 1200 and 1250. Out of about 150 early names in *-lane* 62 are recorded before 1280, 14 before 1200 or *c.* 1200, 19 between *c.* 1200 and 1250, 29 between 1250 and 1280. This may seem to indicate that names in *-street* on the whole belong to an earlier stratum than those in *-lane*, but the greater percentage of early names in *-street* may be due to special circumstances. Roads with names in *-street* were in general more important than the lanes and more likely therefore to appear in early documents. Further names in *-street* are frequently found attached to names of parishes, as St. Alban Wood Street, while names in *-lane* are only rarely so used. These parish-names sometimes afford very early examples of names in *-street*. Thus the only 12th-century forms of Broad Street, Cannon Street, Monkwell Street are found in such parish names. Not one parish name with a name in -*lane* attached to it is recorded at that early date.

Very likely some street-names found so late as the 13th or 14th century belong to an early stratum, though in most cases it is impossible to find conclusive arguments in favour of a 12th-century or earlier date. But sometimes there are circumstances that suggest an early date. Knightrider Street is a peculiar case. In the 14th and 15th centuries two separate sections of a long thoroughfare had that name, recorded from 1322, in a shorter form possibly from 1298. A middle section in the 13th century and later was known as Old Fish Street, but is now Knightrider Street. It is probable and generally assumed, that the middle section was originally Knightrider Street like the other sections. If that is right, the conclusion seems warranted that the name Knightrider Street goes back to the 12th or early 13th century.

Broad Street is normally *Brad(e)strate* and the like from about 1200 till the 16th century. The shortening of the originally long *ā* of the first syllable must have taken place before OE *ā* had become ME *o* or developed to a sound near it. This shortening can hardly have been later than the early 12th century.

Street-names containing font-names of English origin probably belong to an early stratum, at least the 12th or early 13th century, since most English font-names went out of use early. Some such street-names first appear comparatively late, as Desborne Lane (1253), Golden Lane (1291–2), Wolsy Lane (1307). A name such as Ing Lane (*Englenelane* 1282) gives the impression of being an early name.

The question may be discussed here why so few street-names are recorded before the year 1200, though the probability is that some street-names in London go back to pre-Conquest or early post-Conquest date. The absence of Old

English examples of such names is accounted for by the scarcity of records. But from the 12th century considerable material is preserved. The manuscripts and charters of St. Paul's contain numerous early charters and other records, and a wealth of early deeds, especially relating to Christchurch Priory in London, are summarized in Ancient Deeds. Several 12th-century charters are found in the Clerkenwell Cartulary. But 12th-century charters only rarely give names of streets. They are generally short, and the situation of land or tenements is mostly indicated by mention of the parish or the like. Often a street is referred to only in general terms, such as 'the king's highway' or the like, its identity being indicated by the context. Many streets are thus mentioned without the name. The important early deeds found in PaulsMSS, pp. 60–68, are a disappointment to the student of City street-names. In the document of *c.* 1130 (PaulsMSS 66) indicating the measurements of the lands of St. Paul's, a few street-names are mentioned, but they are all given in Latin translation (*uicus judeorum, uicus piscarius, uicus fori, strictus uicus.* Other early deeds in the collection mentioned give a few London place-names, but not all of them names of streets (e.g. *Cornhilla* 1115, *forum rerum venalium* or *forum* for Cheap t. Hy 1). It is sometimes due to mere chance that an early example of a street-name has survived. The earliest instance of Fleet Street in Harben dates from 1274. There is an example in a Patent Roll of 1270, but also *vicus de Flete* in a Salisbury charter of *c.* 1188, which shows that the name goes back at least to the 12th century. Birchin Lane is well evidenced from 1260 on, but the only earlier example of the name is found in an original charter of *c.* 1193–5.

The problem then arises to what extent we are permitted to reckon with London street-names having come down from the Old English period. A definite answer to this question cannot be given, but some suggestions may be offered.

Names recorded at the very beginning of the 12th century may generally be supposed to have survived from Old English time. Cheap (or Westcheap) and Eastcheap are recorded very early in the century and are doubtless Old English survivals. The form *Westceap* in a forged late Old English charter (really of the early 12th century) looks as if it had been taken from a genuine Old English document. Aldermanbury and Cornhill are both found in the second decade of the 12th century and are in all probability of Old English origin. Old Fish Street is found *c.* 1130 and is doubtless an ancient name.

Special circumstances point to an early date for Birchin Lane and Cannon Street, though not found till the later 12th century. Both have as first element occupational terms (OE *beard-ceorfere* 'barber' and *candelwyrhta* 'chandler'), which are unrecorded in Middle English and probably went out of use very early. As a matter of fact neither word is recorded in Old English either. Both street-names are probably of Old English origin.

The names containing OE *æðeling* 'prince' very likely go back to the Old English period, though Addle Street is first found in 1244 and the old name of Watling Street (*Athelinge-strete*) *c.* 1213.

Attention has been drawn to the fact that names such as Milk Street, Honey Lane, that is names with a word denoting a commodity produced or offered for sale in the street as first element, are particularly common on both sides of Cheap. Here belong (the original) Old Fish Street, which has been shown to be a very ancient name, and probably of pre-Conquest origin, further Bread Street (*c.* 1150–79), Milk Street (*c.* 1140), Wood Street (1156–7), Distaff Lane (12th), Honey Lane (*c.* 1200). It may be suggested that these names and also some belonging to the same type but found in other parts of the City, as Lime Street (1170–87), Chicken Lane (*c.* 1185), Cock

Lane (*c.* 1200), form a chronological group and are relics of an Old English system of streets where names of this type were a characteristic feature. It is at any rate very probable that for instance Bread Street, Milk Street, and Wood Street are Old English names.

VIII. STREET-NAMES AND EARLY LONDON HISTORY

Not a few street-names give information on early London.

Some contain allusions to the nature and condition of road-ways, as comparative width or the like, as Broad Street, *Smalelane*; *Fulelane*, Stinking Lane; Addle Street (CripI). These names are often uncomplimentary.

Of considerable interest are street-names which offer information on the localization of early trades and trades-people. On street-names indicating a product or article for sale in the street see pp. 72 ff, 104 ff. Many of these are evidenced early and very likely to some extent go back to Old English times, as Bread Street, Wood Street, Old Fish Street, Distaff Lane. But names of a similar kind also arose in later periods, as Lad Lane (recorded *c.* 1300), Bladder Street and Giltspur Street (found in the 16th century). To this group may belong two names with a French first element, *Viterilane* (1294 &c.) and Budge Row (1342 &c.).

In connexion with these may be discussed names such as have an occupational term as first element, Cordwainer Street and the like. These names prove that people following the trades indicated by them formed a considerable proportion of the inhabitants of the streets at the time when the street-names were formed. The names tell us nothing about the population in a later period. It is therefore important to try as far as possible to establish the dates of these street-names.

Few names in *-street* belong to this group. There is first

Cannon Street 'the street of the chandlers', which is found early and very likely of Old English date. Had the name arisen in the 12th century, Chandler Street would have been a more probable name. Cordwainer Street, like Cannon Street, was an important road, which gave its name to a ward; the name probably arose in the 12th century. Roper Street (*c.* 1270 &c.) was only an alternative name of Thames Street; it may well have come into use about the middle of the 13th century. Paternoster Street (1265 &c.), the old name of College Hill, was really named from Paternosterchurch (St. Michael Pater Noster Royal) and need not indicate that paternosterers were numerous in the street itself. *Rennerstrete* (late) and Knightrider Street are difficult to judge; it is doubtful if the first element is really occupational.

More numerous are names in *-lane* belonging to this category. Ancient names, partly very likely Old English ones, are Birchin Lane, Ironmonger Lane, *Huettawiereslane*. Soper Lane is probably a 13th-century name. Later evidenced and very likely of later origin are Billiter Street (olim B. Lane), Carter Lane, Crocker Lane, Hosier Lane (FarrE), Limeburners' Lane, Roper Lane, Spurrier Lane, all recorded about 1300. Sporon Lane (*Sporones lane* 1268–9) is very likely a modification of earlier *Spurierelane* (with AF *esperoner* for English *spuriere*). Hosier Lane (Cordw) has supplanted earlier Cordwainer Street. Needlers Lane was probably at an earlier date called *Newstrate*. The last-mentioned two names probably arose in the 14th century. The remaining names in this group are more or less doubtful.

Most names in *-row* belong here. They are all comparatively late, and some are alternative names of sections of old streets. Names in *-row* may generally be supposed to give information about the trades followed in the streets about the time when the names are first recorded.

Street-names giving information on agriculture and farming in early London

Agricultural pursuits were frequently carried on in early urban communities, which in many cases had grown out of a country village. 'There was an agricultural element in all medieval towns', Salzmann remarks, *English Life in the Middle Ages*, p. 72. He points out that important and ancient towns like Coventry or Leicester were practically surrounded by three great 'open fields' and that the burgesses of Norwich and Oxford insisted on their pasturage rights, which the freemen of Oxford retain to this day.

In the ancient south Swedish, originally Danish, city where this is written, Lund, agriculture played an important role till not so very long ago. A map of 1704 shows the city surrounded by its open fields and meadows, which were many times more extensive than the town within the walls. The burgesses who held land in the various fields are enumerated. It is stated that corn was grown in these fields and that the meadows yielded sufficient pasture for the cattle during summer time. It must be supposed that the cattle were kept in the town itself, at least during the cold season.

There are two important direct statements concerning agriculture in early London. The first dates from 896 and is found in the Anglo-Saxon Chronicle (Parker MS) and relates that in the autumn of this year King Alfred encamped near London while the citizens reaped their corn, so that the Danes might not prevent them from the harvest.[1] Page, *London*, p. 41, renders the passage somewhat freely thus: 'that the people might harvest the crops of corn, vegetables and other food

[1] The passage in the Chronicle runs thus: 'þa þæs on hærfæste þa wicode se cyng on neaweste þare byrig, þa hwile þe hie hira corn gerypon, þæt þa Deniscan him ne mehton þes ripes forwiernan'. ASC (A) 896.

raised on the lands dependent upon the city.' The Chronicle
only mentions corn, and there is no reason to take vegetables
and the like to be included. There were plenty of gardens within the walls where vegetables could be grown. The passage
quoted shows that the Londoners about 900 must have grown
their own corn and that they may even have been self-support-
ing as regards corn; further that their arable was at least in the
main outside the city wall. No doubt the suburbs, the later
Farringdon, Aldersgate, Cripplegate, Bishopsgate wards without the walls and Portsoken ward, represented the cornlands
of early London, though it is possible that some parts beyond
the suburbs provided corn for London.

The other statement is found in William FitzStephen's
Description of London in the 12th century, held to have been
written in 1174 (Kingsford, p. 387). The section with the head-
ing *De Pascuis et Sationalibus* among other things contains
these passages, which are important for our purpose: 'On the
north side are fields for pasture, and open meadows, very
pleasant; among which the river waters do flow. . . . The arable
lands are no hungry pieces of gravel ground; but like the rich
fields of Asia, which bring plentiful corn, and fill the barns of
those that till them with a dainty crop of the fruits of Ceres.'[1]
There follows an account of wells about London, among which
are mentioned Holywell, Clerkenwell, and St. Clement's well,
which were outside the City boundaries, even outside the
suburbs. The pastures to the north may well have been partly

[1] The passage runs as follows in the original Latin: 'Item, a Borea
sunt agri pascui, et pratorum grata planities, aquis fluuialibus inter-
fluis. . . . Agri vrbis sationales non sunt ieiunæ glareæ, sed pingues
Asiæ campi, qui "faciant lætas segetes"; et suorum cultorum repleant
horrea "Cerealis mergite culmi".' Quoted from Stow ii. 220; translation from Strype's edition of Stow given by Heuser, *Alt-London*,
pp. 11 ff. A more modern translation is found in Stenton's *Norman
London*, p. 27, where the words *Agri vrbis . . . Asiæ campi* are rendered
thus: 'The corn-fields are not of barren gravel, but rich Asian plains.'

at some distance from the City, and so may the arable land. But it is very likely that in the middle of the 12th century the suburbs were still partly arable and pasture land. At any rate FitzStephen seems to imply that agriculture was still to no small extent carried on by London people.

There is a third statement which has often been quoted, namely the regulation that the sessions of the Husting of London were suspended for one month during harvest-time (Liber Albus i. 321). So far as I know, there is nothing to show when this regulation came into force, but one would suppose that it was a relic from an early period. There was a similar suspension of the sessions of the Husting for one month after the feast of St. Botolph (17 June), the reason given being that citizens had to be present at Boston Fair and were prevented from attending to business at the Court. This regulation was not cancelled till 1416 and was in force long after the fair had lost its importance.[1] Similarly the suspension during harvest-time may have remained in force after the need for it had ceased. The arable land we may suppose to have been mainly in the suburbs, but many wealthy London citizens had land in the counties surrounding London, Middlesex, Bucks, Essex, Kent, Surrey, and it may be it was partly the harvests in these country estates that needed the presence of the owner.

The testimonies to London agriculture discussed refer to the area outside the city wall, the suburbs. There is no unequivocal and direct reference to such pursuits within the wall. Yet some writers are of opinion that even the interior parts of London were formerly to some extent arable or pasture land. Page, *London*, p. 128, holds that the centre of trade and traffic in early London was at the Bridge and in Eastcheap, and that the lands surrounding this area were still largely agricultural in the 10th century. On p. 270 the same author says that 'London of

[1] See CW i, p. ix.

the thirteenth century was much like a modern country town. Within was a good deal of open land, which, near the Walbrook in Coleman Street and Broad Street Wards, was probably pasture.'

It is not likely that agriculture played an important part in the life of London citizens generally in the 13th or 14th century or later. Within the walls there can hardly have been much arable land, but there may have been some in the suburbs. Animals were doubtless kept to no small extent even within the City, to judge by various notes in early records, and gardens were frequent. Page, op. cit., p. 270, points out that most houses had gardens and many larger houses had orchards and shrubberies. FitzStephen makes special mention of spacious gardens in the suburbs.

We come to street-names or other names which may contain allusions to agriculture or farming in early London.

A possible early case is *Warmanacre* (cf. p. 38), recorded from 1044 and possibly going still farther back. The name means '*Wærmann*'s acre' and *acre* may well refer to a tilled field. The place was somewhere in Tower ward.

Another early name is *Cornhill*, recorded from *c.* 1100. The name means 'corn hill', which may be 'hill where corn was grown'. See further on pp. 186 f. If this is right, it is probable that the name arose early in the Old English period. Even if, as Dr. Wheeler thinks,[1] some Roman houses were still standing on Cornhill at the time of the Saxon settlement in London, parts of the hill may have been open land in the later part of the Anglo-Saxon period.

Among names found later particular interest attaches to Seething Lane, recorded from about 1250, but very likely a good deal older. The name means 'lane where chaff was plentiful'. If, as suggested on p. 104, the chaff came from corn threshed

---

[1] *London and the Saxons*, pp. 98 ff.

and winnowed in the lane, the corn may be supposed to have come from fields outside the wall.

Oat Lane (Aldersg), first found in Stow, cannot well mean 'lane where oats were grown', more likely 'lane where oat-mongers lived'.

Not a few street-names tell us that domestic animals were kept in the City. It goes without saying that horses were common there, and no street-names referring to horses have been met with. Many street-names belonging here are found in Farringdon Without, and this part of the City may have remained partly rural for a long time.

A few street-names seem to testify to cattle (horned beasts) having been kept, but the meaning of these names is not in all cases quite clear.

Cow Lane (FarrE), found from 1416 on, means 'cow lane', but the exact sense may be rather 'lane along which cows were driven to or from pasture', than 'lane where cows were kept'. The name is common in old English towns, as in Coventry (1335), Nottingham (1296), Cambridge (1348).

Rother Lane is not a case in point; see p. 154.

Milk Street (CripI), found from *c.* 1140, is very likely an Old English name, which indicates that cows were kept and milk was produced in the street in Old English time.

Addle Street (CripI), olim *Addelane* (1304 &c.), may well have had the special meaning 'lane full of cow-dung' or the like. OE *adela* seems to have been used especially of stinking urine (OED). OSwed *ko-adel* means 'cow urine' and MLG *adel, eddel* 'liquid manure'. This is, of course, a doubtful case.

That pigs were frequent in early London, is a well-known fact. There are numerous regulations concerning pigs in the City. Thus an ordinance of 1277–8 (LBA 216) enjoined that places and lanes should be cleared of every impediment, as ladders, pigsties, &c., and 'that no pig be henceforth found by the streets or lanes of the City or suburb, nor in the ditches of the City; and if found they shall be killed by whoever finds them. . . . Whoever wishes to feed his pigs, let him feed them in the open (*in franco*) away from the King's highway [or] in his house, under heavy penalty.' See also Liber Albus i. 270, where the same regulation is given in French. This ordinance seems to have had no effect, for it was repeated in 1297 (Riley, *Mem.* 35) and later, for instance in 1388 (Riley, p. 509). In 1291–2 four persons were elected to take and kill such swine as were found wandering in the King's highway (LBC 5). In 1322 a baby one month old is reported to have been bitten in her cradle with fatal effect by a wandering sow (Cor 56 f.). The pigs were probably not kept by London people in their houses, as the regulation of 1277–8 may seem to imply, but in pigsties on the premises. But pigsties seem often to have been erected outside houses in the street. There was a complaint made against a citizen of Derby in 1276 (RH i. 61), who had built a pigsty in the King's highway 12 feet long and 6 feet broad, the encroachment having been made seven years earlier. The regulation that pigs were to be kept in the open (*in franco*) is not quite clear. Page, *London*, p. 270, suggests that pasturelands within the City may be meant.

Some London street-names are memorials of the custom of keeping pigs, the two Huggin Lanes (CripI and Queenh), both *Hoggenelane* in early records and first found in 1234–5 and 1329–30 respectively, also the later Hog Lane. The last was in Portsoken and Bishopsgate wards without the wall.

Several street-names testify to poultry having been kept. There are two lanes called Chick(en) Lane, one in Farringdon Without (found from the late 12th century), one in Tower (first recorded in 1235). Others are Duck Lane in Farringdon Without and Aldersgate (1410) and Goose Lane in Cordwainer (*c.* 1300). Cock Lane in Farringdon Without (found from *c.* 1200) probably means 'lane where cocks were reared', but the probability is that the cocks were fighting cocks.

Honey Lane in Cheap, found *c.* 1200, indicates that bees were formerly kept in the street.

Gardens are referred to by some early names.

Blanch Appleton was the name of a manor and district in Aldgate, north of Mark Lane. The first reference found is *Blanckesapeltuna* 1168–75 St. Benet of Holme 166, and not much later is *Blanchesapeltuna* 1177 ADA 7295 (belonging to the soke of Robert de Valoniis). Later examples are *Blaunchapelton* 1305 Mayors 217, 1326 Cor 161, 1349 CW i. 569, *Blanch apleton* (manor) Stow, *Blaunch Chappleton* 1628 (1636) CW ii. 758. According to Page, *London*, p. 152, it was a part of the soke of Weremansacre. Whatever the status of Blanch Appleton in later times, it is clear that the name contains OE *æppeltun* 'apple orchard' and that the place originated as an orchard, probably one of considerable extent. *Blanch* will be the name of an early owner, very likely a lady called Blanche.

Harbour Lane [Thames Street–the Thames] in St. Martin Vintry, perhaps identical with the later Bell Wharf Lane, is *Herbierlane* 14th PaulsMSS 16 b, *Herberlane* 1421 f. Plea, *Erberlane* 1437 (1439) CW ii. 487, *Harbour Lane* t. Eliz Harben. The first element is OF *herbier* 'garden', whence English *arbour*, formerly 'a flower-garden'. The lane must have been named from a garden. This garden is probably not identical with that which gave its name to a house in Walbrook, called *le Herber* 1392 Pat, *lerber* 1368 CW ii. 122 &c.

IX. EARLIER WORK ON CITY STREET-NAMES AND THE PLAN OF THE PRESENT BOOK

A good deal has been written on City street-names, but only part of the literature on them has been accessible to me. Many contributions are doubtless to be found in early descriptions of London or of special London districts or parishes. Harben in his Dictionary gives many suggestions in sources of this kind, most of them hardly worthy of attention. The following publications used by the present writer may be mentioned.

Stow's *Survey of London* (1598, 1603), as its title indicates, is foremost a topographical work and as such a source of the greatest importance. Explanations of names are frequently, but not regularly, given. Stow not only had an accurate and extensive knowledge of the London of his time, which was probably not greatly different from medieval London, but he was also an assiduous student of early records and thus familiar with the older forms of street-names. This special knowledge sometimes caused him to adopt old name-forms long since disused as the correct and current ones, as when he calls Billiter Street *Belzettars* (or *Belsetters*) *lane*, though he admits in one place that the contemporary form was ('corruptly') *belliter lane*. But his studies of early documents enabled him in many cases to give correct etymologies of names whose explanation is by no means self-evident, and his familiarity with City topography and history gave him the clue to the meaning of several names. Not a few of Stow's etymologies must be rejected, however. Some obviously erroneous ones are still accepted by modern writers. Clunn, *The Face of London* (1951), for instance, follows Stow in deriving Birchin Lane from Birchover Lane, Birchover being the name of an early owner, or in explaining Lothbury from the loathsome noise of pewterers and metal-workers. Stow is a source of first-rate importance for the history of London streets and their names.

The introduction to Riley's *Memorials of London* (1868), pp. xi ff., contains a good deal of early material for street-names, taken from the London City Letter-books, and also some contributions to their explanation. Riley criticizes some of Stow's statements or etymologies.

The copious notes by Charles L. Kingsford in his edition of Stow, vol. ii, pp. 269–388, published in 1908, are a mine of information on early London and its street-names. They are based on an examination of early records and contain important material collected from them. Etymologies are only occasionally given, and not all of them are convincing. A supplement, *Additional Notes*, was published in 1927.

William Heuser's *Alt-London* (1914) contains a brief chapter headed 'Die Altlondoner Ortsnamen' (pp. 5 ff.), in which a few street-names are discussed, some explanations being good, others less so. He quotes some early forms from the London records on which he based his important study of the early London dialect. Seething Lane is apparently first explained in the main correctly by him.

Arthur Bonner, 'Some London Street-names. Their Antiquity and Origin', in *Transactions of the London and Middlesex Archaeological Society*, N.S. ii (1917), pp. 185–216 (Names of the Eastern City), 287–320 (Names of the Western City). The two papers deal with a considerable number of City street-names, and the history of many among them is illustrated by a very valuable collection of early forms taken from a variety of sources, while other names are dealt with briefly. The lists of early forms often show considerable agreement with those in Harben's *Dictionary of London*, the reason being that on the whole the same material was used by both writers. Harben's Dictionary was published only a year later than Bonner's articles, and its editor cannot have made use of Bonner's material and results; at any rate nothing indicates that he did so. For not a few names Bonner gives fuller material and more information than Harben; St. Mary Axe, Sherborne Lane, Cannon Street, Tower Royal, Bucklersbury, Cheapside may be mentioned by way of examples. And though his papers on the whole may be said to have been superseded by Harben's

monumental work, which deals with the whole material, yet
they deserve the serious attention of students of London street-
names and form a valuable supplement to Harben's book.

Bonner ranks above Harben as an etymologist. He was apparently not a trained philologist in the proper sense, but he
had a good deal of experience as a place-name student, as
shown by many other articles of his on place-names, and his
papers on City names contain several apt new explanations and
suggestions. But not a few of his etymologies must be rejected.
It should be added that some of the explanations were suggested in private communications by Dr. Henry Bradley, thus
that for Seething Lane.

Bonner's papers did not become accessible to me till my
book was finished in manuscript. I have not considered it
necessary to rewrite any of my articles, but a few slight addi-
tions have been made and references to Bonner inserted here
and there.

Louis Zettersten's *City Street Names* was first published in
1917, and a revised and augmented edition followed in 1924
(92 pp. as against the 64 pp. of the first ed.). The first edition
has the subtitle 'The origin and history of the names of
Streets, Lanes, Alleys and Courts of the City of London',
which in the second edition has been replaced by the more
modest and accurate 'The names of the Streets, Lanes, Alleys
and Courts of the City of London'. The late Mr. Zettersten,
a Swede by birth, was a man of business who spent a great
part of his life in London and took a lively interest in City
names. His book, as he candidly states, 'only pretends to be a
resumé of what learned historians have gathered'. He specially
acknowledges his debt to Bonner's *Some London Street-Names*,
a debt which is still more apparent in the second edition than
in the first. Early name-forms are given only occasionally and
have generally been taken from Bonner (thus the long list of

forms under Seething Lane). In the second edition the author gives a list of chief references; it is noteworthy that Harben's Dictionary is not among them.

Zettersten's book does not satisfy the demands of a modern place-name student as an etymological study. The history of names is not worked out in any detail. Etymologies have largely been taken from the works of earlier writers, and not a few among them are unsatisfactory. But the handsomely got-up volume contains a valuable and convenient survey of the name-material and, in spite of its shortcomings, has distinct merits.

Henry A. Harben's *Dictionary of London* (1918) is the most important contribution to the topography and history of London published hitherto and is indispensable to every serious student of London street-names. It includes in dictionary form all wards, parishes, churches, streets, lanes, alleys, courts, and historic buildings in the City, and gives full historical information on them and their names. The history of names is illustrated by very copious material from early sources. Indeed this early material for many names is practically exhaustive, while for others it is not sufficient. An immense amount of work has been devoted to the identification of the streets or lanes referred to in early records, and a firm basis has been laid for further research.

Harben's book is the outcome of more than thirty years' study and labour. It was originally projected as an edition of Stow's *Survey of London* to be accompanied by copious notes and illustrations. This plan was abandoned when Kingsford's edition appeared in 1908, but Harben decided to make use of his vast materials for the Dictionary. The original plan has left distinct traces in the references to and quotations from Stow found everywhere in the book. The Dictionary was not completed at Harben's death in 1910, and the final revision was undertaken by I. I. Greaves, who acknowledges valuable help from Sir Lawrence Gomme.

The editor in the preface describes Harben as a man of varied and profound knowledge, a scholar and an antiquarian, whose legal training disposed him to weigh conflicting evidence with a calm and impartial judgement. There is nothing to show that Harben was a trained philologist, and the etymological part of his work is not of the same high standard as the topographical or historical. He is often content to quote suggestions by earlier scholars, especially Stow, many of them altogether unacceptable to a modern name student, and his own suggestions more than once show that he was an amateur in the field of etymology.

J. E. B. Gover, *The Place Names of Middlesex* (1922). The book contains a number of City place-names, altogether just over a score. Only one street-name proper is included, Bury Street, but some among the names came to be used to denote streets (as Cornhill, Dowgate, Walbrook) or as the first element of such (as Abchurch, Aldersgate). There are several good etymologies. Thus Fenchurch is taken to contain the word *fen*, and Gracechurch and Walbrook to mean 'church surrounded by lawns' and 'brook of the Britons' respectively.

Edward H. Sugden, *A Topographical Dictionary to the Works of Shakespeare and his Fellow Dramatists*, Manchester, 1925. The volume, which fills nearly 600 closely printed pages, deals in the first instance with places mentioned in the dramatic works of Shakespeare and his contemporaries, but other books from the same period have also been searched, and London streets given as the address of publishers on the title-page of early printed books are included. The number of London streets noticed in the book is very considerable, and a great deal of valuable information concerning them is collected, for instance on inns or other houses situated in them, on trades or pursuits carried on there, on notable events associated with them, on prominent residents. The book provides a very large number of literary references to London streets from Shakespeare's time. The material collected contains very valuable information also on the history of London street-names. But the usefulness of the book as a source is somewhat impaired by the fact that the street-names are often abbreviated or modernized, so that it does not always appear what exactly is the form of the original. The book hardly contains any results of independent etymological research, and the occasional explanations of names given are generally second-hand and sometimes uncritical.

Gertrude B. Rawlings, *The Streets of London. Their History and Associations* (1926). The little book contains a select list of London street-names, but not a few other names have been included, as Hyde Park, Islington, Kensington. There is no limitation to the City; indeed the City street-names dealt with are not very numerous. Etymologies are given only occasionally and most of them have been taken from the works of predecessors, especially from Bonner, sometimes rather uncritically. The book has its value as a convenient survey of the material.

Dr. Hjördis Bohman's treatise *Studies in the ME Dialects of Devon and London* (1944) is a valuable contribution to the early London dialect, which is based to a great extent on street-names. It offers very full and carefully sifted material for certain groups of names, namely such as contain the Old English vowels *æ* and *y* and the diphthongs *ea*, *eo*, *ie*. Thus all names in -*street* are included. But etymology plays an unimportant role in the book, and very few new explanations are suggested.

In view of the survey just given it may be asked if a new book on the subject is called for, especially as Harben's Dictionary offers sufficient information on a great number of names to satisfy most readers interested in London street-names and contains a wealth of material for the majority of old names from which a trained name-student may be able to draw conclusions as to the etymology. But Harben's book has long been out of print and is now very scarce; it will be accessible to most students only in public libraries. A brief new survey of City street-names with etymologies should therefore be welcome to many. And as has been pointed out already, many of Harben's etymologies are unsatisfactory, and some that may be on the whole correct can be formulated more exactly and definitely. Further, though on the whole not so very much is to be added to Harben's collections for the majority of names, yet even the sources utilized by him contain not a few important forms overlooked or disregarded by him, and a good deal of fresh material is to be found in sources published in Harben's life-time but not used by him, and especially in sources published later than 1910, the year of Harben's death. Many such additional forms are of importance etymologically and chronologically. To take an example, the earliest instance of Chicken Lane (FarrE) given by Harben is dated 1280, but there is an example in a Final Concord of 1197 (printed in 1892), and the recently published Clerkenwell Cartulary has contemporary or even slightly earlier examples.

For the present book I have made use of all the material excerpted by Harben and at my disposal. Few printed texts of importance have been inaccessible to me. I have further laid under contribution a considerable number of records apparently not used by Harben, as the publications of the Selden Society, cartularies of non-London monasteries, early diaries, such as those by Machyn, Evelyn, and Pepys, and the like, and a good many later publications, such as Mayors' Rolls, Coroners'

Rolls, and Plea Rolls for London, late series of Patent Rolls, Pipe Rolls, Episcopal Registers.

The relation between the present book and Harben's Dictionary must be indicated somewhat more in detail. My book is in all essentials the outcome of independent research and is not an abbreviation of Harben's. I have derived a great deal of information from Harben concerning the identification of old street-names, on early London topography and the like. Early forms have been taken from his book only when the sources were inaccessible, for instance the few forms derived from unprinted sources (mostly charters of St. Paul's) and occasional forms from early maps, which I have not been able to consult. My debt to Harben is always acknowledged in such cases.

Otherwise, if forms given by me are also found in Harben, they have been taken direct from the sources. Harben's book was not accessible to me[1] when I started my collection of material for London street-names, and I preferred to form my own opinion independently of predecessors. If one wants to become familiar with the place-nomenclature of a district it is much safer to go to the sources oneself than to rely on collections made by another. My re-examination of the sources has frequently given additional information beyond that in Harben.

The present book does not claim to contain all the street-names of the City of London. Names found later than about 1500 are included only if they present some particular interest or denote streets of special importance. The names that interest me are the early names, on the whole those which go back to medieval times, and the attempt has been made to make the

---

[1] Harben's Dictionary, so far as I know, is found only in one Swedish public library; that copy is much in demand and had been lent to another scholar. I have later managed to acquire a copy of my own of the important work.

collection of these as full as possible. But the chief aim has not been so much to collect names as to investigate and determine the principles of name-giving. Many names allow of more than one explanation. Thus Love Lane may have as first element the word *love* or the known surname *Love*. Harben seems to favour the second alternative. But since there were at least three lanes called Love Lane and one would suppose that the meaning of the name is the same in all cases, it is highly unlikely that *Love* is here the surname. In order to bring out clearly the different types of names used in early London the names have been arranged systematically according to the nature and meaning of the first element, that is so far as names are compounds with a word for street as second element. Some questions of a more general nature are dealt with in the Introduction.

Since the chronology of street-names is of considerable interest and importance, pains have been taken to find as early instances of each name as possible.

The history of names is illustrated by fairly full material from early sources, but owing to considerations of space only a number of important examples have been included, generally the earliest form or forms on record, in the case of names now obsolete often the latest example(s) noted, examples that are of special importance for the etymology or else illustrate the linguistic development of name-forms and the like. Many streets (or, better, lanes) were named from persons; the attempt has always been made to identify the person or at least the family. The information of this kind is a good deal fuller than that given by Harben. The etymology of family names or other names that form the first element of street-names has often been indicated when not self-evident.

In the etymological part the form of the head-word of the various articles has sometimes been somewhat difficult to determine, and absolute consistency has not been aimed at. For names still in use or used till lately the head-word is the modern form printed in bold Roman type, the spelling being as a rule that preferred by Harben. For names now obsolete and recorded only rarely (many once only) the (earliest) form, printed in bold italics, serves as head-word. But there are numerous now obsolete names that were in common use in medieval and early modern English times. For such, a more or less fictitious head-form, generally agreeing with the latest form(s) found (often that used by Stow), has been placed in the front of the article; examples are Gayspur Lane, Soper Lane.

A note on the situation of streets is generally placed directly after the head-word.

Etymologies are generally brief, and it has not been intended to point out and discuss suggestions by previous students unless they seemed at least worthy of consideration. In the case of self-evident etymologies references to earlier scholars have not been considered necessary.

In the various sections street-names are generally given in alphabetical order, but in a few cases a different arrangement has been preferred, especially with a view to bringing together names of similar or related meaning. For names in -*hill* a topographical order has been found advisable.

CITY STREET-NAMES

I. NAMES IN -*STREET*

A. Streets named from external characteristics

Streets named from some external characteristic, as relative width, the nature of the roadway, or the like, are few.

Broad Street extended from Stocks Market, where the Bank and the Mansion House are now, to London Wall. A later continuation beyond the wall is New Broad Street. The eastern part of the original street is now Old Broad Street, the western portion being known as Threadneedle Street. The three churches of St. Bartholomew, St. Benet Fink, and St. Christopher, which are now in Threadneedle Street, were formerly in Broad Street.

The name means 'the broad street'. It gave its name to a ward, which, however, was called Lothbury ward in 1285–6, the name *Bradestrete* not being found till 1293 (LBC 12). The normal forms are *Bradestrate* or *-strete* down to the 16th century, e.g. *Bradestrate c.* 1212 Clerkenwell 285, *Bradstrete* 1255 Cl, 1422–3 Plea, *Bradestrete* 1279 *RHT* m. 2, 1305 Mayors, 1321 Misc, 1550 Pat, *Brastrete* (ward) 1422 CW ii. 429, *Bradstret* (ward) 1523 LP. Apart from isolated *Brodestrate c.* 1215–30 Clerkenwell 345, 1291 CW i. 100, *-strete* 1301 StAug 346 (p), the *o*-form has not been noticed till about 1500: *Brodestrete* 1513 LIpm, *Brodstrete* 1544 LP.[1] The name is recorded with certainty *c.* 1200 or early 13th PaulsMSS 23 b (St. Peter de *Bradestrete*) and 1229–41 PaulsCh 298 (St. P. de *Bradestrat'*), but St. Peter le Poor is apparently referred to as St. Peter Broad Street as early as 1181 (PaulsMSS 68 b); if so

---

[1] We may note Germanized forms such as *Breydstrate, Breytstraet* 1468 f. Hansisches Urkundenbuch ix.

'Broad Street' is modernized. The form of the name, however, indicates that it must have been in use a good deal earlier. The original long $\bar{a}$ of the first element (OE *brād*) was shortened before the rounding of OE $\bar{a}$ to $\bar{o}$, and the latter change began early in London, probably not later than the first half of the 12th century.

The same name is found in other old towns, as Worcester (*Brodestrete c.* 1230). In some cases the name probably meant 'main street' like *broadway* (a 1613 OED), and this is clearly the meaning when Bishopsgate Street is called *the Kinges brode stret* in 1549 (ADA 13043); for a similar case see p. 188 (London Wall). It is unlikely that this is the meaning of Broad Street in the City, which was not really a thoroughfare, but ended at the city wall. Also the great age of the name tells against such a meaning. The synonymous name *Bredegade* is common in Denmark (Matthiessen, p. 53). *Bredgatan*, one of the main streets of Lund, is *lata platea* in 1289, *Brethægatæ* in 1315.

Threadneedle Street [the Bank–Bishopsgate Street] is *Three needle Street* 1598 Stow, *Thred-needle-street* 1616 (1640) Ben Jonson, *Christmas*, 1632 (1640) id., *Magnetic Lady* (cf. Sugden), *Thridneedle Street* in 1656 (Kingsford, *Add. Notes*, 9), *Threed Needle Street* in 1666 and 1677 (Harben). It has been explained from a sign-board with three needles on it or from the arms of the needlemakers' company, which are stated to have borne three needles (Harben). But it is unlikely that the name should not be connected with that of the children's game *thread-needle*. The game is described thus: the children stand in two long rows, each holding the hand of the opposite child, the last two forming an arch. The other children run under the raised arms, and when all have passed under, the first two hold up their hands, and so on again and again. The game is known in various parts of England and is said to be played in the streets of towns, often on a special day. See EDD. It is worth noting that Samuel Pepys saw morris-dancing in the neighbouring Leadenhall Street in May 1663 (Diary iii. 108). The game is first noticed in 1751 (OED), but may well be a couple of centuries older. The broad Threadneedle Street may have been found particularly suitable for the game. The earliest form *Three Needle* may be a simplification of *Threadneedle*; *threed* and *thrid* were common forms of *thread* in early Modern English.

An old name meaning 'the narrow street' is found *c.* 1130 PaulsMSS 66 b: (in) *stricto uico*, stated to be by *domum Herlewini*. In the same document *domus Herlewini*, doubtless the same house, is described as in Cheap. The ward has been identified as Bread Street. If so, *strictus vicus* may be the present Bread Street, which is certainly remarkably narrow in our days, or Friday Street. See also pp. 39 f. on *via arta*.

Cateaton Street, now **Gresham Street** [Cheap, ColemSt, CripI; Old Jewry–Milk Street]: *Cattestrate* 1271 Pat, *Cattestrete* 1278 ExchJews, 1281 Ch &c., *Cattestreet*, corruptly *Catteten streete*, *Catton streete* Stow, *Cateaton Street* 1837 Dickens, *Pickwick*. Alternative names are *Cattonlane* (alias *Cattestrete*) 1449 (1475–6) CW ii. 574, *Catlen Strete* (bis) 1548 Pat, *Catteton* [*streate*] 1588 LIpm. It is not clear how some of the variants are to be explained. *Catlen Strete* may be for *Cattelane Strete* and *Catteten* possibly a corruption of *Catlen*. The name will mean 'street where cats were frequent'. Identical is no doubt Cat Street in Oxford (*Cattestrete c.* 1215 ff. Frideswi. 310 &c.). Cattedown Street in Plymouth was formerly *Cat strete* and the like (*c.* 1493 &c.), but here Cat was probably the name of a fort or the like, referred to as *la Catte* 1249 &c. (ERN 328 f., PND 234 f.).

B. Streets named from some article or commodity produced or offered for sale there

Bread Street [Cheapside–Old Fish Street or Knightrider Street] was an important street, since it gave its name to a ward (*Warda de Bredstrate* 1285–6 CW i. 702). It is first found as *Bredstrate* 1163–70 FacsCh 53 (p), *c.* 1150–79 PaulsCh 175, later as *Bredstret* 1204 Ch, *Bredstrat'* 1220–1 (1241–2) PaulsCh 303, *Bred Strate* 1223 ADA 1631, *Bredstret'* 1224 Cl. The name means 'street where bread was baked and sold'.

Old Fish Street. There were two streets successively so named.

(1) **Old Fish Street** [BreadSt; by Cheapside]: *uicus piscarius* (bis) *c.* 1130 PaulsMSS 66 b (in warda Radulfi filii Algodi, probably BreadSt), *vetus piscaria* (*pisconaria*) late 12th, early 13th ib. 24 b, 26 a, *Eldefistrate* 1286 CW i. 76 (in St. Vedast). The first fish-market is placed in the map appended to Stenton's *Norman London* in West Cheap, a little west of the head of Friday Street. The exact position is not known, but from references in PaulsMSS it can be seen that it was at least partly in St. Vedast parish and near St. Paul's. St. Vedast is mainly north of Cheapside, but extends south of it so as to embrace a strip of Bread Street ward along Cheapside, roughly the part on both sides of the head of Old Change, which is frequently referred to as in St. Vedast (e.g. 1293–4, 1297–8 CW i. 111, 131).

Vetus piscaria is mentioned in a series of grants summarized PaulsMSS 24 b, beginning with one by the Dean and Chapter to William Fitz Isabel of land in the market in St. Vedast formerly held of them by Robert son of Gosbert.[1] The date is

---

[1] The land will be identical with that in *uicus piscarius* held of St. Paul's by Robertus filius Gosberti *c.* 1130 (*Essays presented to Tout*, p. 59). *Uicus piscarius* must then be (1) Old Fish Street, not its later namesake.

c. 1170 or 1160–80, since Hugh de Marny was dean at the time. The 'market' will be the fish-market, and the land doubtless included the 'tenement in the parish of St. Vedast before the wall of St. Paul's *in veteri piscaria*' which was granted, apparently in 1196, by William Fitz Isabel to Roger Pentecoste in lawful marriage with Margaret his daughter, and very likely the land *in veteri Piscaria* granted in 1196 on the same occasion by Roger son of William Fitz Isabel to the said Roger Pentecoste and Margaret. In 1243 Dionisia daughter of Margaret granted to St. Paul's land which belonged to William Fitz Isabel her grandfather '*in veteri Piscaria* opposite to the tower (*berefridum*) of St. Paul's', and apparently about the same time William Fitz Roger, doubtless a son of Roger Pentecoste, sold to Simon Fitz Mary his right in a void piece of ground formerly belonging to Margaret relict of Roger Pentecost 'at the corner of Westcheap, opposite to the tower (*berefridum*) of St. Paul's *sicut itur de foro secus veterem pisconariam*'. There is further a grant of a different piece of land by the Dean and Chapter to Ralph *fenarius* '*in veteri piscaria* over against the wall of the cemetery of St. Paul's' (*c.* 1180–90 PaulsMSS 26 a).

From the information here collected it can be concluded that the old fish-market was at the western end of Cheap by the wall of St. Paul's and St. Paul's Churchyard and opposite to the belfry of St. Paul's. The latter was east of St. Paul's and north of St. Paul's School, thus near the head of Old Change. The road running from Cheap near the old fish-market may have been Old Change itself. The Old Fish-market might thus have been north or east of the belfry, and my first impression was that it was in Old Change, but on the whole it is more likely that it ran east and west and was a part of Cheap or a continuation of it towards St. Michael le Querne. It is probably placed a little too far east in the map referred to.

The only instance of the English name is *Eldefistrate* 1286 in the will of Henry Frowick, who had shops in the street. The property is very likely identical with the piece of ground in St. Vedast at the west end of the great street called *Westchepe* opposite to the great bell-tower (*campanale*) of St. Paul's, which was given in 1249 to Henry de Frowike (PaulsMSS 25 a). It is curious that the name *Eldefistrate* was used so late as 1286 of the original Old Fish Street, but the name may have been taken over from an earlier deed.

No other safe references to this street have been noticed.

(2) **Old Fish Street** [BreadSt, Qu] ran east and west parallel to Cheapside from Queen Victoria Street to Knightrider Street; it is now called Knightrider Street.

In the earliest records it is generally referred to by names such as *Piscaria* or *Pisconaria*, really 'the Fish-market', for instance *Piscaria* 1170–87 ADA 2423, 1202–3 PaulsCh 106, early 13th ADA 2496 &c., *Piscenaria* 1202–16 PaulsCh 108, *Pisconeria* 1212–14 ADA 1677, *pisconaria* 1231–41 PaulsCh 206. Another name-form is *Westpiscaria* t. R 1 ADA 1695, 1252 ib. 1487, where *West-* is added for distinction from the fish-market in Bridge. Sometimes the street was called New Fish Street for distinction from (1) Old Fish Street, as (St. Nicholas) *apud novam piscariam* 1206 or 1207 ADA 2332, (St. Mary Magdalen) *in noua piscar'* 1285 Harben, the new Fish-market t. R 1, Hy 3 PaulsMSS 22 b. A further name is *uicus piscatorum* 1192–8 P, which means 'the fishermen's (or fish-mongers') street' and may indicate that an alternative English name was *Fisherestrete*.

The name *vetus piscaria* in reference to this street turns up comparatively late, the earliest safe examples having been found 1295 ff. BM, 1299 ADB 2238, but is very common in later records, e.g. 1306 LibCust 120, 1321 Pat &c. Apparently *vetus* (*old*) is here used in contradistinction to the newer fish-market in Bridge.

The English name shows similar variation: *Westfihistrate* (vicus regius) 1230–40 Clerkenwell 344 (by St. Nicholas Coldabbey); *Fihstrate* 1272–3 BM i. 480 (id.), *Fishstreete* 1312 Abbr, *Fisshstrete* 1422 Plea (LoEngl 129), *Fychestret* 1549 Grey Friars; *Eldefistrate* (p) 1281 LBB 8 (a probable example), *Old Fistrete* 1293–4, *Eldefisstrete* 1300–1, *Eldefihstrete* 1305 CW i. 112, 151, 169, *Heldefihstrete* 1305 Mayors, *Eldefysshstrete* 1325–6 Cor 149, *le Olde Fysshestrete* 1550 Pat, *Oldfishstreete* 1609 ADA 5778, *Old Fish Street* 1662 Pepys ii. 306.

(2) Old Fish Street must be a later name than (1) Old Fish Street and probably arose in the 12th century.

Fish Street, now **Fish Street Hill** [Bridge]. The old name was Bridge Street, which remained long in use by the side of Fish Street; cf. also p. 31 and Fish Street Hill. The earliest instances found are (St. Margaret the Virgin *prope*) *piscariam* 1284 Pat, (St. M. in) *Fhistrete* 1317–18 ib., *Fysshstrete* Chaucer, *Pardoner's Tale.* Later are *Fysstrett* 1561–2 Machyn 275, *Fishstreet* Shakespeare, *2 Hy 6,* iv. 8, 1, *Fish Streete* 1666 Pepys v. 263. An alternative name was New Fish Street: *Newe Fysshestrete* 1545 MxFF ii. 60, *Bridgestreete* alias *Newfishstrete* 1572 (1580) CW ii. 704, *Bridgestreete,* commonly called *New Fishstreete* Stow i. 211, *New Fish Street* 1661 Pepys ii. 133, *Fishstrete* alias *Newfishstreete* 1593 LIpm.

Both names mean 'street where fish was sold'.

Lime Street [Aldg, Langb, LimeSt; Leadenhall Street–Fenchurch Street] gave its name to a ward. The earliest references noted are (Fulcred de) *Limstrate* 1170–87 ADA 1949, *Limstrate* 12th ib. 5853, *c.* 1200 ib. 2358. The name indicates that lime was formerly burnt and sold here. Kingsford points out a deed of *c.* 1200 (ADA 11559) which mentions

Ailnoth *calcerius* ('lime-burner') as a 12th-century tenant in the ward.

Milk Street [CripI; north out of Cheapside]: *Melecstrate c.* 1140, *Melcstrata c.* 1160 PaulsMSS 18 a, *Milkestrete* 1153–67 (1241–2), *Melcstreð* 1163–87 PaulsCh 214 f., *Melcstrate* 1211–12 (13th) Clerkenwell 252, *Melcstrat', -stret'* 1214 Ch, (vicus de) *Milkstret* 1260 Cl, *Mulcstrate* 1279 *RHT* m. 2. The name means 'street where milk was sold', but probably more exactly 'street where milk was produced and sold'. *Milk* was OE *meoluc, milc.* The name is clearly old, probably of Old English origin, and need not indicate that cattle were kept here in the later Middle Ages. Milk Street in Exeter is *Melkstrete* t. Hy 2 (PND).

Silver Street [CripI, FarrI; west out of Wood Street]: *Selvernestrate* 1279 CW i. 42, *Silvernestret* 1318–19 LBE 101, *Selverstrete* 1301 Cor 29, *Selverstrate* 1306–7 CW i. 183, *Silverstrete* 1311–12 ib. 228, 1357 ADA 2457 (lane). Stow says the street took its name 'of siluer smithes dwelling there', and this is no doubt correct, but the history of the name is not clear. The two early examples with the longer form *Selverne-* (*Silverne-*), the first the oldest on record, seem to indicate that the first element was not OE *seolfor* 'silver', but the adjective *seolfern* 'of silver'. Possibly from this adjective was derived an Old English *seolfern* meaning 'silversmith's work, silver articles' or the like. We might possibly compare the surname (Symon) *Gildinsmith* 1275 Oriel Records 78 (an Oxford citizen), apparently meaning 'goldsmith'. Cf. also p. 19. The name Silver Street is common; according to PNW, p. 22, there are no less than eight instances in Wilts, and there are Silver Streets in Cambridge and Cheshunt. But very likely the name was partly transferred from London, since examples are generally late.

Silvergate in Lincoln is found t. Hy 3 (BM). Dr. Reaney (PNCa) doubts if the meaning of the name is really 'silver street', but hardly with justice so far as the examples in towns are concerned.

Wood Street [CripI, FarrI; north out of Cheapside]: *Wodestrata* 1156–7 Fr, *Wodestrate* 1163–76 (13th) Clerkenwell 86, *Wudestrate* 1160–81 PaulsMSS 21 b. It is called *vicus regius* 1282 ExchJews, but the lane of *Wodestret* 1324 Cor 99. The name means 'the street where wood was sold', as suggested by Kingsford. The sale of wood was later removed to wards on the Thames, especially Castle Baynard, but in earlier times wood was probably brought into the City mainly by land. Wood Street is not an uncommon street-name, occurring in Calne, Kingston-on-Thames, and elsewhere, but in some cases it probably meant 'the street leading to the wood'. The southern and the northern parts of Wood Street were sometimes distinguished as Great and Little Wood Street, as *Little Wodstrett* 1547, *Great Woodstret* 1577 LIpm.

Some further names may belong to this group.

Bladder Street [Aldersg, FarrI, formerly the name of the east part of Newgate Street] is first mentioned by Stow, who says it took its name 'of selling bladders there'. This is probably correct, since bladders were an article of some importance in early times and would be obtainable in the street, which was one of the chief butchers' quarters. A later name is *Blow Bladder Street* (1663 &c., Harben). *Blow* is very likely the old past participle of *blow* vb., meaning 'inflated'.

Giltspur Street [FarrE, extending from West Smithfield to Newgate Street]: *Gyltesporestrete* (alias *Knyghtryders Strete*) 1547 LP, *Gyltspurstreate* 1564 LIpm, *Guilt spurre* (*Giltspurre*)

or *Knightriders streete* Stow ii. 22, 24. Gilt spurs are frequently
mentioned in early deeds and may have been made in Giltspur
Street. But a gilt spur may have been the sign of some spurrier
or spurriers in the street. If the street was named from such a
sign this example rather belongs to the first group.

Hart Street [Tower and Aldg; Mark Lane–Woodroffe Lane]
is rarely found in early records, the only cases noted before
1500 being *Herthstrete* 1348 (1352) CW i. 659, 1380 (1381–2)
ib. ii. 227, *Hertstrete* 1405 Pat. But *Novtstrate* 1285 CW i. 72
(in St. Olave, Tower) may well have been misread for *Hert-
strate*.[1] *Hertstrete* is found also 1535 LP, 1549 Pat. Harben is
no doubt right in identifying the first element with the word
hearth, but does not explain the name further. Possibly hearths
were made and sold in the street. Or more likely *Herthstrete* is
elliptical for *Herthstonstrete*. Hearthstones, flat stones forming
the hearth, were doubtless a sufficiently important article for a
street to have been named from them. The change of *Herthstrete* to *Hertstrete* has an exact parallel in early forms of the
word *hearthstone*, which is *hert-ston c.* 1325, *hartstone c.* 1475
(OED).

C. Streets named from a person or persons

The first element of names in -*street* is sometimes a word
denoting a person or a group of persons or else a personal name.
It is sometimes difficult to say if a first element was originally
in the singular or plural; see pp. 8 ff.

In some cases the first element is an occupational term,
probably in the plural. This group has much affinity with that
last dealt with.

---

[1] *H* and *N*, *e* and *o*, *r* and *v* are often much alike and easily misread
one for the other. Cf. Bevis Marks, p. 199.

Cannon Street [Cand, Walbr] originally extended from Walbrook to Eastcheap, but in a late period the name was applied to a considerable extension west as far as St. Paul's. The earliest forms found are *Candelwrichstrete* 1180–7 PaulsMSS 16 b, *Candelewrithstrete* 1182–3 PaulsCh 180, and forms such as *Kandelwrihtestrate, Candelwrictestrate, Candelwrithestrate, Candelewrite Strate* are common *c.* 1200 and later (e.g. ADA 1957, 1961, 2025, 7821). The first *r* was lost owing to dissimilation, as in *Candelwithtestrate* 13th ADA 11939, and *ht* became *c(k)*, as in *Kandelwiccestrate* 1241 PaulsCh 269. In the 14th century and later the usual form was *Candelwik-strete* or the like, which was doubtless supposed to mean 'street where candlewicks were made'. In the 15th century and later appear forms such as *Canwyke strete* (e.g. *c.* 1430 Lydgate, London Lickpenny), *Canwikstrete* 1498–9 ADB 2282, *Cane-wike Strete* 1550 Pat. The further development is not quite clear. *Canyngesstrete* occurs 1480 Stonor, *Canning-street* 1662–3, 1666 Pepys iii. 69, v. 419. The modern form has been first noted in Pepys (*Cannon Street* 1667, Diary vi. 304), but *Cannon-street* is found on the title-page of a book printed in 1664 (Character-Books 74). The street gave its name to a ward, which in medieval sources is generally called *Candelwykestrete* ward and is now Candlewick ward. The first element of the name has long been seen to be an unrecorded OE *candelwyrhta* 'candle-wright, chandler', which is not found in Middle English either and was doubtless at an early date superseded by the French *chandler*. The street-name must be very old. In the 13th century and later the street does not seem to have been a chandlers' quarter. Cannon Street in Birmingham (1733 &c. PNWa) was doubtless named from the London street.

Cordwainer Street [Cheap, Cordw, Vintry] ran south out of Cheapside to Thames Street, but its upper end is now Bow

Lane and the remainder Garlick Hill. The name varies in the
earliest records between *Corueiserestrate*[1] (1216–17 Clerkenwell 341, 1222 Cl) and *Cordewanere-strete* (1230 ADB 1971).
A document of 1260 has *Corveyserestrate*, but in the endorse-
ment *Kordewanerstrate* (ADC 1929). From about 1280 forms
such as *Cordwanerestrete* are regular. The street gave its name
to Cordwainer ward, in early sources regularly *Cordwaner-
strete* ward or the like. It is called a high street or highway in
1356 ff. (Cl), but a lane in 1321–2 (Cor 42). The part nearest
Cheapside fairly early ceased to be called by the old name;
cf. Hosier Lane and Bow Lane (p. 159). But the southern part
continued to be called Cordwainer Street till the 16th century.
The part by St. James' Vintry is *Cordewanerstrate, -strete*
1297, 1419 (1421–2) CW i. 130, ii. 427, *Cordwalstrete* alias *Garlickhith* 1550 Pat; that by St. Mary Aldermary, *Cordewanerstrete*
1462 LBL, 1497 CW ii. 595, *Cordewennerstrete* 1550 Pat,
Cor(d)wainer streete Stow i. 250. The name must be of post-
Conquest date, the first element being French, ME *corviser* or
cordwaner from OF *corveisier, cordoanier*, both 'cordwainer'.
The cordwainers may have been leather-sellers (importers of
cordwain and merchants) or shoemakers or both. From about
1300 the place of the cordwainers in the street seems to have
been taken by hosiers and perhaps pepperers. *Cordwainer* is
recorded as a by-name (*Randolf se cordewaner*) c. 1125–30
Earle 257.

Roper Street [Dowg], an alternative name of Thames Street
in Dowgate by All Hallows the Great, found from the 13th
till the 15th century, e.g. *Roperestrete* 1271 ADA 10402, 1456
Pat, *Roperstrate* 1307–8 CW i. 197, *vicus regius cordariorum*
1291 CW i. 99. An alternative name was Ropery, which probably as a rule denoted a district, but sometimes a street, as

---

[1] *Corneiserestrate* in the printed editions.

(street called) *la Roperie* 1307 LBC 207. *Roper* means 'corder' and Dowgate was the chief ward of corders.

For occasional formations of this type see Sporon Lane, Paternoster Row, and Tower Royal, also Newgate Street. The following are doubtful cases.

Rennerstrete 1453 (1456) CW ii. 530 (high street so called) is the present Pye Corner in FarrE. *Renner* meant 'one who runs a race, a racer', also 'a swift horse'. The name possibly refers to a street in which running-matches or horse-races took place.
Bermonnestrete (St. Martin in B.) *c.* 1225 Gloucester Cart. i. 391 was possibly a variant name of Thames Street in Vintry. St. Martin Vintry is usually St. Martin Bermanchurch and the like in early sources. On *berman* 'porter' see *Baremane-lane*, p. 111.

Names containing various other designations for persons

Addle Street [CastleB], now called **Addle Hill** (q.v.), ran south from Carter Lane to Upper Thames Street. It is *Adhelingestrate* 1244 Harben, *Athelingestrate* 1279–80 CW i. 46, *Athelingstrete* 1322 ib. 298, *Athelyngestret* 1324–5 Cor 110, *Adlingstreet* 1591 LIpm; *Athelstrete* 1392 Pat, *Addle streete or Lane* Stow ii. 17. Identical with this name is the old name of Watling Street.

Watling Street [BreadSt, Cordw, FarrI; east from St. Paul's Churchyard]: *Aphelingestrate c.* 1213, 1231–8 ADA 1499, 1934, (lane called) *Athelingstrate, -strete* 1289, 1303 ib. 2526, 2522. The later name is first found in 1307 (*Watlingstrate* CW i. 186) and is regularly used from that time on with small varia- tion in form. Stow has *Wath(e)ling streete*, with *th* no doubt from the old name *Athelingstrete*.

The first element of both names is clearly OE *æðeling*, as

seen already by Leland, who speaks of *Nobilium via Atheling-streate, Watelingstreate corrupte.*[1] OE *æðeling* usually means 'king's son, one of royal blood', sometimes more generally 'a highborn person'. It is unlikely that the so-called barons of London can be referred to, as has been suggested.[2] There is no reason to suppose that early aldermen were residents especially in Addle Street or Watling Street and highly improbable that these City magnates were ever called athelings. The meaning of *æðeling* in the names is doubtless the usual Old English one of 'prince of the blood'; one or more princes will have had land in the streets in Old English times. No doubt the name in both cases dates from the Old English period. The original form may have been OE *Æðelinges* or *Æðelinga strǽt.*

The later name Watling Street can hardly be an old name of the street now so called. It is unlikely that two relatively so similar names as *Athelingestret* and *Watlingestret* should have been used side by side. The name *Athelingestret* and that of the famous Roman road of Watling Street were sufficiently alike for medieval people to have identified them and taken the former name to be a corruption of the latter.

Knightrider Street [CastleB, BreadSt, Qu; Addle Hill–Queen Victoria Street, formerly somewhat farther east]. The middle part was formerly Old Fish Street (q.v.), but originally no doubt Knightrider Street; cf. p. 30. The earliest references are *Knyghtridestrete* 1322 CW i. 297, (lane called) *Kyynght-riderestret* (sic) 1325 Cor 125 (both Holy Trinity the Less). Later examples generally have forms such as *Knyghtridere-strete* (e.g. 1349 CW i. 560), *Knyght Riderestrete* (1362 ADC 2734), *Knyghtride strete* (1356 Cl), but there is one instance of *Knyghtriderlane* (CW i. 617). An earlier form is possibly

[1] Quoted from Kingsford, p. 352.
[2] Heuser, *Alt-London*, p. 8.

Riderestrate, mentioned 1298 CW i. 137 as adjoining St. Mary Mounthaw. This parish was south of St. Nicholas Cole Abbey, which was in Old Fish Street, but an outlying portion of St. Mary may have reached Old Fish Street or Knightrider Street. *Riderestrete* would mean 'the street of the horsemen' and might refer to a street often used by such. Knightrider Street is difficult to explain. Stow's picturesque suggestion (i. 245) that it was so called 'of Knights well armed and mounted at the Tower Royall, ryding from thence through that street, west to Creede lane, and so out at Ludgate towards Smithfield, when they were there to turney, iust, or otherwise to shew actiuities before the king' is hardly calculated to convince a modern scholar. A word *knightrider* is unrecorded and if it existed it ought to have meant either a horseman serving a knight or a knightly horseman, a knight. Possibly the original name was *Riderestret*, to which *knight* was prefixed. Early Middle English *rider* was used as a synonym of *knight*; people may have thought *Riderestret* meant 'knights' street' and prefixed *knight* so as to make that meaning clear.

Giltspur Street [FarrE] is called alternatively *Knyghtryders Strete* 1547 LP, *Knightriders streete* by Stow, a name doubtless transferred from Knightrider Street.

Lombard Street [Langb, Bridge, Walbr; Mansion House– Gracechurch Street]: (Jhosep de) *Lumbardstret* 1318 LBE 96, *Lumbardestret* 1318 Pat, *Lumbardestrete* 1321 Misc. On the old name see p. 98. The street was named from Lombards dwelling there.

Names containing personal names

These are few, apart from late names.

Coleman Street [Lothbury or Gresham Street–the city wall]: (ecclesia sancti Stephani in) *Colemanestrate* 1181–3

(1241–2) PaulsCh 233, *Colemannestrate* t. R 1 ADA 2124, *Cole-manestrate* 1205 Cl, *Colemanestrat* 1235 Ch, *Colemannestrete* 1279 *RHT* m. 32. The street gave its name to a ward: *custodia de Colemanestrete* 1224 Selden 60, p. 3. Riley's suggestion that the street was named from coalmen or charcoal burners is not satisfactory; *coalman* is first recorded in the 16th century. Kingsford's and Page's identification of the first element with that of *Ceolmundingchaga*[1] in a charter of 857 is rightly rejected by Harben. The name cannot well mean anything else than 'Coleman's street' (thus Bonner alternatively), but it is perhaps most likely that *Coleman* is here the saint's name and that St. Stephen Coleman Street was originally dedicated to St. Coleman. The parish is once referred to as St. Stephen Coleman (1276 ADA 1999). If this is right, the name Coleman Street may really be elliptical and mean 'the street by Coleman's church'.[2]

Colmanstrete (alias *Fanchirchestrete*) 1407 (1408) CW ii. 378 must be an occasional name of Fenchurch Street derived from St. Katherine Coleman, which is in Fenchurch Street.

Friday Street [BreadSt, FarrI; Cheapside–Knightrider Street] may be discussed here. The name is old, early instances being (Gifard de) *Fridaiestraite* 1138–60 PaulsMSS 20 a, *Fridei-strate* t. Hy 2 ADA 2176, *Fridai-strate* 1201 ib. 2182, *Frideie-strate* 1205 ib. 2180, *Frideistret* 1213–15 EpCant, *-strate*

---

[1] Cf. on this name, p. 37.

[2] Kingsford, p. 336, apparently identifies *Colemannecheriche* in a late 12th-century Clerkenwell charter (no. 257 in the printed edition) with St. Stephen Coleman Street, while the editor of the Cartulary takes St. Mary Colechurch to be meant. Neither is satisfactory. *Cole-manchurch* is a common early side-form of All Hallows Colemanchurch in Aldgate, and *Colemannecheriche* in the Clerkenwell charter will have the same meaning. It is noteworthy that the Clerkenwell charter is witnessed by Roger Huscarl, who was a witness of a grant in All Hallows Colemanchurch of about the same date (ADA 1883).

1238–9 Clerkenwell 350. Later forms show little variation. The name contains the word *Friday* (OE *Frīg(e)dæg*). *Friday* occurs as a font-name and as a surname (e.g. William Friday 1281 LBB 5), and the street may have been named from an inhabitant with this name. The early forms *Fridaiestraite*, *Frideiestrate* may indicate that the first element was originally in the genitive form (OE *Frīgdæges*), and this to some extent tells in favour of the OE personal name *Frīgdæg*. But it is also possible that the first element is the day of the week, and Stow may be right in his suggestion that the street was 'so called of fishmongers dwelling there, and seruing Frydayes market' (i. 351). The Germanized form (in) *Fridagesstraten* 1469 Hansisches Urkundenbuch ix is noteworthy.

Little Britain [Aldersg, FarrE; Aldersgate Street–West Smithfield]: *Brettonestrete* 1329 CW i. 350, *Britten Strete* 1547 LP, *Britaine* (*Briton*, *Briten*) *street*(*e*), *little Britaine streete* Stow, *Petybryttayne* 1548 Pat, *Lyttell Bretton* 1601–2 Harben, *Little Brittain* 1673 Character Books 146. The name is generally stated to be due to dukes of Brittany having lodged there (Stow, CW i. 350 &c.), but nothing has been adduced in support of this statement, which appears to be a guess. One Robert le Bretoun in 1274 was left by James de Abbyngwrth, Canon of London, all his tenements and houses in St. Botolph without Aldersgate (CW i. 19). There can hardly be any doubt that the street was named from him. *Bretoun* means 'Breton, of Brittany', but it was a surname.

Grub Street [CripE; north out of Fore Street; since 1830 **Milton Street** from an early owner]: *Grubbestrete* early 13th PaulsCh 249, *-strat c.* 1250 ADA 11863, *-strate* 1281 CW i. 55, *Grobstrat a* 1243 PaulsMSS 8 a, *Grobbestrate* 1277–8 CW i. 29, *le Grubbestrete* 1331 (1332) CW i. 376. It is possible, though not very probable, that the first element is ME *grub* 'larva of an insect, caterpillar, maggot, worm' (*c.* 1420 &c. OED), the name meaning 'street infested by caterpillars or worms'. More likely the street was named from an inhabitant. *Grubbe* is a known surname in London. The will of one Edward Grobbe, probably of Tower ward, was enrolled in 1277–8 (CW i. 32), and a Peter Grubbe, fishmonger of London, is mentioned in 1378 (MxFF i. 153). A Grub Lane (*Grubbeslane* 1460) is found in Hitchin. From this was possibly taken the surname (William de) *Grubbelane* 1328 LBE 233, 1332 Subs (of Cheap), but Grub Street seems to have been alternatively called Grub Lane (*Grublane* without Cripplegate 1373 Pat). The surname *Grubbe* may be derived from ME *grub* 'a short, dwarfish fellow' (a 1400–50 OED) or more likely from the well-evidenced Danish surname *Grubbi* (1284 &c.).

Late and partly doubtful examples of names in *-street* derived from surnames are the following three.

Noble Street [Aldersg, FarrI; north from Gresham Street]: *Noble streete* Stow. Harben suggests that Noble may have been the name of an owner. The surname *Noble* is known in early London: Thomas le Noble 1322 Cor 60 (surety Aldersg).

Panerichstrete 1553 Pat, identical with *Peneritch* (*Penerith*) *street*(*e*) Stow i. 260 (apparently an old name of the east part of Pancras Lane), *Penny-rich-street* 1616 (1640) Ben Jonson, *Christmas* (cf. Sugden). Harben thinks *Peneritch* is miswritten for *Pencritch* and this a corruption of *Pancras*, and in support of this may be adduced *Pancridge Church* for St. Pancras Mx in Ben Jonson's *Tale of a Tub* ii. 2, 104. But more likely *Pencrich* is a surname taken from Penkridge in Staffs. Cf.

Stephen de Pencrich 1304 CW i. 166, Sir Edmund Pencrich, rector of St. Edmund the King (Langb) 1380–1 CW ii. 219.

Throgmorton Street [BroadSt; Old Broad Street–Lothbury]: *Throkmorton* (*Throgmorton*) *Street* 1598 Stow. According to Harben named after Sir Nicholas Throckmorton (1515–71, diplomatist, a relative of Catherine Parr), but it is not clear for what reason. Sir Nicholas had a house in St. Katherine Cree (Aldg), where he died according to Kingsford.

The following late names may be placed here.

King Edward Street [Aldersg, FarrI; north out of Newgate Street], formerly Stinking Lane, was named after Edward VI in 1843.

King William Street [south from Lombard Street to London Bridge] was built in 1829 and named from King William IV.

Queen Victoria Street [Mansion House–Blackfriars Bridge], a new street opened in 1871.

Queen Street [Guildhall–Thames], a street built after the fire in 1666 and named after Queen Catherine, and **Prince's Street** [Bank–Threadneedle Street] of the same date.

D. Streets named from their situation

Various groups can be distinguished.

Fore Street [CripE; Red Cross Street–Moor Lane, now extending to Finsbury Pavement]: (highway called) *le Forstrete* 1330–1 ADA 7930, *le For(e)stret* 1338 (1348) CW i. 504, *le Vorestret* 1361 CW ii. 18, *Foreststrete* (sic) 1421 Plea. The name, which regularly has the definite article in the 14th century, will mean, as apparently suggested by Harben, 'street in front of the wall'. The street runs outside and along the city wall. The name is unique in having an adverb as its first element. There are Fore Streets also in Edmonton and in Hertford, but both were formerly High Street.

Farringdon Street [FarrE], which joins Fleet Street at Ludgate Circus, was built over the Fleet Ditch (or River) in the early 19th century, and was apparently named from Farringdon ward.

Streets named from some prominent natural feature

Fleet Street [FarrE; Ludgate Circus–Strand]: *vicus de Flete c.* 1188 (14th) SalisburyCh 45, *vicus de Fletebrigge* 1228 LibAlb 86, *Fletestrete* 1271–2 CW i. 12, 1279 *RHT* m. 2. 'The street leading to Fleet river.' The Fleet ran into the Thames at Blackfriars.

Froggemerestrete 1363 Pat [probably BroadSt]. Apparently named from a pond *Froggemere* 'frog pool'. A surname *Froggemere* is unrecorded in London.

Thames Street, the longest street in the City, extending from Castle Baynard to Tower wards, is now divided into Lower and Upper Thames Street. There is abundant evidence that the name Thames Street was used for all the different parts of the long thoroughfare, but some sections were alternatively or temporarily known by special names; see p. 28 and cf. Roper Street p. 80 and Stockfishmonger Row p. 169. The name means 'the street on the bank of the Thames', as shown by the early instance *vicus super Ripam Tamis'* 1222 Cl. Other early examples are: *la rue de Thamise*[1] t. John EHR xvii. 500, *Tamisestrete* 1275 CW i. 25, *Temestret* 1308 ib. 202. The form

[1] The document is in French.

of the name shows a good deal of variation as does the name of the river itself. Thames Street follows the line of the Roman wall on the south side of the City (Page, *London*, pp. 270 ff.).

Moor Street, now **Moor Lane** [CripE; Fore Street–Chiswell Street] was named from the Moor, the marshland north of the city wall referred to in very early post-Conquest records.[1] The name will mean 'the street by or leading to the Moor'. There is much variation between the name-forms, but Moor Street is earlier and more common. Both usually have the definite article till the end of the 14th century. We find *le Morstrate* 1310 CW i. 212, *la Morestrete* 1348–9 ib. 529, 1398 (1404) ib. ii. 358 &c., *le (la) Mor(e)lane* 1331–2 ib. i. 373, 376, *Morelane* 1401 (1403–4) ib. ii. 356, *Morelane* or *Morestrete* 1502 (1510) ib. ii. 615, *More Lane* 1548 Pat, *More lane* Stow.

Monkwell Street [CripI, FarrI; Silver Street–the city wall]: (St. Olave *de*) *Mukewellestrate* late 12th PaulsMSS 23 a, *Mukewellstrete* c. 1200 ib. In the 13th century similar forms are common, but *Mogewelstrete* occurs 1279 *RHT* m. 2, *Mogwellestrate* 1287, 1290 CW i. 82, 91, and forms in *Mug-* are common in the 14th century and later (*Mugwellstrete* 1544 LP, *Mugwelstrete* 1550 Pat). The form *Monkwell* may well be due to an erroneous etymology by Stow, who calls the street *Munkeswell* (*Monkeswell*) *streete* and explains the name from a well near which the Abbot of Garendon had a cell. *Mukewelle* was evidently the name of a well, very likely that mentioned by Stow, which gave rise to the name of a place (terra de *Mukewell'* 1206 Ch), whence a well-evidenced surname: Algar de Muchewella t. Hy 1 PaulsMSS 61 a, Robert de Mukewell' 1200 f. P, John de Mogwelle, rector of St. Olave Silver Street 1318–19 LBE 101. St. Olave itself is called St. O. de *Mocwelle*

---

[1] *þæne mor wið-uten Crepelesgate* 1068 (copy) EHR xi. 742.

(*Mokwelle*) 1303 LibCust 230, 233. Harben prefers to derive the street-name from the surname. *Mukewelle* might be supposed to mean 'the dirty well', but *muck* is probably a Scandinavian word and was hardly used in London in the 12th century or earlier. Nor is it likely that a well in the City would have been permitted to become so dirty as to deserve such a name. Wells in the district outside the City were frequently named from persons, as Clerkenwell, Everard's Well, Fag's Well (cf. ELPN 146). *Mukewelle* is probably '*Muc(c)a*'s well'. OE *Muca* and *Mucca* are evidenced, and the first element of Muckton (Li), Mugginton (Db), and Mucking (Ess) are derived from one of these names. Derivation from a personal name such as *Muca* is suggested also by Bonner.

Streets named from City gates

Aldersgate Street [north from the gate]: *Aldredesgate Street* (no doubt for *vicus de Aldredesgate*) 1260 ADA 1953, *magnus vicus de Aldredesgate* 1266 Cl, *Aldresgatestrete* 1303 LBB 129. *Aldersgate* means 'the gate of one Ealdred'.

Aldgate Street. This name is no longer used, but *Alegatestrete* was a common street-name from the early 13th century on. It denoted in the first place the street leading west from Aldgate to Leadenhall Street or farther west, secondly very often the street leading east from the gate. The former as far as Leadenhall Street is now Aldgate, the latter being Aldgate High Street. Besides *Alegatestrete* was used to designate various other streets converging on Aldgate, as part of Fenchurch Street and Jewry and Crutched Friars. See further Harben under Aldgate High Street. Examples of the name are: *via quæ Anglice dicitur Ealsegate c.* 1095 MemStEdm i. 43, (Edward of) *Alegatestrat* t. Hy 3 ADA 7319 (A. High Street), *regalis via extra Alegate* 1275 RH 413 (id.), *via regia infra Alegate* ib. 407

(not to be identified), *Alegatestrete* 1282 ADA 1950 (A. High Street), *Algatestrete* 1544 LP (id.), *Aldgate street* Stow (Aldgate), *Aldgate Street* 1668 Pepys vii. 390. *Aldgate* is *Alegate* 1108 (copy) LBC 73 and commonly. The first element may be OE *ealu* 'ale'. The early form *Ealsegate* is probably corrupt.[1]

Bishopsgate Street [Bish; Cornhill–the City boundary]: *Bis(s)hopesgatestrete* 1275 RH 426, 1360 Cl.

Ludgate Street, since 1865 **Ludgate Hill** (q.v.): *Lutgatestrate* t. R 1 Harben 373, *Ludgatstrete* 1359 PaulsMSS 49 b, *Ludgate Street* 1676 Character Books 86. The street extended west from St. Paul's Churchyard to Ludgate and Old Bailey. *Ludgate* is *Ludgate* 1164–79 PaulsCh 169, *Luthgate* 1195–1215 ib. 209, 1189–90 (13th) Clerkenwell 6, *Hludgate* early 13th PaulsCh 208, *Lutgate* 1312 MxFF 83. It is evidently, as alternatively suggested by Harben, OE *ludgeat* 'a back door, postern', found in early Old English glossaries, as *ludgaet* Epinal, *ludgæt* Corpus. If the not infrequent forms in *Lut-* are trustworthy, the first element might be a derivative of OE *lūtan* 'to bow, incline', the word meaning 'gate where one has to bow one's head in order to enter'. A change of *t* to *d* before *g* may have taken place early.

Newgate Street [FarrI and FarrE; Cheapside–Holborn Viaduct]. It is curious that there does not seem to have been a customary name of this important street. The present name is first exemplified in a plan of Grey Friars of 1617[2] (LMAS v.

---

[1] *Ealse-* cannot well be the genitive of an OE personal name *Ealh*, as suggested by Stevenson, EHR xii. 491. The regular *Ale-* in 12th- and 13th-century sources tells definitely against such a derivation.

[2] According to Harben the plan is a copy of an original of 1546, and in LMAS, N.S. ii. 499, the date of the original is stated to have been of *c.* 15th century. Nothing seems to support either statement, and even

421, N.S. ii. 499). The eastern part was formerly Bladder Street.
Otherwise chiefly occasional descriptions are found, as *vicus
regius versus Newgate* 1275 RH 404, *strata regia que ducit de
Westchep versus Neugate* 1279 *RHT* m. 3, the road on the
north of St. Michael at Corn 1305 Mayors 220, *Vicus Carnificum Occidentalium in Parochia Sancti Nicholai* 1324 LibCust
276, the broad highway of the King *que ducit a macellis usque
Neugate* 1349 PaulsMSS 10 b. See also pp. 29 f.

Hog Street, now **Royal Mint Street** [Ports; east from Tower
Hill]. The forms of this name vary in a curious way. In the
14th century the usual forms are *Hegge-* and *Hoggestrete*, and
Harben is rightly inclined to prefer the form *Heggestrete*,
found for instance 1365 Pat, 1365 ADA 2647 (termed a highway or a high road). *Hoggestrete* occurs 1321 Cor, 1366 Cl,
Hogstreete Stow i. 125. Alternatively also *Hogglane* is found
1542 LP, *Hoglane* alias *Rosemarylane* 1633 PNMx 157. If
Heggestrete is the old form, *Hogge-* will be due to misreading
of *e* as *o*. This *Hogge-* was later associated with the word *hog*,
and *Hoggestrete* (with hard *g*) developed. *Hegge-* would seem
to be the word *hedge*. But in the 13th century the street is
evidently referred to as *Hachestrate* 1223–48 ADA 2543 f., as
(via regia que vocatur) *Hacchestrate* (juxta Est Smethefeld)
1275 RH 413 (Ports, thrice), *Hacchestrete* 1275 ib. 426 (thrice).
This *Hache-* cannot well be anything else than OE *hæcc* 'a
half-door, a small gate or wicket'. The hatch was no doubt
Tower Postern, which used to be near the place where Hog
Street began, and the street was named from it. *Hachestrate*
may have been associated with the word *hedge*; possibly there

if the plan is a copy, there is nothing to prove that the name *Newgate
Street* was in the original. Harben probably misunderstood the following passage in LMAS v. 421: 'The original was drawn in 1617, and
has defined upon it buildings indicated in a MS. survey of the year
1546.'

were hedges along the street. Or there was a change of *ch* to *dg* analogous to that in *Mengenelane* and the like for *Menchenelane* (Mincing Lane).

In PNMx, pp. 157 f. the form *Hoggestrete* is taken to be correct, the street being named from pigs. *Hacchestrate* is identified with the later St. Katherine's Way. This is not convincing.

The late name Rosemary Lane (found 1608 &c. according to Harben), must have been derived from the name of the shrub, at least ultimately. The modern name, first found in the 19th century, was taken from the Royal Mint by the lane.

Streets named from various buildings or structures

Bridge Street [Bridge; old London Bridge–Eastcheap]: *vicus de ponte* 1193–1212, *vicus pontis* 1235–55 Clerkenwell 200, 360, *Brygestrate* 1226–7 ADA 1893, *Bruestrete* 1200–34 Book of Seals 122. The name was in common use till about 1500 and is found still later, as *Bryggestrete* 1501 (1504) CW ii. 608, (highway of) *Briggestrete* 1514 LIpm (St. Margaret), *Brigestrete* 1545 LP (St. Leonard Eastcheap), *Brydgestrete* 1550 Pat (St. Margaret), the highway upon London Bridge called *Bridgestreate* 1555 Pat, *Bridge Street* 1661 BM ii. 478. The name was superseded by Fish Street, later Fish Street Hill; cf. pp. 31, 75.

Cowbridge Street [FarrE], perhaps a variant name of Chicken Lane: *Coubrugestret* 1331, *Coubryggestrete* 1407 CW i. 370, ii. 375, *Cowbridge street or Cow lane* Stow ii. 29. Named from a bridge over the Fleet (Holborn), called *Cubrege* 1252–65 Clerkenwell E, *Cowbridge* Stow. *Cowbridge* is self-explaining.

Tower Street, now **Great Tower Street** [Tower; Tower Hill–St. Margaret Pattens] is mentioned 1259 CW i. 3 (Tower Street, no doubt for *vicus Turris* or the like). Genuine English forms are: *la Tourstrate* 1287 ADA 1708, 1295 CW i. 122, *la Tourstret* 1329–30 ib. 354, *la Tourstrete* 1347 Pat, *Tourstrete* 1423–4 LoEngl 183. Cf. p. 20.

Basinghall Street [Bas, ColemSt; Gresham Street–London Wall]: *vicus regius* (in St. Michael Bas) 1277 ADA 1857, the street of *Basingeshawe* 1279 Pat, high road called *Basingeshawe* 1280 ib., *Bassings hall streete* Stow. The name very likely means 'the street of Bassishaw ward', but may mean 'the street by the manor of Bassishaw'. Bassishaw appears as *Bassingshage* (par.) 1160–81 PaulsMSS 20 b, *Bassieshaghe* 1189–99 ADA 1952, *Bassiishag'* (ward) 1230 P, (St. Michael de) *Bassingehawe*, *Bassihawe* 1218–22 PaulsCh 118 f., *Bassinghag'* 1268 ExchJews. The name means 'the town house or hostel of the Bas(s)ings', the Bas(s)ings being probably the people of Basing or Basingstoke in Hants; cf. Staining Lane for a similar name. OE *haga* is evidenced in the special sense 'town house' or 'hostel', which does not seem to have survived the Old English period; hence Bassishaw is probably an Old English name. If so, the usual opinion that Bassishaw was named from the London family of *Basing(es)* cannot be correct. Members of the family are recorded in London from the late 12th century.

High Timber Street [Qu; south from and east parallel with Upper Thames Street] was named from a wharf in St. Mary Somerset, called Timberhithe in early sources, as *Tymberhethe* t. John EHR xvii. 483. The street is first referred to as the road into *la Tymberhethe* 1272 ADA 2684, later as the street called *Tymberhuth* 1317 ADA 2676, *Tymberhuthe-strete* 1297 ib. 2346, *Tymberhethelane* 1343 ib. 2613, *Tymberhythstrete* (regia via) 1549 Pat, *Timber Hithe* or *Timber street* Stow ii. 10. The modern name is recorded from 1677 (Harben). *Timberhithe*

means 'timber harbour'. From this a street-name was formed
by the addition of *street* or *lane*. Later *Timberhithstret*, whose
th would disappear before *s*, was misunderstood as 'Timber
High Street', which was changed to High Timber Street. This
explains the initial *High*, which has no early authority.

Royal Street. See p. 198.

Here may be briefly mentioned a few late names.

College Street [Dowg, Vi; College Hill–Dowgate Hill],
formerly Bow Lane and Paternoster Lane, was named from
Whittington College (founded in the reign of Henry VI). The
modern name appears to be first found in 1831 (Harben).

Gresham Street [CripI, Cheap, ColemSt, Bas; west from
Old Jewry] was formerly Lad Lane and Cateaton Street. The
present name seems to be first recorded in 1845 (Harben). It
was taken from Gresham College, founded in the late 16th
century.

Leadenhall Street [Aldg, LimeSt; Cornhill–Aldgate] was
formerly Cornhill or Aldgate Street. The first reference found
is *Leaden Hall Street* 1605 HMC, Salisbury MSS xvii. 523.
Pepys has the name *Leadenhall Street* 1663 ff. (Diary iii. 108
&c.). Leadenhall (*La Ledenehalle* in *Garscherch* Street 1296
CW i. 128, *le Ledenhalle* 1322 Cor 49) was a large house which
was later acquired by the City and made into a market. The
hall will have had a leaden roof.

Rose Street [FarrI; Newgate Street–Paternoster Square],
first mentioned in 1708, but called *Rose Alley* in the 17th
century (Harben), was named from *la Rose*, formerly *la
Katerine Whele*, a tenement (tavern) near *Dicereslane* or *le
Redye*, mentioned 1423–4 CW ii. 434 f. *Dicereslane* and *le*

Redye were earlier names of Rose Street. *The Rose Taverne* (in Newgate Market) is mentioned 1566 LIpm. The name is fully dealt with by Bonner.

Streets named from churches

Colechurch Street, now **Old Jewry** [Cheap, ColemSt], is mentioned 1246 Ch; later references are *vicus de Colechirch* 1271 Pat, *Colechurchstrete* 1278 ExchJews, *Colcherchestrete* 1291 Orig, *Col(e)cherche* Street 1329-30 (1542) LIpm, *Colechirchelane* 1280 Ch, 1281 Pat, *Colchirchlane* 1293-4 CW i. 113. The street runs by St. Mary Colechurch, which was doubtless named from an early owner or incumbent, as suggested already by Stow. The font-name *Cole* was used in early London; cf. ELPN 78.

Fenchurch Street [Langb, Aldg, Bridge; a continuation of Lombard Street] is recorded from the first half of the 14th century (street of *Fanchurche* 1337, *Fancherch* Street 1348-9 CW i. 424, 520). Genuine English forms are *Fancherchestret* 1377-8 CW ii. 200, *Fanchirchestrete* 1384 ADA 2181, *Fanchurche Strete* 1510 LP, *Fanchersse strete* 1553 Grey Friars, *Fanch Churchstrete* (sic) 1560 LIpm. For a possible earlier name of the street see Aldgate Street. *Fenchurch* has as its first element OE *fen* 'fen', generally in the East Saxon form OE *fæn*, ME *fan*. The form *Fanchurch* (*Street*) is still used alternatively by Pepys. The derivation of *Fen-* from Lat *fenum* 'hay' preferred by Bonner, Harben, and others is ruled out by the early form *Fan-*.

Gracechurch Street [Bridge, Langb, Bish; Cornhill-Fish Street Hill]: *vicus de Garscherch* t. Hy 3 PaulsMSS 14 b, *Garscherchestrate* 1284 LBA 83, *Greschirchestrete* 1326 Cor 160, *Graschirchestrete* 1423-4 LoEngl 183, *Graschestret* 1501

Grey Friars, *Grasse* (*Grasse church*) *streete*, *Grastreete* Stow. It was named from St. Benet Gracechurch according to Harben. *Gracechurch* (late OE *Gerschereche*) means 'grass church'. There was a market for corn, possibly also for hay and greens, here, and Stow says the church was named 'of the Herbe market there kept' (i. 213). The evidence for a herb-market here is hardly satisfactory, and the age of the name renders a different etymology preferable. The church may have stood in a grassy plot, or its roof may have been made of turves. The first element of the name was associated with the word *grace*, whence *Gracestrete* 1557 LIpm and the modern form, which appears so early as 1437 Pat (*Gracechirche strete* alias *Graschirche strete*). In the 16th and 17th centuries a very common form was *Gracious Street* (e.g. Pepys i. 304 &c.). Other spellings are *Graciousstreate* 1510 (1526) CW ii. 631, *Gracious-street* Dekker, *Shoemakers Holiday* III. iv. 43, *Gracious Streete* 1666 Evelyn, *Diary*.

Paternoster Street, now **College Hill** [Cordw, Vi]: *vicus de Paternosterchirch'* 1232 Cl, *Paternosterstret*(*e*) 1265 Pat, 1334 CW i. 395. Named from Paternosterchurch, now St. Michael Paternoster Royal: *pater noster chirche* 1199 Ch, (St. Michael of) *Paternosterchierch* 1219 ADA 2388, *Pater Noster cherche* 1241-2 ib. 7824. *Paternoster Street* is probably elliptical for *Paternosterchurch Street*, and *Paternosterchurch* appears to mean 'the church of the paternosterers or makers of rosaries' (Harben).

Streets named from crosses

Red Cross Street [CripE; south from Barbican]: *Redecrochestrete* 1275 CW i. 23, *Redecrouchestrete* 1341 Pat &c., *le* (*la*) *Redecrouchestrate* 1318, 1329 CW i. 279, 351, *Redcrosse Strete* 1502 Pat, *Redecross-strete* 1509 LP. The street is described as that leading to the Red Cross in 1279 (CW i. 41),

and the Red Cross is referred to as *Rosy Cross* in St. Giles'
1204 MxFF 8, as *rubea crux* 1230–1 Clerkenwell 298, t. Hy 3
PaulsMSS 11 b (here also *Barra Rubee Crucis* early 13th).
Harben suggests that the Red Cross was a house. No doubt it
was a cross, perhaps a boundary cross, though the rent of the
Red Cross is mentioned 1274–5 CW i. 23.

White Cross Street [CripE; north from Fore Street]:
Whitecruchestrete 1226 MxFF 17, *Whitecrouchestrate, -strete*
1309–10 CW i. 210, 1366 Pat &c., *Whitecrosse Strete* 1502 Pat.
Named from a white cross, mentioned in the 13th century. In
this and the preceding name the word for cross was originally
ME *cruch, crouch*, replaced *c.* 1500 by *cross*.

Here may be discussed the old name of **Lombard Street**:
Langburnestrate 1285 CW i. 74, *Langbournestrete* (high street)
1311–12 ib. 226, *Langebournestrete* 1312 LBD 249. From 1318
on the name is regularly *Lombardstrete* and the like (see p. 83).
An earlier designation is 'the street (*regius vicus*) running to
Longebrod' 1252 Ch, and a form *Longbord strete* is found
according to Kingsford (p. 307) in a document of the 14th
century, which may have followed one of the (early) 12th
century. This street-name was taken from an early form of the
name *Langbourn*, which is still preserved in the name of the
ward, but the original name of the ward was (ward of) *Langebord* 12th ADA 5853. A corruption of this is (ward of) *Lange-
ford* 1285–6 LBA 209 f. *Langebord* (*Longebord*), probably in
combination with *street*, lost its final *d* and the second element
was associated with the word *bourne* 'a stream', whence *Lange-
bourne*. The original *Langebordstrete* meant 'the street leading
to Langebord' (cf. the example of 1252 supra). *Langebord* must
have been at one end of the street, either at Stocks Market or
near Gracechurch. The name contains the words *long* and

board (OE *bord*) 'board, plank' or 'board, table'. A possible meaning would be 'the long table(s)', referring to some stall(s) to place wares on. There were market-places at both ends of the street, and some sort of erection for the purposes of one of the markets might have had the name *Langebord*. Bonner's and Harben's opinion that *Langebord-* is the tribal name *Langobard* cannot be accepted.

E. Various

New Street. See Chancery Lane and Needlers Lane, also Soper Lane.

Laffullestrete 1179 Papal Bull (LMAS, N.S. viii. 207), the context being *in Laffullestrete Laffullecherche*. According to B. W. Kissan *Laffullecherche* (*Laffulchirche* in a document of 1200) is identical with St. Mary Bothaw, and *Laffullestrete* would then seem to be the later Turnwheel Lane. Kissan adduces names such as *Fulelane* and thus takes the correct form of the name to have been *La Fulestrete*. This is not convincing. The double *f* and the double *l* would both be irregular in so early a text, and it is improbable that a church situated in Foul Street would have been called 'the Foul Church'. More likely the street was named from the church, and *Laffulle-cherche* will have as first element OE *gelēaffull*, ME *leafful*, *læfful* 'full of belief, believing, faithful, holy'. The Old English adjective is combined with such words as *gaderung* 'community', *boc* 'book' (*geleaffulle bec* 'holy books'). *Laffullecherche* might mean 'holy church' or 'the church of the faithful', even 'the church of (all) saints'. *Laffullestrete* would be elliptical for *Laffullecherche-strete*.

Bury Street [Aldg; south from Bevis Marks]: *Burye street* 1508 (1538) LIpm, *Berry Street* 1677 map (Harben). Harben thinks the street was named from the Abbot of Bury, to whom

Bevis Marks belonged, but if so the name would rather have been Abbot Street. More likely *Bury* means 'Bury Abbey' or is elliptical for *Burysmarkes*, the earlier and more correct form of Bevis Marks.

II. NAMES IN -*LANE*

Names in -*lane* are a good deal more numerous than those in -*street*, not only because there are more lanes than streets in the City, but also because lanes change their names far more readily than streets. For many lanes several different names are recorded.

A. Lanes named from some external characteristic

A special group is formed by names with an adjective as first element.

Broad Lane [Vi] ran south from Upper Thames Street opposite St. Martin Vintry, but is now merged in Queen Street. It is *le Brodelane* 1335 CW i. 404, 1375 (1376) ib. ii. 191, *Brodelane* 1343 LibCust 450, 1522 LIpm, *Brodelayne* 1545 LP, *Brode lane* Stow, who remarks that it was broader than other lanes.

Smalelane in St. Sepulchre [FarrE] is mentioned *c.* 1250 ff. ADA 2616 ff., 2391. It is possibly identical with the present Fleet Lane. The name means 'the narrow lane' (OE *smæl* 'small, narrow, thin').

Fye Foot Lane [Qu; Upper Thames Street–Lambeth Hill, now merged in Queen Victoria Street]: *fiue foote lane* Stow, *Fyvefootelane* 1609 ADA 5778. Stow tells us it was but 5 feet in breadth at the west end. Cf. Finamour Lane, p. 136.

Crooked Lane [Cand, Bridge; King William Street–Miles's Lane]: *la Crokedelane* 1278, 1280 ADA 2001, 2129 &c., *Crokedelane* 1281–2 CW i. 57 &c., *venella torta* 1303 LBC 192. The lane used to be winding, but has now been straightened.

Dark Lane, later **Dark House Lane** [Qu; south from High Timber Street]: *le Derkelane* 1355 (1357) CW i. 697 (St. Michael Qu), *Dark Lane* 1677, 1755 Harben.

Long Lane [Aldersg, FarrE; West Smithfield–Aldersgate Street]: *Long Lane* 1530 LP, *Longlane* 1532 ADB 3622, *Longe Lane* 1543 LP. Stow refers to it as 'the lane truly called Long' (ii. 28).

Fowle Lane [Bill, Tower; St. Mary at Hill–Harp Lane by St. Dunstan], now **Cross Lane**. It is first recorded as *Fowle lane* by Stow (i. 134). There was formerly a lane with the same name farther east in Tower ward, by St. Olave. It is *Fule-lane* 1265 ADA 2652, *Fullane* 1294–5 LBA 200, 1302 ADA 2700. The name means 'the foul (i.e. dirty or evil-smelling) lane'.

Stinking Lane, from 1843 **King Edward Street** [Aldersg, FarrI; north out of Newgate Street]: *Styngkynglane* 1228 ff. (15th) MonFranc i. 495 ff., *Stukandelane, Stigandeslan'* (sic) 1275 RH 404, 429, *Stinkendelane* 1285 Harben, *stinking lane* Stow. The form of 1228 ff. (*Styngkyng-*) is doubtless modernized. The lane was in the butchers' quarter and its name is self-explanatory.[1] A euphemistic variant is *Fowle Lane* 1617 LMAS v. 421.

Turnagain Lane [FarrE; west out of Snow Hill]: *Wendageyneslane* 1293 Harben, *Wandayeneslane* 1308–9 CW i. 204

---

[1] Bonner, relying on *Stigandeslan'* (1275), takes the name to mean 'Stigand's lane', the remainder of forms being corrupt. No doubt *Stigandes-* is a wrong form, due to association with the personal name *Stigand*.

&c., *Wendaʒeneslane* 1328 ib. 335, *Wendeagayneslane* 1349 ib.
574 &c., *Wyndeagayne Lane* 1544 LP, *Windagaine lane* (alias
Turnagaine lane) Stow. The later name appears as *Turne-
ageyne lane* 1415 LoEngl 232, *Turnagayn Lane* 1559–60
Machyn 225. A turn-again lane is a blind alley, a cul-de-sac.
The old name contains a form of OE *wendan*, ME *wende* 'to
turn' and ME *aʒeines*, *ageines* 'against', here in the sense 'again,
back'. The lane ended at Fleet River and was a cul-de-sac.

Names with a noun (substantive) as first element

Addle Street [CripI; Silver Street–Aldermanbury], formerly
Addelane and the like, as 1304 ADA 2451, 1305 CW i. 172 &c.
Variant forms are *Adellane* 1360, 1385 ADA 2455, 2459 &c.,
Addellane 1347 LBF 181, *Aldlane* 1550 Pat, *Adlane* or *Adellane* 1559–60 LIpm. The modern name turns up in the 16th
century: *Adelstrete* 1537 LP, *Addelstrete* 1557 Pat, *Addle-
streete* Stow. The probability is, as suggested by Bonner, that
the name contains OE *adela* 'filth, liquid manure'. It looks as
if Stow had considered this derivation, but rejected it because
in his time the street had fair buildings on both sides. The
street may have had a different look in the 13th century or
earlier. Cf. also p. 55. The name is similar to, but etymologically quite distinct from, the common Danish street-name
Adelgaden, which means 'the main street'.

Ivy Lane [FarrI; Paternoster Row–Newgate Street]: *Yvi
lane* t. Hy 3 PaulsMSS 9 b, 69 a, *Ivilane* 1280 CW i. 49, *Ivylane*
1329 CW i. 350, *Yvilane* 1305 Mayors 212 &c. For earlier
names see p. 125. Stow says the name refers to ivy growing on
the walls of the prebend houses there.

Pudding Lane [Bill, Bridge; Lower Thames Street–East-
cheap]: *Puddynglane* 1360 Ipm, 1361 Cl, 1372–3 CW ii. 153

(alias *Retherlane*), 1426 LBI 282, *Podynglane* 1452 (1457–8), 1514 (1515) CW ii. 535, 640, *Puddinglane* 1505–6 LIpm, *Poodding Lane* 1549 Pat, *Pudding-lane* 1666 Pepys v. 418. The lane has been alternatively known as Rother Lane and the like and as Finch Lane.

Pudding Lane [Qu], now perhaps **Gardner's Lane**: *Pudding Lane* 1448 PaulsMSS 18 a (east of Timberhithe), *Poddyng Lane* 1544 LP. According to Harben alternatively known as Dunghill Lane.

Stow (i. 211) says the lane in Bill and Bridge was so called 'because the Butchers of Eastcheape haue their skalding House for Hogges there, and their puddinges with other filth of Beastes, are voided downe that way to theyr dung boates on the Thames'. This is very likely right. *Pudding* was used in Middle English in the sense 'bowels, entrails, guts'. Harben adduces in favour of this that in 1402 the lane was given to the butchers of Eastcheap with a right to build a bridge from which they could cast offal into the Thames (LBI 22). It is also worth noting that a house called the *Podyng-house* was in the lane according to a Patent Roll of 1549. The alternative name Dunghill Lane tells in favour of the other Pudding Lane having the same meaning as that in Bill and Bridge, even though there is nothing to indicate that just butchers' offal was carted along the lane.

Seething Lane [Tower; Tower Street–Crutched Friars] is first recorded as *Shyvethenestrat* 1257 ADC 1202, *Syvidlane* 1258–9 CW i. 2. Later forms show a great deal of variation, as *Sivethenestrate* 1280–1 LBA 150, *Sivethenelane* 1305 Mayors, *Sevethene Lane* t. Edw 1 PaulsMSS 1 b, *Syvthelane* 1322 Pat. Late forms are *Sedyng Lane* 1533 LP, *Sythen Lane* 1544 ib., *Seythin Lane* 1556 Machyn 105, *Sydon lane*, corruptly *Sything*

lane Stow, *Seething Lane* 1660 ff. Pepys i. 192 &c. Forms in
-*lane* are much in the majority. The first element of the name
has been correctly connected by Heuser and by Dr. Bradley
(Bonner, p. 194) with OE *sifeþa, seofeþa* 'siftings, bran, chaff',
also 'useless weeds, tares', a word found as *syvedys* (plur.) in
a 15th-century text. A derivative is ME *sivedy* 'full of bran'.
The name may then contain the genitive plural *sifeþena* or still
better an unrecorded adjective *sifeþen* 'full of chaff' derived
from *sifeþa*. In either case the name means 'lane full of chaff'.
Bonner explains the name from the ancient market for hay &c.
about Fenchurch Street. But more likely the chaff came from
corn that was threshed and winnowed in the lane or in the
courts round it. See further, pp. 54 f. Seething Lane, it may
be noted, is near the city wall.

Two lost names containing names of animals may be added
here.

Cate Lane 1274 PaulsMSS 11 a, *Cattenelane* t. Edw 1 ib.
25 b, 1275 RH 415, 428 (Bill), 1279 *RHT* m. 9, *Cateslane* 1279
RHT m. 30 (Bill). Identical in meaning with Cateaton Street
(p. 71).

Ratones Lane 1327 *PaulsMSS* (Harben), *Ratoneslane* 1343
LibCust 451 (St. Michael Qu), *Raton Lane* 1367 PaulsMSS
5 b (near Timberhithe), *Ratten* (*Rotten*) *Lane* 1549 Pat, perhaps
Rattesalie 1373 Plea (Qu). Apparently identical with Pudding
Lane Qu. The name means 'rat lane', 'lane infested by rats',
the first element being ME, OF *raton* 'a rat'.

B. Lanes named from an article or commodity produced or offered for sale

Some of the names might be placed alternatively in the
preceding section. A name such as Chicken Lane doubtless

indicates that chickens were reared and sold in the lane, but the chickens may have formed a conspicuous feature of the lane or the court-yards round it.

Chick or **Chicken Lane** [FarrE; west out of West Smithfield]: *Chikeneslane* 1181–9, 1196–8 Clerkenwell 81, 87, *Chikennelan'* 1197 FF, *Chikenelane c.* 1198 Clerkenwell 328, 1280 CW i. 50, *Cheke Lane* 1540–1 LP, *Chicke Lane* 1547 LP, *Chicklane*, *Chicken lane* Stow. The name is no longer used.

Chick Lane [Tower; according to Harben now Barking Churchyard]: *Chikenelane* 1235, 1271 ADA 1627, 1640, 1298 CW i. 134, *Chikynlane* 1339 Cor 223, *Chicke lane* Stow.

Both names mean 'chicken lane' and indicate that chickens were reared in the lanes.[1] A similar explanation holds good for most of the following names.

Cock Lane [FarrE; Snow Hill–Pye Corner]: *Cockeslane c.* 1200, *c.* 1210 Oseney, early 13th ADA 1661, t. Hy 3 PaulsMSS 23 b, 1336 LBF 117 &c., *Cokkeslane* 1311 CW i. 224 &c., *Cokkes Lane* 1300 (1305) Mayors 218, *Coklane* 1543 LP, *Cocke lane* Stow. The regular early form *Cockes-* (*Cokkes-*) to some extent tells against the meaning 'cocks' lane, lane where cocks were reared' and in 1300 one William Cok, butcher, had houses in the lane. Yet in view of the early appearance of the name it is unlikely that the first element is the surname *Cock*, and *Cockes-* will be a ME genitive plural form of *cock* the bird; cf., however, also p. 16. Game cocks are probably meant. Cockfighting is mentioned as a favourite pursuit of Londoners by Fitz Stephen in 1174. Cock Lane was known for its houses of ill fame, referred to, for instance, 1300 Mayors, 1338 Plea.

[1] *Chick(e) lane* Stow, *chickine Lann* 1617 LMAS v. 421, a variant name of Stinking Lane, rather means 'lane where chickens were sold'.

Langland's Clarice of Cokkeslane (*Piers Plowman* B, v. 318) was doubtless a courtesan.

Duck Lane, later **Duke Street** and Little Britain [FarrE, Aldersg; West Smithfield–Little Britain]: *Duklane* 1410 Pat, 1544, 1547 LP, *Ducke* (*Duke*) *lane* Stow. The meaning is clearly 'lane where ducks were reared', but the name seems to have been wrongly read with the vowel of *duke* and mis-interpreted. The same is no doubt the meaning of Duck Lane in Westminster, though it is held by the editors of PNMx to mean 'a muddy lane'.

Goose Lane, now **Goose Alley** [Cordw; south of Bow church]: *Goos* (*Gose, Godes*) *lane c.* 1300 (14th, 15th cent.) Sir Beues of Hamtoun, *Goselane* 1336 (1337), 1355–6 CW i. 421, 687, 1351–2 Pat, 1358 Cl, *Gooselane* 1548 Pat, *Goose lane* Stow i. 251. Harben thinks it was named from an early owner, but no doubt the name means 'goose lane'.

Cow Lane, now **King Street** [FarrE; West Smithfield–Snow Hill]: *Cowlane* 1416 CW ii. 410, 1556 LIpm, *Cowelane* 1540–1, 1543 LP, *Cow lane* Stow, *Cow Lane* 1668 Pepys viii. 144. The name may mean 'lane where cows were kept', but perhaps more likely refers to a lane along which cows were driven to and from pasture; cf. p. 55. The same name occurs in other towns such as Coventry, Northampton, Nottingham.

Hog Lane, now **Middlesex Street** [Ports, BishE; Aldgate High Street–Bishopsgate]: *Hog Lane* 1534 LP, *Hoge Lane* 1561 Machyn 263, *Hogge lane* Stow. 'Lane where hogs were seen.' An alternative name is **Petticoat Lane**: *Peticote Lane* 1602 HMC, Cecil MSS xii. 168, *Petticotelane* 1618 Acts Privy Council.

Huggin Lane [CripI; Gutter Lane–Wood Street]: *Hogges-lane* (venella) 1234–5 Clerkenwell 326, *Hoggenelane* 1256 ADA 2240, 1275 CW i. 21, 25, *Hoggenlane* 1259–60 Oseney, 1279 *RHT* m. 2, 1544 LP, *Hoggelane* 1282 ExchJews, 1328 EpLo, *Huggen lane* Stow.

Huggin Lane [Qu; Queen Victoria Street–Upper Thames Street]: *Hoggenelane* 1329–30 CW i. 357, *Hoggenlane* 1375 ib. ii. 181, *Hoggan Lane* 1551 LIpm, *Huggen lane* Stow ii. 1. An earlier name was Sporon Lane. The two forms of *c.* 1260 quoted by Harben do not belong here. Cf. p. 122.

Both names mean 'lane where hogs were kept', the first element being the genitive plural of ME *hogg* 'hog', sometimes *hogge* or *hogges*, sometimes the analogical weak form *hoggene*.

Oat Lane [Aldersg, CripI; east from Noble Street]: *Oatelane* Stow. The name will mean 'lane where oats were sold'. Nigel de Whatele or le Avener ('oatmonger') 1319 Subs (Aldersg 3) may have lived in Oat Lane.

Honey Lane [Cheap; north from Cheapside]: *Hunilane c.* 1200, a 1204, 1204–15 PaulsCh 251, 240, 168, *Honylane* 1274–5 CW i. 22 (p), *Honilane* 1279 *RHT* m. 21 &c. 'Lane where honey was sold', as suggested by Kingsford, but more correctly no doubt 'lane where bees were kept and honey produced'. The same name occurs in other towns, as Great Berkhamsted, Chipping Barnet, Cambridge, Hertford, in the volumes of the Place-name Society generally explained as 'the muddy lane'.

Distaff Lane[1] [BreadSt, FarrI; Friday Street–Old Change,

---

[1] Sometimes called Great Distaff Lane for distinction from Little Distaff Lane, which was the name of a lane running south from Distaff Lane to Knightrider Street.

now merged in Cannon Street]: *Distauelana* 12th Harley Ch (Harben), *Distave Lane* 1200 Abbr, *Distavelane* 1200 Cur &c., *Distaflane* 1270 ADA 1590, 1271–2 CW i. 12 &c., *Dystaves lane* 1298 BM, *Distafeslane* 1305 Cl. The chief forms represent OE *Distæflane* and *Distafalane* with OE *distæf* 'distaff' in the uninflected and in the genitive plural form. Distaffs were an important article and may well have given its name to the lane, the meaning being 'lane where distaffs were made and sold'. This derivation is suggested already by Bonner.

Lad Lane, now part of Gresham Street [CripI ; Wood Street–Milk Street]: *Ladelane c.* 1300 LBC 238, 1335–6 Cl, *Laddelane* 1321 Pat, *Ladellane* 1392 Pat, *Laddellane* 1419 CW ii. 417, *Ladle lane*, corruptly *Lad lane* Stow. It looks as if Stow took the name to mean 'ladle lane', the first element being OE *hlædel*, ME *ladel* 'ladle'. He was very likely right, the name meaning 'lane where ladles were made'. There is a ME word *ladel* (in Usk; see OED) that has been held to mean 'a bypath'. But Professor Arngart, *English Studies* xxxii. 252, gives good reasons for taking the word to mean 'an acorn-cup'. Harben's suggestion that the first element is OE *lād* 'a way, path' is not convincing.

Mede Lane [Vintry]: *Medelane* early 13th LBC 150, 1297–8 LBB 246 (p), 1368 CW ii. 115, *la Medelane* 1317–18 CW i. 275, *Mede Lane* alias *Shepherds Alley* 1543 LP. The lane is stated to have been in St. James' Vintry. The document in LBC 150 is a deed of limitation of metes and bounds of 'Medelane', which was held *c.* 1300 by one Henry Monquoy, a son of Geoffrey Munkoy. The latter in 1281 left to his son Henry his capital messuage in St. James' and had a wharf and lands towards the Thames. No doubt this capital messuage was identical with the property called Medelane in the early

13th century, and Medelane probably ran south from Thames Street. This is corroborated by the identification of the lane with Shepherds Alley in 1543. The latter till the late 19th century ran south from Upper Thames Street to Bull Wharf. Of the words that may be thought of as the source of *Mede-*, *mead* the beverage seems the most probable and the name means 'lane where mead was to be had'.

Harben is inclined to identify Mede Lane with Maiden Lane in Vintry, which runs north of Thames Street, and there is something to be adduced in favour of this. A lane in St. Michael Paternoster Royal is called *Medelane* alias *Maydenlane* 1550–1 LIpm, also *Meadelane* alias *Maidelane* in the same parish, *Meadelane* alias *Maydenlane* alias *Dorsett Lane* 1551 Pat. Either the identification with Shepherds Alley or that with Maiden Lane must be wrong. No doubt that with Shepherds Alley is correct and the other is due to the similarity of form between *Mede Lane* and *Maiden Lane*. Etymologically the two names must be distinct. Against the identification suggested by Harben also tells the fact that Maiden Lane was formerly *Kyrunelane* (1259 &c.); it is improbable that the lane was alternatively called *Medelane*.

Seacoal Lane [FarrE] formerly ran from Snow Hill to Fleet Lane. The name is mentioned according to Riley 1228 P. Later forms vary between *Sacolelane* (1253 Pat), *Sacollane* (1260 Oseney, 1316 CW i. 262 &c.), *Secolelane* (1279 *RHT* m. 3), *Secoleslane* (1285 CW i. 71), and *Secollane* (1304 CW i. 163 &c.). Late examples are *Secolane* alias *Fletelane* 1550 Pat, *Seacole lane* Stow ii. 21 (running into Fleete lane). 'Lane where sea-coal (mineral coal) was to be had.' Riley, *Mem.* p. xvi, suggests that the coal came in lighters up Fleet River.

Viterilane (*Viter' lane*) 1294–5, 1298 CW i. 119, 139 (in St.

Sepulchre, FarrE), *Fytrilane* 1324 ib. 369 may belong in this group. The lane cannot be identified with Fetter Lane, as Kingsford suggests, nor can *Viteri*- be for *Veteri* 'old', as proposed in CW i. 119. There is a ME *vitry* (*vettris*) 'Vitry canvas, a kind of light durable canvas' (*c.* 1425 &c. OED), which may be the first element. *Vitry* from Vitré, a town in Brittany. For occasional *F*- instead of *V*- cf. Foster Lane.

Shoe Lane [FarrE; Fleet Street–Holborn Hill] does not mean what it seems to mean, namely 'lane where shoes were made', but may be discussed here. Though from about 1280 the name normally appears as *Sholane* (e.g. 1279 *RHT* m. 2, 3, 1306 CW i. 181) or *Scholane* (e.g. 1285 CW i. 72), earlier records have forms such as *Sholand: vicus de Solande* 1187–1216, (land in) *Solande c.* 1200, 1206–7 Clerkenwell 299, 271, 245, (houses in) *Sholond*(*e*) 1271–2 CW i. 12, *Sholand* (street) 1272 *Hustings Roll* (Harben), (venella in) *Foland* (*Sholand*') 1275 RH 404, 429, (Stephen de) *Scholaunde* 1283 CW i. 65. *Scholane* is found 1283 CW i. 67 in the will of Roger de *Scholond* and St. Brigid in *Scholane* is mentioned in the will of John le Tuler de *Scholaunde* 1285 ib. 72. It is evident from this material that the early ME form was *Sholand* and that *Sholane* is a modification of *Sholand*, perhaps an ellipsis of *Sholand-lane*. The examples from Hundred Rolls are especially important; here *Sholand* does not refer to a lane. In the 16th century the lane was alternatively Shoe Alley: *Sho*(*e*) *Alley* alias *Sho*(*e*) *Lane* 1565, 1582 (1586) LIpm.

Sholand must be identical in origin with Shoeland Farm in Hendon Mx (*Scholand* early 13th ADA 1496), Shoelands in Puttenham Sr (*Sholand* 1235 &c.), Shoelands in Witley Sr, *Scoland* 1177–86 (in Wandsworth Sr). The first element of these names is taken in PNMx and PNSr to be OE *scōh* 'shoe', a piece of land resembling a shoe in shape being referred to, or else OE *sceolh* 'oblique'. OE *sceolh-land* would have given ME *Sholland* and must be ruled out, but the first alternative is doubtless correct. On field-names in Holland and in Sweden containing words for shoe, boot, or the like, see Schönfeld, *Veldnamen in Nederland*, p. 103, Ejder, *Marknamn och Kulturhistoria*, p. 32. OE *scōland* may have been a technical term for a piece of land of a certain shape.

The name *Shoe Lane* has often been compared with, even derived from *Showelle*, the name of a well situated perhaps near Shoe Lane and mentioned in 1260 and 1262 (see Harben). If the well was in or near Shoe Lane, its name may be explained as elliptical for earlier *Sholand-welle*. Or else the piece of land may alternatively have been called *Sho* 'the shoe'.

C. Lanes named from a person or a group of persons

Names containing a personal noun

First are discussed names containing a personal noun, not a personal name. The first element is generally in the plural.

A considerable group is made up of names with an occupational word as first element. Some doubtful cases are included.

Baremanelane 1285 CW i. 73 (St. Mary Woolnoth and St. Mary Woolchurch), apparently *viculus regius* 1252 Ch (opposite the cemetery of St. Mary Woolchurch). *Baremanelane* must be 'the lane of the bermen or porters' (OE *bǣrman*). According to Harben the lane may be identical with that later called Bearbinder Lane, but the two names seem to have totally different meanings.

Bathesteres Lane 1246–7, 1330 PaulsMSS 1 b, 2 a, *Bathestereslane* 1344–5 CW i. 476 (will of John de Grantham). The name denoted the present Brewers Lane, formerly also called

Grantham Lane, which runs south from Upper Thames Street in Dowgate. John de Grantham, after whom Grantham Lane was named, had tenements in Bathestereslane, All Hallows at the Hay, clearly just Grantham Lane. *Batteslane*, with which Harben wanted to identify the lane is farther east. *Bathestere* may be a derivative with the OE suffix -*estre* of *bath* or *bathe*, meaning 'a bath-keeper, an attendant at a bath'. Stews or hot baths are often referred to in early London records. Alternatively it may be explained as a word *bath-stairs*, meaning 'steps or landing-stage from which people could bathe'. The lane ran down to the Thames, and *stair(s)* is well evidenced in the sense 'a landing-stage, esp. on the Thames in and near London' (1517 &c. OED). Examples are found earlier, as 'a Steyre for esement of all þe commune poeple to wasshe and fete (= fetch) water atte' 1422 LoEngl 127. For an even earlier example cf. *Faukesteire* p. 192. With -*steres* instead of -*staires* we may compare forms of Gofair Lane in Dowgate (*Govereslane* &c.).

Bearbinder Lane [Langb, Walbr; Stocks Market–Swithin Lane and Lombard Street, now **George Street**]: *Berbynderslane* 1338–9 Cor 212, *Berebyndereslane* 1342 CW i. 455, *Berebynder Lane* 1510, 1532 LP, 1548 Pat, *Bearebinder lane* Stow. The first element apparently means 'bearbinder', i.e. perhaps 'bear-tamer, bearward'. There was a *Barebinder Lane* in Poplar (1617), for which connexion with the plant-name *bearbind* 'Convolvulus' is tentatively suggested in PNMx.

Berewards Lane [All Hallows Barking, Tower]: *Berewardeslane* 1285, 1304, 1334 (1336–7) CW i. 71, 163, 418, *Berwardeslane* 1417 (1418) CW ii. 415, *Berwardes lane* 1598 Stow. The name is no longer used.

Berewards Lane later **Hog Lane** [Bish]: *Berewardelane*

1279 *RHT* m. 31, *Berewardes lane* t. Edw 2 PaulsMSS 6 b, *Berwardeslane* 1373 LBG, *Berwards lane*, now *Hogge lane* Stow.

Harben is no doubt right in taking *Bereward* to be ME *bere-ward* 'a bearward or bear-keeper'. The first element is here probably in the singular: 'the bear-keeper's lane'.

Billiter Street [Aldg; Leadenhall Street–Fenchurch Street]: *Belȝeterslane* 1298 CW i. 134, *Belleyettereslane* 1306 ib. 180, *Belleyeterslane* 1468 (1470) ib. ii. 543, *Belleterlane* 1421 Plea, *Belleȝeterestret* 1349 CW i. 587, *Byllyter Lane* 1556 LIpm, *Billitar lane, belliter lane* Stow i. 138, 349, *Billiter Lane* 1667 Pepys vii. 30. The form in -*lane* is practically regular till the 19th century. 'The bellfounders' (or bell-founder's) lane.' ME *belleyetere* 'bell-founder' is recorded as a surname from 1275 on (Fransson).

Birchin Lane [Langb, Cornh; Lombard Street–Cornhill]: *Bercheruere lane* 1193–5 FacsCh 76, *Berchervereslane* 1260, *Bercherverelane* 1285 CW i. 7, 74, *Berchenereslane* 1300 Mayors 103, *Bercheneslane* 1301 LibAlb 242, *Bercher(es)lane* 1372–3 CW ii. 153, *Birchenlane* 1386, 1445 ib. 260, 504, *Birchinlane* 1493–4 LIpm, *Byrchyn lane* 1494, *Byrchenlane* 1549 Pat. The name has been variously explained. Stow's derivation of the first element from an owner named *Birchouer*, though in the main approved by Bonner and Harben, must of course be rejected. Heuser (p. 7) takes it to be a ME *berk-chervere* 'bark-carver', i.e. 'tanner', while Dr. Bohman (p. 302) suggests an OE *beorc-ceorfere* 'birch-carver'. Neither can be accepted. *Bark* was ME *bark* and does not suit formally; birch-carver gives no suitable meaning. As I have shown in a paper in *Studia neophilologica* xvii, pp. 32 ff., the name means 'the lane of the barbers', the first element being an unrecorded OE *beardceorfere*, analogous to G *Bartscherer* 'barber'. ME *cherven*,

kerven (OE *ceorfan*) 'to cut' was used also in the special sense
'to cut hair'.[1] The formal history of the name is peculiar.
Bercheruere lane became *Bercheuelane*, two *r*'s being lost owing
to dissimilation, and *Bercheuelane* was misread as *Berchene-
lane*. Alternatively the first element may be an analogical genitive plural *bercherverne*; for such a form cf. p. 18.

Carter Lane [CastleB, FarrI; Water Lane–Old Change]:
Carterestrate 1295 CW i. 123, *Cartereslane* 1349 CW i. 587,
1373 Plea, *Carterelane* 1397 CW ii. 328, *Carterislane* 1413
ADC 3245, *cartirlane* 1422 Plea (LoEngl 122), *Carter Lane*
1544 LP, *Carter lane* Stow.

Carter Lane [Dowg]: *Carterlane* 1409–10 Hansisches
Urkundenbuch v, *Carterslane* 1421 Plea, *Carter lane* Stow i.
231 (an old name of Chequer Lane, now Chequer Yard).

'The carters' lane.' Two carters, Stephen and Thomas le
Charetter, are among taxpayers in Castle Baynard ward in the
Subsidy of 1319.

Crocker Lane [FarrE; Fleet Street–the Thames at Whitefriars; now lost]: *Cro(c)kerelane* 1277 LBB 267, 1283 CW i.
66, *Crokkereslane* 1291 CW i. 101, 1349 Pat, *Crokers lane*
Stow. *Crocker* is ME *crockere* 'a maker of earthen pots'.

Dicer Lane, now **Rose Street** [FarrI; Newgate Street–
Paternoster Square]: *Dicereslane, Dikereslane, -lan'* 1275 RH
404, 429, 433, *Deysserelane, Dicerslane, Dyceslane* 1279 *RHT*
m. 2, 3, 18, *Discyes lane* (sic) 1282 PaulsMSS 10 a, *Dycers
Lane* t. Hy 3 ib. 60 b, *Dicereslane* 1321 LibCust 344, *Dyceres-
lane* 1394 Pat, *Diserlane* 1411–12 Plea, *Dyser Lane* 1416–17 ib.
(houses of minor canons here). The name may mean 'the lane

---

[1] OED (*carve* i. 1) gives an instance from Cursor Mundi. A 12th-
century instance will be found ASWrits 113.

frequented by dice-players'; if so, the name does not belong in this section. But *dicer* may also have meant 'a maker of dice', and the form *Dikereslane* (twice in RH) makes it doubtful if the first element is the word *dicer* in either sense. The earliest forms point rather to OE *dicere* 'a ditcher'. If that is right the forms *Dicer-*, *Diser-* must be due to Norman influence. For alternative names see Alsies Lane p. 125, *Redye* p. 193.

Goldbeterslane [St. Alban Wood Street, CripI] 1434 Plea. Not further identified. ME *goldbeter* means 'gold-beater'.

Goldhoper Lane, an old name of Pancras Lane [Cordw, Cheap], is found once 1455 PaulsMSS 6 a. The first element may be a ME *goldhoper* 'maker of gold hoops (rings)', which is apparently recorded in the surname (John) *Goldehoper* in a Lincolnshire Subsidy Roll of 1327 (Fransson).

Hosier Lane [Cordw, Cheap] was a name of the upper part of Cordwainer Street, the later Bow Lane. It is *Hosihereslane* 1365 CW ii. 88, (shop in *Corwanerstrete* in) *Hosierlane* 1365–6 ib. 92, 1394 LBH 413, *Hosyerlane* 1472 (1482) CW ii. 583, *Hosyar (Hosyer) Lane* alias *Bowe lane* 1537 f. LP, *Hosier lane* now *Bow lane* Stow. *Corwanerstrete* in the example of 1365–6 supra will refer to the ward.

Hosier Lane [FarrE; King Street–West Smithfield]: *Hosiereslane* 1328, 1349–50 CW i. 332, 626, *Hosierelane* 1333 (1334–5) ib. 400, *Hosierlane* 1338 Plea, *Hosiar lane* Stow.

Both names mean 'the lane of the hosiers'. Cordwainer ward was one of the chief districts of hosiers about 1300 and later. As for Hosier Lane in FarrE, at least John de Flaunden, hosier, whose will was enrolled in 1332, was a tenant there.

Ironmonger Lane [Cheap; Cheapside–Gresham Street]:

Ysmongerelane c. 1190 Bonner, (the little street called) *Ysmongeres Lane* 1213–16 ADA 1988, *Ismongers Lane* 1227, *Ismongerslone* 1280 Ch, *Ismongerelane c.* 1250 Ipm, 1272, 1278 ExchJews, 1280 Pat, *Ismong[er]strate* 1267 Pat, *Ismongernelane* 1326 (1328) CW i. 338, *Irmongerlane* 1422 Plea (LoEngl 125), *Iremongerlane* 1444 ADC 3414, *Ironmongerlane* 1485 ib. 596. 'Ironmongers' lane.' The first element in the earliest instances is ME *ismongere*, which contains the OE form *īsen* (or *īsern*) 'iron', later replaced by *ire(n)* from OE *īren*. *Isen* is a typical early London dialect feature.

Limeburners' Lane [FarrE, now lost]: *Lymbarnereslane* 1308–9 CW i. 204, *Lymbrennereslane* 1349 ib. 541, *Lymebrennerslane* 1415–16 CW ii. 408. Stow says *Limeburners lane* was so called 'of burning Lime there with Seacole', which is evidently correct. The forms vary between *-barnere* from OE *bærnan* 'to burn' and *-brennere* from ME *brennen* the same, perhaps of Scandinavian origin.

Needlers Lane, now **Pancras Lane** [Cordw; Queen Street–Queen Victoria Street]: *Nedlerslane* 1400–1 Pat, *Nedelerslane* 1403, 1472 Pat, *Nederslane* 1505–6 LIpm, *Needlers* (*Needlars*) *lane* Stow. The first element is ME *nedlere* 'maker or seller of needles'. An old name is apparently *Newstrate juxta venellam de Soperes lane* t. Edw 2 PaulsMSS 6 a, *Newestrete* 1347 LBF 160 (in St. Benet Sherehog parish).

Roper Lane, now **Love Lane** [Bill]: *Ropereslane*[1] 1313 CW i. 242, *Roppelane* (sic) 1394, *Roperelane* 1455 (1458) CW ii. 311, 536 (a former name of *Lovelane*). The meaning may be 'the lane of the corders', but *Roper-* may be a surname. A Robert

---

[1] Wrongly identified by Harben. The will is that of Ralph de Beri, cordwainer, who was of Billingsgate ward and probably of St. Mary at Hill. See ELSR 195.

le Ropere, merchant of Billingsgate, is recorded 1319, 1332 Subs (Bill), 1336 Cor (probably of St. Mary at Hill), 1346 LBF 146. The lane may have been named after him, but it is possible that he was a corder.

Soper (or **Soper's**) **Lane**, now part of Queen Street [Cordw, Cheap; Budge Row–Cheapside]: *nouus vicus in parochia sancti Pancracii* (*Panccratii*) a 1218 (1240–1) PaulsCh 117, 1227–37 Clerkenwell 335, *Sopereslane c.* 1246, 1257 ADA 2560, 1509, 2609, *Shoperes lane* 1251 PaulsMSS 3 b, *Shoperlane* 1279 *RHT* m. 2, *Soperslane* ib. m. 3, *Soperlane* 1282 LBA 53, 1283–4 CW i. 68, *Soperelane* 1305 CW i. 170, *Soperlone* 1328–9 Pat, *Sopers lane* Stow. 'The lane of the soapers (soap-makers or -sellers).' ME *sopere* occurs as a surname 1195 P, in the latinized form *Soparius* as early as 1130 P. *Sopereslane* is called a new street in 1257 (ADA 2609).

Spurrier Lane, now **Water Lane** [Tower]: *Sporiereslane* 1295, 1329–30 CW i. 122, 354, *Sporieslane* 1310 LBD 239, *Sporyerslane* (old name of *Waterlane*) 1459 (1461) CW ii. 547, *Sporiar lane* Stow (an old name).

Sporiereslane in *Poletria*, *Sporiereslane* 1301 StAug 346. Not found elsewhere.

Sporon Lane, now **Huggin Lane** [Qu]: *Sporones lane* 1268–9 *PaulsMSS* (Harben), *Sporuneslane* 1269, 1271 ADC 3950, 1910, *Sporounelane* 1295 CW i. 120, *Sporoneslane* 1317 LBE 79, 1351 (1353) CW i. 674, *Sporunlane* 1337–8 CW i. 425, *Hoggan Lane* alias *Sporren Lane* 1551 LIpm, *Spooners lane*, now *Huggen lane* Stow. Identical is no doubt *Sporiere strete* 1291 Orig, *Sporierstret* 1297–8 CW i. 132.

See also **Spurrier Row**. The first name is 'the lane of the

spurriers', and so is the second, if genuine. The third is not so
clear. *Sporoun* occurs as a surname in London. Richard
Sperun (Espurun) was a tenant in St. Matthew Friday Street
c. 1215 (EpCant, Acts of Stephen Langton). Ralph Sporoun
(1319 Will) was a tenant in FarrI, and William Sporoun, goldsmith, a taxpayer in FarrI in 1319, in CripI in 1332 (Subs).
The surname *Sporoun* is very likely a shortening of *sporouner*
(from OF *esperonier* 'spurrier'), which occurs as a surname
(Benedict le Esporouner 1291 LBC 1, a representative of
Farringdon ward). Such a shortening would be particularly
liable to take place in a street-name such as *Sporonerelane*, and
very likely that is the source of Sporon Lane, the meaning
being 'lane of the spurriers'. The variant *Sporierstret* favours
this solution.

Huettawiereslane a 1200 (1241–2) PaulsCh 177, a lost name,
means 'the lane of the whittawers'. The situation is unknown.

Names with a first element denoting a dignity or position
or the like

Chancery Lane [FarrE; Fleet Street–High Holborn] was
first called **New Street** (*nouus vicus* 1185 Templars, *New(e)-
strate* 1227 Ch, 1300 CW i. 148 &c.), and this name occasionally crops up later, even in Stow. Land of John Herlisun in this
lane that had been escheated was devoted by the King to the
foundation of a house for converted Jews, apparently in 1231
(cf. 1232 Ch), and from this Domus conversorum the lane was
sometimes called *Vicus Conversorum* (1253 Cl, 1278 CW i. 36)
or *Converslane, -lone* (1278–9 CW i. 39, 1338 Pat). The House
of Converts was later made use of as a depository of the rolls
of chancery and became the seat of the Chancery; the site now
forms part of the Public Record Office. The lane hence came
to be called the Chancellor's Lane: *Chauncel(l)ereslane* 1338

Plea, 1339 Pat, *Chauncelerlane* 1340 Cl, *Chaunselerlane* 1422
Plea (LoEngl 122), *Chaunceler Lane* 1524–5 LP, *Chanseler
Lane* 1551 Machyn 7. Eventually this name was superseded
by *Chancery Lane*, the earliest instances of the latter form
found being *Chauncerylane* 1454 Pat, *Chauncery Lane* 1531
LP. The modern name need not be a corruption of *Chancellor
Lane*; it may be a new name formed with the word *chancery* as
first element.[1]

[1] The precise history of the name Chancery Lane is not altogether
clear. The early *Chanceller(es)lane* means 'the Chancellor's Lane' and
seems to imply that the Chancellor had his residence or personal office
in the lane when the name arose. If Page is right in stating (*London*,
p. 171) that the Chancellor's household became stationary at Domus
conversorum at the end of the 13th century, the matter is simple. But
according to Stubbs (ii. 282) the Chancellor did not cease to be a part
of the King's personal retinue and follow the court till early in the
reign of Edward III. When Lady Stenton, *English Society in the Early
Middle Ages*, p. 51, says that the first steps were taken in 1265 to pro-
vide the Chancery with what became its permanent home in Chancery
Lane, she is probably referring to the time when the House of Converts was first used as a repository for the rolls of chancery. There is
plenty of evidence that it was so used from about 1294, though, as has
been shown by Agnes Sandys in *Essays presented to Tout*, p. 160, there
is proof that the rolls of chancery were housed in the New Temple in
1289 and 1291. On the early history of the Chancery reference may also
be made to Tout, *The Beginnings of a Modern Capital* (London, 1923),
p. 20.

In view of numerous entries in records to the effect that people
came into Chancery at the House of Converts, or in the Chapel of the
House, and acknowledged a deed or the like (e.g. 1294, 1300, 1323 Cl),
it is evident that the Chancery had an office there. We may also take
it for granted that the keeper of the rolls was resident there at least
during the time when the custody of the rolls and that of the Converts
was in the same hands. Adam de Osgodby, keeper of the rolls 1295–
1316, was appointed custodian of the Converts in 1307 and his successor William de Ayreminne in 1317. But this does not sufficiently
explain the street-name.

It is stated in a Close Roll of 1302 that the newly appointed Chancellor, Master William de Grenefeld, Dean of Chichester, received from
the keeper of the rolls the great seal in the Chancellor's chamber in the

Mincing Lane [Langb, Tower; Tower Street–Fenchurch Street] : *M(e)ngenelane* 12th ADA 5929, *Maninelane* 1189 (1364) Ch, *Mengene lane c.* 1250 Colchester Cart 299, *Menechinelane* 1273–4 CW i. 17, *Menchenelane* 1294–5 ib. 119, *Manionelane* 1295 ib. 121, 1302 Mayors 139, *Menionelane* 1312 CW i. 230, *Mengeoneslane* 1324 ib. 309, *Maioneslane* 1325 ib. 317, *Mynchenelane* 1360 PaulsMSS 49 b, *Mynchenlane* 1456 Pat, *Mynsyon Lane* 1559 Machyn 201, *Minnchinge Lane* 1568 LIpm, *Mincheon lane* Stow, *Minsingelane* 1619 (1621) CW ii. 745, *Mincing Lane* 1677 Ogilby's map (Bonner). The name, as was suggested already by Stow, means 'the lane of the nuns', the first element being OE *mynecenu* 'nun' (ME *minchen* and the like, early Modern English *minchun*). But his statement that the nuns were those of St. Helen's Bishopsgate cannot be correct since that house was not founded till 1212. There may have been a small community of nuns or recluses in Mincing Lane, who possibly later joined the nunnery of St. Helen's. The late change of *ch* to *c* (*s*) is not easy to explain. A common early form had *g* or *i* instead of *ch* denoting the sound of *g* in *singe*.

lodging of the Bishop of Chichester. It looks as if there was a Chancellor's chamber in that lodging before W. de Grenefeld became Chancellor. The lodging of the Bishop of Chichester was in Chancery Lane close to the House of Converts. Some land near that house was granted in 1227 by the King to Ralph, Bishop of Chichester, and he and his successors had an inn (a hostel) with a garden there. The name Chancellor Lane may have been given in reference to the Chancellor's chamber in the Bishop of Chichester's hostel, but since one dean and two bishops of Chichester acted as Chancellor in the period 1302–40 (W. de Grenefeld, dean, 1302–4, John de Langton, bishop, 1307–9, Robert de Stratford, bishop, 1337, 1340) and these may be supposed to have resided in their hostel while in London, the conjecture seems warranted that the name Chancellor Lane began to be used in a period during which the chancellorship was held by a dean or bishop of Chichester. As the new name first appears in 1338, the year after Bishop Stratford had become Chancellor, the lane may have been named after him. If this is right, the new name came to be recorded very soon after it had arisen.

This change is often found in place-names containing OE *hlinc*.

Another name taken from a religious community is **Sakfrere-lane** 1310 CW i. 214, an old name of Old Jewry. A *sack-friar* was a member of the mendicant order called Fratres de Poeni-tentia Jesu Christi or de Saccis, because the friars were clothed in sackcloth. The Friars of the Sack had a church in St. Stephen Coleman Street referred to 1298 Mayors 18. They first appeared in London in 1257 and had settled in Coleman Street by 1271–2 (*Victoria History of London*, i. 513).

Old Dean's Lane, now **Warwick Lane** [CastleB, FarrI]: *Eldedeneslane* 1257, *Venella Veteris Decani* t. Hy 3, *Aldedenes lane* t. Edw 1 PaulsMSS 9 a, b, *Oldeneslane* 1361 EpLond, *eldenlane* 1424 LoEngl 184, *Eldens lane* alias *Warwik lane* 1513 PaulsMSS 9 b. 'The lane of the old Dean.' Named from a dean of St. Paul's who must have had a house here not later than the early 13th century. Ralph de Diceto, dean 1180–1202, may be suggested.

Names with a personal designation of a general meaning as first element

Fetter Lane [FarrE; Fleet Street–Holborn]: *Faytureslane* 1292 *Hustings Roll* (Harben), *Faitereslane* 1312, *Faytoreslane* 1315, *Fayturlane* 1329–30 CW i. 230, 252, 357, *Faytourlane* 1340 Cl, *Faytereslane* 1447 (1459–60) CW ii. 540, *Feweterlane* 1544 LP, 1557 Pat, *Fewterlane* 1556 f. Pat, *Feter Lane* 1568 LIpm, *Fewtar(s) lane* Stow. Stow (ii. 39) says Fewtar lane was so called of Fewters (or idle people) lying there. A more cor-rect form of the word, as pointed out by Kingsford, is ME *faitor*, which meant 'impostor, cheat; esp. a vagrant who shams illness' and the like.

Haggenelane [CastleB], an old name of **Bennet's Hill** (or Paul's Wharf Hill), which extends north from Thames Street by St. Benet Paul's Wharf. The earliest reference is *Haggelane* (by St. Benet) 1202–4 (1241–2) PaulsCh 79. Next follow *Hoggene lane* (sic) 1257–8 PaulsMSS 4 b (not Huggin Lane), *Haggen Lane* 1260 ib. 5 b (by the cemetery of St. Benet), *Haggenelan'* 1275 RH 433 (iuxta ecclesiam Sancti Benedicti), *Haggenelane* 1279 *RHT* m. 17. For the first element the choice is between the words *hag* 'an old woman' and *hag* '(the fruit of the) hawthorn' (found in the dialects of Kent, Bucks, Berks &c.). In all probability it is *hag* (ME *hagge*) 'an ugly repulsive old woman' (Ancren Riwle, Langland &c.). *Haggene-* is the genitive plural form.

Maiden Lane occurs at least thrice in London, but in all cases it has replaced earlier names. The identification of *Maden lane* t. Hy 3 PaulsMSS 25 b is quite doubtful; it may have been a fourth lane with this name. Two Maiden Lanes are still in existence, one in Aldersg and CripI [Foster Lane–Wood Street], formerly **Ing Lane** (q.v.), and first exemplified as *Maydenlane* in 1534 (Harben), the other in Vintry [College Hill–Garlick Hill], formerly **Kiron Lane** (q.v.) and first recorded in 1543 (cf. **Mede Lane**, supra, p. 108), as *Mayden Lane* 1568 LIpm. Maiden Lane was thirdly an alternative name of Distaff Lane, found, for instance, 1500, 1505–6 Pat, 1510 LP. Stow has *Mayden lane* or *Distaffe lane*. He takes *Maiden* in this case to refer to a sign, and Harben gives the same explanation of the other Maiden Lanes. But there is hardly any evidence of inns or other houses having been called the Maiden, and it may well be the name means 'the lane of the maidens'. The exact meaning of *maiden* must remain unexplained. The synonymous *Jomfrugade* in Denmark and Norway is held to refer to prostitutes dwelling in the street.

The name is recorded early in Southwark (Sr): *Maydelane* 1364, *Maydenlane* 1418 PNSr (the present Park Street).

Wyvenelane 1328 (1329–30), 1355–6, 1361–2 CW i. 356, 688, ii. 65, 1366, 1369–70 ADB 2083 f. (St. Mary Somerset, Qu) has not been identified. The name must mean 'the lane of the women (or wives)', *Wyvene-* being the genitive plural of OE *wīf*, analogically formed with the ending *-ena*, ME *-ene*. Cf. p. 18.

Names containing folk-names

Two names at least ultimately contain folk-names (tribal names).

Ing Lane, now **Maiden Lane** [Aldersg and CripI]: *Englenelane* 1282 LBA 154, *Inggelenelane* 1310–11 CW i. 217, *Ingelane* 1320 f. Pat, 1325 Cl, *Engleslane* 1331 (1332–3) CW i. 380, *Inggenelane* 1339 ib. 433, *Ingenlane* 1381–2 (1383) CW ii. 236, (lane of) *Ingestrete* 1412 ADA 2460, *Yengellane* 1550 Pat, *Ingenelane, Inglane, Ingaine* or *Mayden lane, Engain lane* Stow i. 298 ff. Harben hesitates between OE *engel* 'angel' and *Engel* 'English' as the first element, preferring the first alternative. Clearly the name is an OE *Englena lane* 'the lane of the Angles', indicating an early Anglian immigration into London. 'The lane of the English' in contradistinction to a lane with mainly French inhabitants seems less probable. The old word *Engle* would hardly have been used in forming a comparatively late name.[1]

Staining Lane [Aldersg, CripI; Gresham Street–Oat Lane]: *Staningelane* 1181–6 (13th) Clerkenwell 293, t. R 1 ADA 2124,

---

[1] There are, or were formerly, in Southampton two streets called respectively English Street and French Street. The former is referred to as early as 1248 (ADB 3383) and is called *vicus anglicus c.* 1270 BM, *Englisschestrete* 1300 ADB 3385. The latter is mentioned 1250 ADB 3441 and is called *vicus franciscus* 1314 BM.

1275, 1281 CW i. 25, 52, *Stanigelane* 1252–3 Pat, *Stannynge-lane* 1272–3 CW i. 13, *Stanigeslane* 1278 LBB 274, *Steningge-lane* 1279 *RHT* m. 2, *Sanynglane* 1293–4 CW i. 113 (will of Thomas de Stanes). The name is connected with *Stæningahaga* (in London) 1053–65 ASWrits, which is described as belonging to Staines (Mx). *Stæningahaga*, as suggested by Maitland, *Domesday Book*, p. 181, means 'the *haga* (town house, hostel) of the Staines people'. The hostel was close to Staining Lane, as shown by the fact that St. Mary Staining (olim St. Mary de Staningelane) is called ecclesia de *Stanningehage* 1189–90 (13th) Clerkenwell 6. If Staining Lane actually meant 'the lane of the Staines people', it belongs to this group and no doubt arose in the Old English period. But *Staining* may be an elliptical formation from *Staningehage*, so that the name originally meant 'the lane by *Staningehage*'. If so, the name is a formation from a place-name. Anyhow Staining is ultimately a folk-name.

On **Basing Lane,** see p. 133.

A personal designation is probably the first element of **Fosterlan'** 1275 RH 430, the name of a lane in Vintry, which had been obstructed by Stephen Bukerel and Juliana Hardel, thus not identical with Foster Lane. It is improbable that the name contains a form of the word *forester*, since *foster* in this sense is first recorded in OED in certain Chaucer MSS. More likely *Foster-* is OE *fostor*, ME *foster* in the sense 'offspring, progeny' or better OE, ME *fostre* 'a foster-parent, nurse'. Foster might have been a nickname of a person. *Illefoster* was used as a surname in London in the 12th century (ELPN 155).

Names containing a personal name

Not a few names in -*lane* have as first element a Christian name, but some of those placed here may alternatively be explained in a different way.

Alsies Lane, an old name of **Ivy Lane** [FarrI]: *Alsies Lane*
12th PaulsMSS 10 a, 25 b. The form *Alfies lane* quoted by
Harben is miswritten or misread for *Alsies lane.* The lane was
named from an early tenant called *Alsi,* OE *Ælfsige,* a name
recorded in London in the early and late 12th century. The
name Alsies Lane was superseded by *Folkemares lane* t. Hy 3
PaulsMSS 9 b, spelt *Fukemerlane* 1280 CW i. 49. Harben's
suggestion that this name is earlier than Alsies Lane and was
due to the proximity of the ground set apart for the folkmoot,
cannot be accepted. The new name, as pointed out already by
Bonner, is of the same type as the old, the first element being
OG *Folcmar* (*Folcmer*), doubtless in a French form. But it is
possible that it was here used as a surname. One William
Folkmar was a witness at St. Dunstan (?West) t. John (ADA
2503); possibly he gave its name to the lane. Sir John Folkmere,
clerk, is mentioned t. R 2 as a tenant in St. Dunstan West
(PaulsMSS 8 a).

Cecile Lane [FarrI], apparently an earlier name of Dicer
Lane, the present Rose Street, is often mentioned *c.* 1200 and
in the 13th century, as *Ceciles lane c.* 1200 PaulsMSS 11 a,
(street called) *Cescille lane c.* 1213 ib. 8 b, *vicus Cecilie de Turri,*
Cecilies Lane de la Tur, Cecille Lane de Turri t. Hy 3 ib. 9 a,
venella que fuit Cecilie de Turri, venella Cecilie 1231–7 (1241–2)
PaulsCh 113. Cecile de Turri had land in St. Andrew Eastcheap *c.* 1200 (ADA 7256) and houses in or near St. Faith
parish (1199–1218 PaulsCh 115). She was probably a widow
c. 1200 and died soon after. She and Roger her son were
tenants of St. Augustine Canterbury (StAug 314). Her sons
were also Masters Richard and Walter de Turri, who with
their brother Roger granted land in Cescille Lane *c.* 1213
(PaulsMSS 8 b). Her husband was very likely Jordan de Turri,
who was a witness at Blanch Appleton (in Mark Lane) in 1177

(ADA 7295) and in St. Michael le Querne (FarrI) in 1193–4 (PaulsCh 110). He is styled a clerk 1214–21 PaulsMSS 57, where his executors are mentioned. The surname *de Turri* means 'of the Tower' or 'of Tower ward'.

Craddock Lane [Tower, Aldg], according to Stow identical with Church Alley, now Star Alley, is *Cradocheslane* 1170–87 ADA 2406 (All Hallows Staining), (*venella que vocatur* or *vocabatur*) *Craddo(c)keslane* 1275 RH 405, 420, 426. Stow calls it *Cradocks lane* (an old name). *Craddock* is a personal name derived from early Welsh *Caradoc*.

Desborne Lane [Qu], a lane in St. Mary Somerset, according to Stow perhaps one running from Fye Foot Lane to Thames Street. The name is now lost. The lane is referred to as *Daneborgate* 1253 ExchJews 16 (from Thames Street to the Thames), *Denebureghlane* (venella) 1275 RH 433, *Deneburzgate* (venella), *Deneburegate*, *Deneburezgate* (via communis) ib. 418, 427 f. (opposite a house in St. Peter Parvus, Qu, apparently identical with *Denebureghlane*), (via communis) *Deneburgate*, *Deneburlane* 1279 *RHT* m. 1, 17. Later appears the form *Desebournelane* 1348 LBF 184, Pat, LibAlb 625 (stated in Pat to extend from Thames Street to the Thames and to be 7 feet broad except near the Thames, where it was one royal ell broad), *Desbo(o)rne lane* Stow. No doubt the part next to the Thames was originally called *Deneburzgate*, the rest being *Deneburzlane*. The change from *Deneburzlane* to *Desebournelane* is difficult to explain. *Deneburz-* is probably OE *Deneburg*, a woman's name found in *Deneburge hleaw* (947 BCS 834), rather than an OE *Denaburg* 'fort of the Danes'. Page (p. 138) thinks the name points to a Danish settlement. For the change to -*bourne*, cf. Sherborne Lane.

Germayneslane 1313 CW i. 239, also called *Wancelineslane* and Haywharf Lane, was named from German le Cordier, who is mentioned as an earlier tenant in *Wauncelineslane* in 1241 (ADA 2723). *German* is a font-name from OF *Germain*. The street-name must antedate 1241.

Golden Lane [FarrE; north out of Holborn Hill; in St. Andrew Holborn]: *Goldinelane* 1291–2 *PaulsMSS* (Harben), *Goldelane* 1314 CW i. 249, *Goldenlane* 1317 ib. 272 &c., *Gold lane* Stow. Richard son of Golda held land in the vicinity in 1245 (PaulsMSS 25 b), and the lane may have been named from this Golda. The earliest form *Goldine-* may well be from *Goldiue-*, OE *Goldgifu*, a woman's name; *Golda* (or more correctly *Golde*) is then a short-form of *Goldiue*. This would give an easy explanation of the common form *Goldenlane*, which is not to be expected as a development of a late OE *Goldan-lane*, while *Golden-* is a normal later form of *Goldine-*. The supposition is necessary that *Goldiuelane* was read as *Goldinelane*, which became customary.

Gutter Lane [FarrI; Cheapside–Gresham Street]: *Godrun lane* 1180–92 PaulsMSS 23 b, *Godrunelane c.* 1200 Wardon, early 13th ADA 11681 &c., *Godruneslane c.* 1206–7 (13th) Clerkenwell 245, (vicus de) *Goderunlan'* 1251 Cl, *Goderonelane* 1256 ADA 2224, *Gotherunlane* 1256 ib. 1998, 2061, *Goderoneslane* 1300 CW i. 148, *Gotherlane* 1349 (1351) CW i. 652, *Gudrunlane* 1312 (1322–3) ib. 300, *Goterlane* 1380–1 Nicolas Chron, 1410–11 CW ii. 390, *Gutterlane* 1472 LIpm. The first element is a woman's font-name, probably an unrecorded OE *Gōðrūn*, but possibly ON *Guðrún*. See ELPN 41.

Kiron Lane, now **Carey Lane** [Aldersg, FarrI; Gutter Lane –Foster Lane]: *Kyrunelane* 1233–4 ADA 7843, (venella)

Kironeslane, Kyronlane 1275 RH 414, 429, 432, *Kyrounlane* 1359 (1361) CW ii. 52, *Kyrone lane* 1539 LP, *Kery lane* Stow, *Carie lane* 1666 Harben.

Kiron Lane, now **Maiden Lane** [Vi]: *Kyrunelane* 1259 CW i. 3, *Kyroneslane* 1275 ib. 24, *Kyrounelane* 1322 Cor 63, *Kyroun-lane* 1349 CW i. 590, 1465–6 Pat, *Kerion lane* Stow.

The same name occurs in Kingston Sr(*Kyronelane* 1297 &c.), but it can hardly be doubted that the Kingston name was transferred from Kiron Lane in Vintry. The latter ran out of the street formerly called *la Ryole* (cf. Tower Royal, p. 198), which is known to have been named from la Réole near Bordeaux. There is also a street in Kingston called *La Ryole* (1304), which was evidently named from *la Ryole* in London. It is practically out of the question that the Kingston street can have been named independently from la Réole.

There are thus at most two lanes called Kiron Lane in early sources, and it is of course not impossible that originally there was only one, whose name was later transferred to the other. The two lanes are both short ones connecting two more important thoroughfares.

The name has been a good deal discussed. Stow thought Kiron Lane in Vintry was named from one *Kerion*, and this no doubt explains his form *Kerion lane*. Kingsford (p. 325) draws attention to one John Kerion who was a tenant in St. Lawrence (Cand) in 1284. This etymology cannot be accepted. The editors of PNSr suggest that *Kiron* (*Kyroun*) is an unrecorded Old French *cuiron*, derived from *cuir* 'leather' and meaning 'a piece of leather'. Early London street-names containing a word for an object or an article are always formed with an English first element, and a formation with a French first element meaning 'a piece of leather' or the like would be without parallel. If the two Kiron Lanes were named

independently of each other, the suggestion becomes too unlikely to be seriously considered.

I am inclined to believe that *Kiron* represents an Old
English woman's name in -*rūn*, analogous to those found in
Gutter Lane (OE *Gōdrūn*) or Leather Lane[1] in Holborn (OE
Lēofrūn). The first element of *Kiron*, if a native word, must
have had an OE *y*, since the *K*- is hard, and we are then really
left only with OE *cyn(e)*, common in OE personal names. The
OE name would be *Cyn(e)rūn*, which is unrecorded, but a
normal formation. A development of *Cynrūn* to *Kyrun* has
many analogies. We may mention OE *Cyred* from *Cynrēd*,
doubtless found also in the place-names Kerdiston Nf, Kird-
ford Sx, further *Thursday* from OE *punresdæg*, *Thursley* Sr,
probably OE *punresleah*. See my *Studies on English Place and
Personal Names*, p. 43. The chief difficulty about this derivation is the double occurrence of the name.

Mark Lane [Tower; Fenchurch Street–Tower Street]:
Marthe-lane c. 1200, 1241 ADA 2679, 7820, *Marthe Lane*
(street) 1272 ib. 2655, *Martelane* 1276 LBB 263, 1280–1 CW i.
51 and commonly, *Martlane* 1369 LBG, 1423–4 LoEngl 183,
1465–6 Pat, *Martel Lane* 1310 PaulsMSS 46 a, *Markelane*
1481, 1548 Pat, *Marke Lane* 1532–3 LP. Forms like *Marche-
lane* (early 13th ADA 7354), *Marcelane* (1305 Mayors) are
doubtless misread or miswritten for *Mart(h)elane*. The change
from *Mart Lane* to *Mark Lane* is late. In the earliest instance
Markelane is given as a variant of *Martlane*. The Celys, who
lived in Mark Lane, write *Mart(e)* or *Martt(e) Lane* (Cely
Papers, passim, 1478 ff.). Three correspondents, not Celys,
write *Marke Layne* (1482), *Marke Lane* (1486, 1475–88). Stow
says *Marke Lane* is corrupt for *Marte lane* (i. 349). *Mark* for
Mart may be a hypercorrect form; there is a tendency for *kl*

---

[1] Cf. PNMx 119. The lane is outside the City boundary.

to become *tl* in English, as in *Watling Street* from early *Wæclinga stræt*. Popular etymology may have helped the change.

The first element has been derived by Stow and others from *mart* 'market', but this is rightly rejected by Bonner and Harben. ME *mart* 'ox' (from Gaelic *mart*), preferred by Bonner, was a Northern word only. Heuser alternatively suggests derivation from the woman's name *Martha*, F *Marthe*. The early spellings with *th* tell in favour of this. *Martel Lane* 1310 suggests as a possible source the French surname *Martel*, a name well evidenced in early London, but if this was the original first element, we should expect to find occasional forms such as *Marteleslane*. The name *Marthe* has not been met with in early London sources, but an Alanus fil. Marthe is mentioned 1275 RH i. 225 (Rochester). The probable meaning is 'Martha's lane'.

Pentecost Lane [FarrI; north from Newgate Street past St. Nicholas Shambles, now Roman Bath Street]: *Pentecostelane* 1280 f. CW i. 50, 52, *Pentecosteslane* 1290 ADB 2237, 1294 Harben, *Pentecostlane* 1307–8 CW i. 197, 1436 Pat, and commonly, *Penthecoste lane* 1539 LP, *Penthecoste Lane*, *Pintottes* alias *Penticotes Lane* 1594 LIpm, *Penticost* (*Pentecost*) *lane* Stow. 'Pentecost's lane.' *Pentecost*, literally 'Easter', was a fairly common early English font-name. The rare occurrence of the genitive form *Pentecostes* may be due to the preceding *s* (dissimilation). The lane was doubtless named from Pentecost' fil. Fromundi, who was a tenant in St. Nicholas Shambles 1198–1211 and 1211–12 (PaulsCh 265 f., 83).

Philip Lane [CripI; Addle Street–London Wall]: *Philippes-lane* a 1179 (13th) Clerkenwell 303, *Philippes lane* 1170–87 ADA 7926 f., *Phelip(p)eslane* 1277–8, 1280 CW i. 31, 47 &c.,

Felipeslane 1291 LBA 135, *Philippeslane* 1301 Cor 30, 1382 Plea, 1414 (1416) CW ii. 409, *Philiplane* 1539 LP. Named from an early owner, but *Philip* was a common name, and the eponym cannot be identified.

Stephen Lane, now **Churchyard Alley** [St. Magnus, Bridge; Thames Street–the Thames]: *Stepheneslane* 1329 CW i. 347, 1343 LibCust 447, 1455 (1456) CW ii. 529 (alias *Chirchawlane*), *Steveneslane* 1349 (1351) CW i. 654, 1373–4 ib. ii. 158 (olim for *Churchehawlane*). Harben suggests that the lane was named from Stephen de Oystergate, who held land in the vicinity in the 13th century. More likely it was named from Stephen Lucas, stockfishmonger, who was a taxpayer in Bridge ward in 1332 (Subs) and whose will was enrolled in 1349. He had a tenement in St. Magnus. As Harben points out, the lane had been turned by one Adam Lucas before 1343. *Chirch-haw* is an old word for *churchyard*, found for instance in Chaucer.

Sygrymeslane 1337 ADA 11539, *Segeryneslane* 1566 LIpm [in St. Dunstan, Tower], perhaps the present St. Dunstan's Hill or a lane near it. A doubtful case. *Sygrym* (*Segeryn*) is OE *Sægrim* from ODan *Segrim*, found as *Sagrim*, *Segrim* in DB, as a family name in RH. But in the name under discussion it may be the family name. No person with this font-name or surname has been noticed in London, but one Segrim the Weaver was a citizen of Oxford *c.* 1200, and Segrim occurs as a surname there (see Fridesw, passim). King's Lane in Cambridge was formerly *Segrim(m)eslane* (1279 &c.). The surname *Sagrim* is evidenced in Middlesex: Alice Sagrim in Edgware 1277 LMAS, N.S. vii. 171, Richard Sagrim in Hendon 1321 ib. vi. 580.

Wancelineslane 1235 ADA 1791, *Wauncelines-lane* 1241 ib. 2723, identical with *Germayneslane* (supra), *Batteslane* (infra), and Haywharf Lane. *Wancelin* is doubtless a French font-name derived from OHG *Wenzil*. An earlier owner of land in the lane than German le Corder must have had that name.

Wolsy Lane [Dowg]: *Wolsislane* 1307 LBC 204, 1311 CW i. 220 (All Hallows the Less, Dowg), *Wolsieslane* 1317 CW i. 273, 1343 LibCust 448 (between the houses of John de Pulteneye and Bartholomew Dewmars), *Wolsylane* 1379 Pat, *Wolseslane* 1421, *Wolsilane* 1422–3 Plea, *Wolsy Lane* 1527 (1537–8) CW ii. 643, *Wolfes lane, Wolsey lane* (obsolete) Stow. The name goes with *Wolsiesgate* 1300 Mayors, 1301 LibAlb 242, *Wolsyesyate* n.d. ib. 697, the name of a water-gate. The lane is identified by Harben as one between Cold Harbour Lane and Haywharf Lane. It was named from a person called *Wolsi* (OE *Wulfsige*). The name is recorded in London in 1137 (Round, *Commune of London*, p. 100). One *Wlsius cognomento Lickescoppe* of London is mentioned in a spurious charter of 1067; see 1335 Ch.

Names containing a surname or family name as first element

Many names in -*lane* have as first element a surname or family name. A few of the names in the preceding subsection possibly belong here.

Armenterslane 1343 LibCust 448 (held by John de Westone), *Erment(i)erslane* 1421 f. Plea (Dowg). Identical with Weston Lane (infra) and perhaps with Coldharbour Lane, which runs from Upper Thames Street to the Thames in All Hallows the Less (Dowg). The lane was named from John de Armenters, draper, wool-exporter, sheriff, alderman of Langbourn 1300–6, whose will was enrolled in 1306. He was a resident in All Hallows the Less. See ELSR 167. The surname was taken from Armentières in France.

Arundellane 1421 (1432–3) CW ii. 461 (apparently in All Hallows the Less, Dowg), not further identified. No doubt named from an inhabitant with the surname *Arundel*, but no such person is known in the neighbourhood.

Basing Lane [BreadSt, Cordw; Bread Street–Bow Lane]: *Basinglane* 1275 CW i. 20, *Basingelane* 1279–80 ib. 46, 1303–4 Mayors 155, *Basingestrete* 1303 LBC 191, *Basiggeslane* 1307 ib. 204, *Basingeslane* 1324 CW i. 309, *Bassingeslane* 1310 LBD 231, *Basyngelane* 1325 Cl, 1550 Pat, *Bassynglane* 1361 Cl, *Bassinglane* 1544 LP. The lane was doubtless named from the Basing family, as suggested by Kingsford and Harben. Peter de Basinges (1275 Will) had a house in Basing Lane (parish St. Mary Aldermary) and the lane may have been named from him, but there were earlier members of the family in London. Peter was a son of William de Basinges, mercer (mentioned 1218, 1223 Cl). The family will have come from Basing in Hants. The lane is now merged in Cannon Street.

Batteslane 1311–12 LBD 312, 1508–9 CW ii. 614 (alias *Heywharfe Lane*), *Battyslane* 1496–7 LIpm. Later called Haywharf Lane (q.v.), earlier *Wancelineslane*, *Germayneslane*. The lane took its name from Gerard Bat (sheriff 1232–3, 1235–6, alderman, mayor 1240–1) or other members of the family. Gerard son of Peter Bat had property by *Wancelineslane* in 1235 and 1241 (ADA 1791, 2723). *Bat* is probably an English nickname derived from OE *batt* 'a cudgel'.

Brickhill Lane [Vi; Upper Thames Street–Greenwich Street]. The earliest reference appears to be *Brikels lane* Stow. The lane seems to have been named from one John Brickel or Brykles,[1] who in 1440 left houses in the lane or a neighbouring

---

[1] Doubtless identical with John Brykelys (Brikelys), draper, who held land in Vintry in 1409–10 (Hansisches Urkundenbuch v).

lane, according to Harben. No other early references to the lane have been met with. The surname will have been derived from Brickhill in Bucks.

Campion Lane. See Haywharf Lane, p. 153.

Cousin Lane [Dowg; south from Upper Thames Street in All Hallows the Great]: *la Cosyneslane* 1305–6 CW i. 175 (will of Johanna Cosyn, who had houses there), *Cosineslane* 1338, 1342 ib. 430, 459, *Cosynlane* 1379 LBH, *Cosyne(s)lane* 1384–5, 1414 Pat, *Cussyn Lane* 1510–11 &c. LP. Several persons with the surname *Cosyn* (from ME *cosin* 'cousin') had land in All Hallows the Great about 1300, two with certainty in Cousin Lane. Peter Cosyn (1291–2 Will) evidently lived in the parish. Johanna Cosyn (supra) was not the widow of Peter. William Cosyn de Sutton, whose will was enrolled in 1345 (dated 1340), had houses in Cousin Lane. He was a taxpayer in Dowgate in 1292 (Subs), a sheriff 1305–6, alderman of Queenhithe 1306–15. He may well have been a son of Peter. Cousin Lane will have received its name from the Cosyns mentioned.

Coventreslane [probably Vi] 1343 LibCust 450. Evidently named from one or more vintners with the surname *Coventre* resident in Vintry, as Henry de Coventre (alderman of Vintry, resident in St. James' Garlickhithe, will enrolled in 1282–3), Stephen de Coventre, son of Henry (1310 Will), Edmund and Thomas, sons of Stephen.

Cressynghamlane 1432 (1436) CW ii. 480 [St. James', Vi], 1438 (1441) ib. 492 (land and wharf between this lane and *Stodyeslane* in St. Martin and St. James' Vi mentioned). Perhaps the present Anchor Alley. The lane was no doubt named from John de Cressyngham (1339 Will) or his son John (1364–

5 Will; of St. James' Vi, apparently a joiner). Cressingham is a village in Norfolk.

Dibleslane 1301, *Dibeleslane* 1310 CW i. 153, 213 [St. Michael, Qu], *Dybleslane* 1422 Plea (LoEngl 127), *Debillane* 1459 (1465–6) CW ii. 553. The lane ran down to the Thames, perhaps near the wharf called *Dibbleswharf* 1364 Cl. The lane and wharf were named, as noticed by Harben, from William Dible, who is mentioned 1265 Pat as the king's enemy and an earlier tenant on the Thames near Castle Baynard. He will be identical with William Dibel (Dybel) who was a surety in Castle Baynard 1275–6, 1276, 1277 (LBB 258 ff.), and a juror there in 1279 (*RHT* m. 19). This suggests that the lane and wharf were in the western part of Queenhithe ward near the boundary of Castle Baynard. *Dible* may be from F *diable*; the surname *le Diable* occurs 1230 P (Cambs).

Dorkynggeslane 1343 LibCust 450 [perhaps Vi]. Doubtless named from Richard de Dorking of St. Martin Vi, probably a vintner, whose will was enrolled in 1321–2.

Fatteslane 1279 *RHT* m. 12, 1295, 1315, 1343 CW i. 122 (with note 2), 257 (St. James' Garlickhithe), called the lane of Richard le Gras 1259 ib. 3. The lane ran to the Thames, but cannot be definitely identified. It was no doubt named from the Richard le Gras (or Grassus) who was a prominent citizen in London in the early 13th century, a son of his being taken as a hostage for the City's loyalty in 1223 (Cl), and appears as a witness in St. Martin Vi *c.* 1230 (Clerkenwell 339). Stephen le Gras was a sheriff 1210–11 and alderman of Vintry. The surname varied between the French form *Gras* (F *gras* 'fat') and the English *Fatt*(*e*); it must remain an open question which was the original form of the name. The English word appears as a by-name in Old English (*Æðestan Fætta* 1049–58 KCD 804).

Finamour Lane, an old name of Fye Foot Lane [Qu]: *Fynamoureslane* 1316 CW i. 263, *Finimore lane or fiue foote lane* Stow. The lane must have been named from a person with the surname *Finamour* (a name of French origin). Henry Finamour was a surety in 1281 (LBB 4) and John Fynamour a tenant in St. Clement Danes in 1379 (MxFF i. 154). On the name see Bardsley under Finnemore.

Finch Lane [Cornh, BroadSt; Cornhill–Threadneedle Street]: *Finkeslane* 1231–45 Clerkenwell 347, 1261–2 HMC 4th Rep 449, *Fynkeslane* 1274–5 CW i. 22, 1293 LBC 14, 1337 Cor 192, *Fynghis Lane* 1305–6 CW i. 177, *Fyncheslane* 1376 CW ii. 189, *Fynke Lane* 1548 Pat, *Finke(s) lane* Stow. The correct form of the first element was probably *Fink*, the alternative *Finch* being at first a Norman spelling with *ch* for *k*. In the name of the parish of St. Benet Fink the form with *k* is regular. The lane and parish were named from Ælfwin (Ailwin) Fink (*c.* 1165–90), a moneyer, who is mentioned as an earlier tenant in *Finkeslane* in 1261–2, or James Finke, an earlier tenant in 1231–45 (cf. supra).

Finch Lane, now **Pudding Lane** [Bill]: *Finches lane* 1333 BM, *Fyncheslane* alias *Pudynglane* 1415 Pat, (the highway lately called) *Fynkeslane* 1449 ADA 1723. Presumably named from a person with the surname *Finch*, possibly an ancestor of Thomas Fynche, tailor, who was a tenant of St. Mary at Hill church in 1479–81 (StMary 94). On the surname *Finch* (*Fink*) see Bardsley and ELPN 149 f. The source is OE *finc* 'finch', which appears to have had a side-form with unpalatalized *k*. But *Fink* is conceivably from Du *vink*, MDu, MLG *vinke* 'finch'.

Fresshfisshlane 1430 (1449) CW ii. 517 (boundary of land in St. Peter Paul's Wharf, Qu, CastleB). Possibly an alternative name of Lambeth Hill (Harben). *Freshfish* is a well-evidenced surname in London, though not in Queenhithe or Castle Baynard; cf. ELSR 328. Alternatively the name may mean 'lane where fresh fish was sold'.

Gayspur Lane, a former name of the north part of Aldermanbury [CripI]: *Gaysporelane* 1332 (1333) CW i. 386, 1339 Plea (St. Mary Aldermanbury), *Gayspor Lane c.* 1450 PaulsMSS 2 b, *Gayspor(r)e Strete* 1550 Pat, *Gay spurre lane* Stow. *Gayspur* is a surname. One Fulk Gayspore was a tenant in Bill in 1319 (Subs). Walter G. was a juror in All Hallows Barking (Tower) in 1327 (LBE 278). Gayspur Lane was probably named from some other person with the surname. *Gayspur* will mean 'bright (showy) spur', '(a person) with bright spurs'.

Gofair Lane, now **Cross Lane** [Walbr, Dowg; Bush Lane–Suffolk Lane]: *Gofairelane* 1313 CW i. 239, *Gofayrlane* 1318 ib. 280, *Gofairlane* 1448 Pat (all St. Swithin, Walbr); *Govayrlane* 1339 CW i. 435, *Govereslane* 1348 (1349) ib. 544, 1456 Pat, *Gofairlane* 1409–10 Lappenberg 34 (all Dowg). Several persons with the surname *Gofaire* ('go fairly') are mentioned in early London sources; cf. ELPN 152. Roger Gofayre was a juror for Walbrook in 1275 (RH 423). Elias Gofaire (1309–10 Will) had rents in St. Swithin.

Grantham Lane, now **Brewers Lane** [Dowg; south from Upper Thames Street, west of Dowgate]: *Granthameslane* 1343 LibCust 449 (obstructed by John de Grantham), *Granthamlane* 1382 LBH, 1421 Plea, *Grantamlane* 1499 LIpm, *Granthams lane* Stow ('so called of Iohn Grantham, some time Maior'). John de Grantham (1344–5 Will) was a sheriff 1322–3, alder-

man of Cornhill and Cordwainer, mayor 1328–9. He had
property in All Hallows the Great in *Bathestereslane* (q.v.).
The surname was taken from Grantham Li.

Greenwich Lane, now **Greenwich Street** [Dowg, Vi;
south from Upper Thames Street]: *Grenewichislane* 1279–80,
Grenewichlane 1283–4 LBA 203, 157, *Grenewicheslane* 1309
LBD 215, *Grenewichelane* 1421 Plea, *Grenewiche Lane* 1497
CW ii. 599, 1550 Pat. Doubtless named from a person with
the surname *Grenewich*. The surname is well evidenced in
London, and one John de Grenewich has been found as a
surety in Dowgate ward (1324 Cor 85). He is too late to have
given the lane its name, but some person connected with him
may have been resident there in the 13th century. According
to Stow the lane was in his time *Frier lane* ('of such a signe
there set vp'). An earlier example is *Frere Lane* (in All Hallows
the Great) 1549 Pat.

Hadestokeslane 1297–8 CW i. 130 [St. Michael, Qu]. Probably named from William de Hadestok (son of Augustine de
Hadestok), whose will was enrolled in 1295–6, and who was
alderman of Tower *c.* 1267–1288 and owner of houses in St.
Michael, or (and) his brother Simon de Hadestok, who was
alderman of Queenhithe *c.* 1267–87 and owner of a house in
the ward. The surname was taken from Hadstock Ess.

Hardeleslane 1431 (1464) CW ii. 551 [St. Martin, Vi].
Harben quotes a reference of 1352 to 'the lane late of John
Hardell' in a grant to John de Stodeye; this indicates that the
lane is identical with Stodies Lane (q.v.), now Little Cheapside. He suggests that the lane was named from Ralph Hardel
(mayor 1258) and his family. But no doubt the lane took its
name chiefly from John Hardel, who was of St. Martin and

doubtless a vintner. His will was enrolled in 1346-7. However, Richard, his father (1301 Will), was likewise of St. Martin, and one Robert Hardel is mentioned as an earlier tenant in the same parish in 1311 (LBD 189). *Hardel* is from OF *hardel* 'youth; good-for-nothing'.

Palmerslane 1343 LibCust 450, *Palmereslane* 1437 (1439), 1442 (1448) CW ii. 487, 516 (St. Martin, Vi), *Palmers lane*, now called *Anchor lane* Stow. Cf. *Cressynghamlane* supra. Clearly named from Henry le Palmer, vintner, who was a taxpayer in Cheap in 1319, in Vintry in 1332, and was living in 1352 (LBF 249). Cf. ELSR 297. *Palmer* from ME *palmer*, AF *palmer*, *paumer* 'a pilgrim'.

Parkerislane 1427-8 LBK 75, 'þe lane by-side þe hous sumtyme John Parkers' 1422 Plea (LoEngl 128). The lane, which runs south from Upper Thames Street in Queenhithe ward, is now **Stew Lane**, so called from a stew (hot baths) for women mentioned LBK 75. John Parker, who is otherwise unknown, must have died before 1422. *Parker* is from AF *parker* 'park-keeper'.

Philpot Lane [Bill, Langb; Eastcheap–Fenchurch Street]: *Philpot Lane* 1480-1 ADC 6563 (alias Lane of St. Andrew Hubbard), 1498-9 (1504), 1532 (1553) CW ii. 607, 656. Named, as pointed out by Stow, from Sir John Philpot, who was a grocer and had land in Bridge Street, Pudding Lane, and elsewhere. His will, dated 1381, was enrolled in 1389. He was a sheriff 1372-3, mayor 1378-9 and alderman of Cornhill 1372-84, the year of his death. *Philpot* is from *Philipot*, a French diminutive of *Philip*. The lane is called *vicus Sancti Andreæ* 1231 LibAlb 94, *venella Sancti Andree Hubert* 1252-65 Clerkenwell F.

Pikardeslane [St. Martin, Vi] 1279, 1285 ADA 2330, 2341, *Pycardeslane* 1284 CW i. 68. Possibly named from Richard Picard (Pycard), who was a sheriff of London 1253–4 and 1260–1 (PaulsMSS 10 b, ADA 1605, 1625 &c.). The surname means 'the Picard'.

Pope Lane [Aldersg, now perhaps St. Ann's Alley, which runs west from Noble Street by St. John Zachary]: *Popes lane* t. Edw 1 (?) PaulsMSS 13 b, *Popes Lane* 1334 ib. 49 b, *Pope lane* Stow. *Pope* is a well-evidenced surname in London in the 13th century, but the only persons to be considered here are Hugh Pope, a horse-dealer, mentioned 1281 ff. LBA 46 &c., 1296 LBB 62, and Walter Pope, his brother (1281 LBA 46). There is no information about their abode, however.

Popkirtle Lane [St. Pancras, possibly an old name of Pancras Lane]: *Popcurtles-*, *Pupekertillane* 1275 CW i. 23, *Popekerte-lane* 1276 ib. 27, *Puppekirtel(es)lane* 1324, 1344–5 ib. 309, 476, *Puppekirtlane*[1] 1436 (1445–6) CW ii. 506, *Puppekirtillane*, *-kirtyllane* 1477 (1489), 1505–6 ib. 590, 612. These are all the examples noted. An etymology of the name has not been attempted before, except that Dr. Bohman (p. 194) suggests that it may contain OE *cyrtel* 'kirtle', which is evidently correct. *Popcurtel*, as indicated by the forms with genitival *s*, is a surname, originally a nickname, which is to be compared with the surname *Pokekertelle* found in 1224. William Pokekertelle (alias Prutkirtel) was a juror in Bassishaw in that year (Selden 60). *Pokekertelle* means 'poke the kirtle', 'one who pokes a kirtle', the first element being ME *poke, pouke, puke* 'to poke'. *Popcurtel* is at least an analogous formation, perhaps with ME *poppe* 'to pop, strike, knock' as its first member, but it is

---

[1] Venella de *Puppekirtlane* (*Pupkirtlane*) in the copy of the will in EpCant (A.D. 1434).

possible that it is a modification of *Pokekertel* or that there was a ME *pope*, *pupe* 'to poke' by the side of *poke* and *pote* (*pute*). However this may be, Popkirtle Lane was hardly named from William Pokekertelle.

Pourteslane 1368–9 CW ii. 124, *Poorteslane* 1392 Plea, *Porteslane* 1398 Plea, 1401 (1407) CW ii. 374, 1408 Pat. The lane was in St. Dunstan Tower and was at right angles to Tower Street. Harben suggests identity with Preist Alley. The lane must have been named from an early inhabitant with the surname *Pourte*. This well-evidenced name was generally borne by people associated with other wards than Tower, but Gilbert Purte was a surety in Tower in 1276 (LBB 262) and Thomas Pourte, whose will was enrolled in 1307, owned a rent just in St. Dunstan.

Pyellane [St. Michael, Qu, apparently the present Huggin Lane] Stow ii. 5. John Pyel (Piel), merchant (mercer), wool-exporter, is often mentioned in records, e.g. 1346 ff. Cl, 1362 LBG. He was a sheriff 1369–70, alderman of Castle Baynard 1369–78, mayor 1372–3. His will of 1378 was enrolled in 1382. *Piel* might be OF *piel*, F *pieu* 'stake'.

Reygateslane 1343 LibCust 450 [Vi?]. One John de Raygate was a taxpayer in Vintry in 1292 (Subs), and a William de Reygate was a juror ibidem in 1325–6 and 1341 (Cor 140, LBF 256). The lane may have been named from the latter. The surname was taken from Reigate Sr.

Sermon Lane [CastleB; Carter Lane–Knightrider Street]: *Sarmoneres lane* t. Hy 3 PaulsMSS 13 a, *Sarmonereslane* 1333 (1334) CW i. 396, *Sarmoneruslane* 1373 Plea, *Sermon lane* 1557–8 Pat, Stow. The name is correctly explained by Harben, who adduces a reference to the land of Adam Sermocinarius in the vicinity (1228 *PaulsMSS*). A tenement formerly belonging to Adam le Sarmoner is mentioned 1279 PaulsMSS 19 b. ME *sermoner* (AF *sarmuner*) means 'a preacher of sermons'. *Sermocinarius* is a synonym derived from Lat *sermocinor*, the same as *sermonor* 'to speak'. *Sarmoner* is a surname, originally perhaps a nickname.

Sevehod Lane [Cheap, the lost name of a lane in St. Lawrence Jewry and St. Martin Pomary]: *Seuehodeslane* 1354 CW i. 679, *Sevehodelane* n.d. PaulsMSS 16 b, *Sefhodlane* 1377 (1378) CW ii. 201, *Sevenhodlane* 1394 ib. 308, *Sevehodeslane* 1406 Pat, *Sevehodenelane* 1412 CW ii. 395, *Sevenfotelane* 1456 ADA 2186. The last form is probably due to popular etymology; possibly the lane was narrow. The lane was named from a family resident there. Harben mentions Robert Schevehod 1277 LBB 266 (of St. Martin Pomary), Henry Sevehod 1283 LBA 79 (of Ironmonger Lane), also a later Robert Seuehod of the same district (A.D. 1352). There are other examples of the surname. One Robert Senehod (sic) was a juror in Cornhill in 1275 (RH). The explanation of the surname is not easy, except that -*hod* is ME *hōd* 'hood'. An attempt at explaining the first element on the supposition that it had initial *Sh*- is made in ELPN 165 f. Connexion with *Sephardim*, the title of one of the two branches of the Hebrew race, suggested by Sharpe and quoted by Harben, is of course not to be seriously considered. Some forms may indicate that the first element of the surname is the numeral *seven*.

Southamlane 1383 Pat, 1383 LBH 225 (by Thames Street, doubtless in Dowg and Cand) was very likely an occasional name of Laurence Pountney Lane. The lane was named from John Southam, stockfishmonger, whose will, dated 1382, was enrolled in 1394–5. He was of St. Lawrence Pountney, and alderman successively of Dowgate, Tower and Langbourn 1377–82.

Stodies Lane, formerly *Hardeleslane*, now **Little Cheapside** [Vi]: *Stodyes lane* 1394 Harben, *Stodyeslane* 1438 (1441) CW ii. 492 (St. Martin and St. James', Vi), *Stodies lane* Stow. Named from John de Stodeye, vintner, of St. Martin. He was alderman of Vintry 1352–76, a sheriff 1352–3, mayor 1357–8, and died in 1376. The surname is from Stody Nf.

Suffolk Lane [Dowg, Walbr; Laurence Pountney Hill–Upper Thames Street]: *Suffolke Lane* (in All Hallows the Less) 1596 (1600–1) CW ii. 727, Stow. Named from the family of Suffolk, who held the manor of Rose, earlier Poultney's Inn. William de la Pole, duke of Suffolk, bought the property, which in 1495 came to Edmund de la Pole (Harben).

Townsend Lane, now **Bull Wharf Lane** [Qu, the boundary of Queenhithe ward on the east]: *Townesend lane* 1562 MxFF ii. 118, *Townes end(e) lane* Stow. Richard Townesende had a lease of a messuage and wharf in St. Michael Qu in 1544 (LP). *Townsend,* from *atte Tounesende* 'at the end of the village', is a common surname.

Trig Lane [Qu; Upper Thames Street–the Thames]: *Tryggeslane* 1422 Plea (LoEngl 129), *Trigge lane* Stow. The lane was named from one or more of the persons with the surname *Trigge* resident in Queenhithe in the 14th and 15th centuries, as William Trigge, fishmonger 1319–20, 1325 LBE 115, 201, W. Trige 1344–5 LBF 116; John Tryg, fishmonger of Old Fish Street, often mentioned *c.* 1360–85, and Andrew Tryg, fishmonger 1378 Riley, *Mem* 425 (LBH). *Trig* is ME *trig* 'faithful' from ON *tryggr*, ODan *trygg*.

Warwick Lane, olim **Old Dean's Lane** [CastleB, FarrI; Newgate Street–Paternoster Row]: *Werwyk Lane* 1474–5 Paston iii. 127, *Warwyke lane* 1506 (16th) Grey Friars, 1554 Machyn 66, *Warwicke lane* Stow. At least ultimately named from the earls of Warwick. One earl of Warwick was a tenant in Old Dean's Lane already in 1368 (Plea); see further Kingsford 351. But the lane may have got its name in reality from Warwick Inn, a house built by one of the earls, as suggested by Stow. Warwick Inn seems to have been in existence in 1458.

Weston Lane [Dowg]: *Westoneslane* 1357, 1363–4, *Westonnes-lane* 1401, *Westonlane* 1377–8, 1379 Pat (All Hallows the Less, formerly *Armenterslane*). John de Weston, draper of Dowgate, was a taxpayer in Dowgate in 1332 (Subs) and a representative of the ward in 1338 (LBF 23).

Weyland Lane, later **Pillory Lane** [Ports]: *Weylandes-lanende* alias *Pylorylane* 1421 Plea. Thomas de Weylond (Weylaund), a judge and chief justice, who was removed from office in 1289 and banished in 1290, his estates being confiscated, had land in London. According to a statement of 1289 in Misc he (and his wife) had held a messuage in Smith-field without Aldgate, and it is obvious that the lane here under discussion was named from him. It is interesting to note that the name lived on so long. *Weyland* is doubtless from Wayland (hundred) Nf.

Windgoose Lane, now **Wingoose Alley** [Dowg; south from Thames Street to the Steelyard]: *Wendegoslane* 1279 *RHT* m. 15, 1300–1, 1339 CW i. 149, 435, 1343 LibCust 449, *Wande-goselane* 1308 CW i. 199, *Wendegoselane* 1327 ib. 327, *Wynde-goslane* 1382 Pat, *Wendegooslane iuxta Thamisiam* 1391 Lappenberg 24, *Wyndegooslane* 1421 Plea, *Wyndegoselane* 1475

Pat, *Wynges Lane* 1515 LP, *Wendegaynelane* 1458 (1477–8) CW ii. 577, *Wyndagayngooslane* (sic) 1422–3 Plea, *Windgoose* or *Wildgoose lane*, now *Windgoose Alley* Stow ('for the most part builded on'). Numerous instances will be found in Lappenberg, pp. 24 ff. (1382–1509). Harben does not consider the early forms and only discusses the form *Wende- gaynelane*, which in his opinion indicates that the lane was a cul de sac. This may be so, but it rather looks as if this form and that of 1422 (supra) are corrupt. Kingsford, who mentions Benedict Wandegos, an owner of land in St. Botolph Bishops- gate in the 12th or early 13th century (ADA 1623), takes *Windgoose* to be of German origin. It is clear that the lane was named from a person with the surname *Wendegos* (*Wandegos*), which is evidently an English nickname containing the word *goose* (ME *gōs*) and apparently a form of OE *wendan*, ME *wende* 'to turn' &c., but it is not easy to account for such a name. *Wendegos* might possibly be a jocular counterpart of *Turnbull*.

Wirehalelane 1458 (1477–8) CW ii. 577 (St. Mary at Hill, Bill), was clearly named from John de Wirhale of St. George Eastcheap, whose will was enrolled in 1371, or his son William Wirhale, goldsmith, mentioned in his father's will. The sur- name is of old standing in London, the forms showing a good deal of variation, as *Wilehale*, *Wirhale*, and the like. It was taken from some as yet unidentified place.

Woodroffe Lane, apparently now **Cooper's Row** [Aldg, Tower; Crutched Friars–Trinity Square]: *Woderouelane* 1260 ADA 2656, 1285 Ch, 1290 ADA 2402, *Woderovelane* 1283– 4, 1291 CW i. 68, 98, *Woodroffe lane* Stow. *Woderove* was a common surname in early times in London (see ELPN 172), but the only known bearer that could have given its name

to the lane is Reginald Woderone (for -*roue*) 1230 P. He paid
tallage in London in that year, but nothing further is known
about him. He may, of course, have lived near Woodroffe Lane.
The surname is an old plant-name, *woodruff* (OE *wudurōfe*,
ME *woderove*) 'Asperula odorata'. But the total absence of
forms with a genitive -*s* renders it doubtful if the name of the
lane does not after all contain the plant-name itself. Woodruff
may have grown in some places (gardens) in the lane or it may
have been sold there. It was a medicinal plant and was also
used for ornamental purposes. In Records of St. Mary at Hill,
p. 81, are mentioned under 1477–9 *Rose-garlondis and wodrove-
garlondis* as used, apparently for the decoration of the church,
on St. Barnabas's Day.

D. Lanes named from their situation

(Great) Shire Lane [FarrE; north from Temple Bar, now
lost]: *Shirelane* 1544 LP, *Shyre* (*Shere*) *lane* Stow ('diuideth the
Cittie from the Shire'). The lane is called Shere Lane in
PNMx 183; *shire* was often pronounced as 'sheer' in early
modern English. The lane was on the boundary of and partly
outside the City liberty.

Names from some prominent physical feature

These are few.

Beech Lane, now **Beech Street** [CripE, a continuation of
Barbican from Red Cross Street to White Cross Street]. At
present Beech Lane is a name given to a side-street from Beech
Street. Beech Street is actually *Bechestrete* 1285 CW i. 74, but
le Bechlane 1279 *RHT* m. 20, *Bechelane* 1333 (1334–5), 1345
(1348), 1348–9 CW i. 402, 504, 525, *Beechelane* 1340–1 ib. 443,
Bechen-lane 1396 Pat, *Berchenlane* (sic) 1430 (1439) CW ii.
489, *Beech Lane* 1618 Acts Privy Council. Stow suggests that

Beech lane was named from Nicholas de la Beech, Lieutenant of the Tower t. Edw 3, and points out that there were no beech-trees in the lane in his time. Harben says it was named after the family 'de la Beche', while Kingsford suggests connexion with the name of a spring called *Wittewellebech* in 1181–2 &c. (Clerkenwell 2 ff.). These suggestions cannot be accepted. The lane was named from a locality called *la Beche*. Henry de la Beche, son of Geoffrey de la Beche, tanner, had land in 'la beche' in St. Giles', by the street called 'la beche' in 1257 (ADA 2263). It is clear that the surname of these two persons was taken from the place or street. As for Nicholas de la Beech it is unlikely that he belonged to an old London family, and in his case the surname probably had a different origin. The probability is that *the Beche* was the name of some land by the lane, which came to be called *the Beche*, later *Bechestrete* or *Bechelane*. *Beche* is probably from OE *bēce* 'beech' in the plural form, so that the name meant 'the beeches'. Occasional *Bechenlane* apparently represents a ME *Bechene-lane*, with the first element in the genitive (plural) form in -*ene* (OE -*ena*). Alternatively *Beche* might be from OE *bece* 'valley, stream', found in place-names such as Land-, Waterbeach and very likely in *Wittewellebech* (supra), though the spring so called was in Clerkenwell. In favour of this tells the fact that there was a watercourse in Beech Lane, referred to as *cursus aque* 1279 *RHT* m. 20. But the vowels of *beech* and *beach* (from OE *bece*) were not the same in the Middle and Early Modern English periods, and the spelling Beech coupled with Stow's remark on the absence of beech-trees indicates that Beech Lane was pronounced with the vowel in *beech*.

Fleet Lane [FarrE] runs from Old Bailey to Farringdon Street, which is on the line of Fleet River, but formerly also south along the Fleet past Fleet prison. The name is *Fletelane*

1544 LP, *Flett Lane* 1552 Machyn 16, *Fletlane* 1567 LIpm.
The lane is very likely identical with *Smalelane* (q.v.) and
seems to be described variously as 'parva venella regia'. . .
from the bailey without Newegate 'usque Flete' 1264–5 ADA
7829, the little lane behind the Flete prison 13th ib. 7842 and
the like. The name may mean 'the lane leading to Fleet river',
but 'the lane leading to Fleet prison' is a possible alternative.

Moor Lane. See **Moor Street**, p. 89.

Water Lane [All Hallows Barking, Tower; Tower Street–
Lower Thames Street]: *Water Lane* 1425 Plea, *Water lane*
Stow ('runneth downe to the Water gate . . . in Thames
streete'). An earlier reference to the lane is *þe Watergatestrete
anynst Berelane* 1422 Plea (LoEngl 129). Beer Lane runs
parallel to Water Lane. The watergate in question is mentioned
as early as 1276 (LBB 262). *Watergate* also occurs as the name
of the lane continuing Water Lane south from Thames Street
(lane called *Watergate* 1547 Pat). In this case Water Lane
may be elliptical for Watergate Lane. An earlier name was
Spurrier Lane.

Water Lane [FarrE; Fleet Street–the Thames]: *Water lane*
1540 LP, Stow. This may be 'the lane leading to the Thames'
or perhaps more especially 'the lane used in fetching water or
in watering animals'.

Names from various buildings or structures

   Names derived from inns or from churches, for reasons that
will appear later, are dealt with separately.

Bordhaw Lane [St. Mary Colechurch, Cheap]: *Bordhawe-
lane* 1305 CW i. 170, *Borchawelane* (sic) 1472 Pat, *Bordhawe* (lane) 1323 CW i. 302, *Burdellane* 1405–6 ib. ii. 365,

Bordhangly lane (sic) Stow. Named from a locality, called *la Bordhae* 1252 Ch (p), *la Bordhawe* 1257 PaulsMSS 17 b, *Bordhaghe* 1275 CW i. 25. The name may have meant 'a timberyard', as suggested by Riley, or 'an enclosure made of boards'. Derivation from *bordel* 'brothel' is excluded.

Bow Lane, now **College Street** and **Little College Street** [Vi, Dowg]. The lane ran west from Dowgate Hill past the Walbrook to College Hill. But also a lane that branched off south to Upper Thames Street, the present Little College Street, was formerly Bow Lane. The name is in the main correctly explained by Bonner and by Harben under College Street. *Bowe* (OF *Arche*) was originally the name of an arched bridge over the Walbrook. An arch of a bridge (and a bridge formed by one arch) is in early English known as *bowe* (OE *boga* 'a bow'). In Bow Lane the word was probably in the plural. *Bowe* is not recorded as the name of the bridge itself, but the lane leading to it at an early date came to be called *Bowe*, later *Bowelane*. It is (the lane called) *les Arches* 1275–6 ADA 7823, (a little lane called) *Le Arche* (upon Walebrok) 1298–9 LBC 35, (lane called) *le* (or *la*) *Bowe* 1307, 1318 CW i. 190, 277, *Bowelane* 1327–8 ib. 329 &c., *la Bowelane* 1317 LBE 78, 1339, 1354 CW i. 435, 681, *Boghelane* 1362 Pat, *Bowlane* 1485 (1510) LIpm, *Bowelane* 1558 Pat. An alternative name was *Eldebowelane* 1343 LibCust 450, *Elbow lane* Stow and later (see Harben). The meaning is 'old Bow Lane', but the name was naturally often taken to mean 'elbow lane' seeing that the lane had a definite bend, thus by Stow. It is not clear if 'old' was added for distinction from Bow Lane in Cordwainer ward or to designate one part (if so, the present College Street) as against another (Little College Street). In view of the late appearance of the other Bow Lane the second alternative is to be preferred. The name College Street dates from the early 19th century. *College* is Whittington College, founded in the time of Henry VI.

Dowe Lane 1526, 1536 &c. LP, *Dowlane* 1560–1 LIpm, is no doubt, as suggested by Harben, for *Bowe Lane*. The capital *B*- was probably misread as *D*-, but association with *Dow*- in *Dowgate* may have helped the change.

Bretask Lane [All Hallows the Less, Dowg; name now lost]: (venella vocata) *Bretaske* 1343 LibCust 448, *Bretask Lane* 1343–4 Plea, probably *Brodaxlane* 1421 f. Plea. A house in the lane called *la Bretask* is mentioned LBF 1 (note); it is called *le Bretasse* 1334 CW i. 397, probably *the Brodeax* 1422 Plea. The source of the name is *brattice*, ME *brutaske*, *bretage* from OF *bretesque* and the like, MLat *breteschia*. The meaning was 'a temporary breastwork, parapet, or gallery of wood erected on the battlement of a fortress' (OED). The form *Brodeax* will be due to popular etymology. The name Bretask Lane may be compared with the Brittox in Devizes (*la Britasche* c. 1300 PNW).

Coldharbour Lane [Dowg; Upper Thames Street–the Thames]: *Coldeharburgh Lane* 1461, *Coldeherborughlane* 1468–9 Pat. Named from a tenement called *the Coldhakber* (sic) 1307 Mayors 261, *Coldherberghe* 1317 LBE 108 and often. *Cold harbour*, the source of a common place-name, is generally held to have meant 'a wayside shelter', *harbour* being ME *herberwe* 'shelter, lodging', but the exact meaning is disputed. For earlier names see *Armenterslane*, Weston Lane.

Coneyhope Lane [Cheap; north from the Poultry by St. Mildred]: *Conohop Lane* 1292 CW i. 106, *Conynghoplane* 1328 ib. 332, *Conyhopeslane* 1422, *Conyhooplane* 1424, *Cony-hopplane* 1425–6 LoEngl 125, 184, 190. The lane was named from a locality, which is first recorded in a surname, (Wlward de) *Cuninghop* 1182 StAug 521 (an earlier tenant), (William de) *Cunighehope* 1170–87 ADA 2719, and next as an addition to the names of St. Mary Coneyhope and St. Mildred Poultry: (parrochia Sancte Marie in) *Cuningchep* (sic) 1192–4 P, (St. Mary de) *Conehop* 1279 CW i. 41, (St. Mildred near) *Conhop* 1292 ib. 107. The name is not easy to explain definitely. Stow's suggestion, accepted by Harben, that it refers to a sign of three conies hanging over a poulterer's stall at the end of the lane, does not seem immediately convincing. Neither Stow nor Harben were aware of the high antiquity of the name, and the sign referred to by Stow hardly dated from the middle of the 12th century. So much is certain that the name contains the word *cony* 'a rabbit', found from 1292, in the form *conyng* c. 1302, a French loanword. The form *Cuningchep* must mean 'rabbit-market', and one would suppose that the form in -*hop* had a somewhat similar meaning. But the only known word *hop* that can be considered here seems to be *hoop* (OE, ME *hōp*) 'a band'. Stow was evidently thinking of a sign-name of the common type *the Bell on the Hoop*, on which reference may be made to OED under *hoop* and *cock-a-hoop*. Ale-houses (breweries) often and taverns sometimes had signs consisting of a hoop and some other object, often the figure of an animal. But the regular type is that just indicated (*le Cok on the Hop* and the like) and *le Cony super le hoop* is actually evidenced in Cornhill 1455 (1458) CW ii. 536. This type of name is comparatively late; the earliest instance in OED is dated 1402. But it occurs occasionally in the 14th century, the earliest example found being *Crowe on the Hop* 1323 PaulsMSS 1 b. Still it is a far cry from c. 1180 to 1323. If *Coneyhope* is really an early instance of the type in question, we must assume that it represents an archaic variant of it, meaning 'the hoop with the rabbit', and this would have been the sign of a place where

rabbits were sold. It can hardly have been the sign of a temporary stall or even a single shop, but the locality called *Conyhop*
may have been a part of Cheap (Poultry) set aside for dealers
in rabbits and marked by a special sign. Two curious names of
houses may be discussed in this place as possible analogies of
Coneyhope, namely Caponhors and Cat and Fiddle.

Capon(es)hors was the name of a tenement in Cannon Street
in the parish of St. Mary Abchurch. It is first recorded as a surname: (Thomas de) *Kaponeshers* (*Koponeshers*) 1275 RH 421,
423 (juror Cand), *Capuneshors* 1278 LBB 276 (of St. Mary
Abchurch), *Caponeshorse* 1282 LBA 52. The tenement is called
Caponeshors 1291 LBA 135, 1337 CW i. 424 (St. Mary Abchurch),
Capouneshors 1324–5 CW i. 312, *le Caponhors* 1395–6 (1399)
CW ii. 340, *Caponhors* 1373–99 BM, *Litelcaponhors* 1327 CW i.
323 (St. Mary Abchurch), *Capilhors* 1368 CW ii. 121 (ib.). The
same name is found in Merton (Sr): *Caponeshors* 1258–9 CW i.
3 (will of Felicia la Colnere of London). The testatrix owned
property in Merton and in St. Nicholas Lane (Langb, Cand),
which runs near and parallel to Abchurch Lane. In all probability Caponeshors in Merton took its name from the tenement
in London. It would be an odd coincidence if this curious name
had arisen independently in London and in a Surrey village as
the name of a house belonging to a lady who was evidently
resident near Caponhors in London. If this is right, the name
must have been in existence about 1250, probably earlier.
An etymology of this name has not been given, so far as I
know, except that R. R. Sharpe in a footnote in Calendar of
Wills ii. 121, derives *Capil-* from *capul*, *caple* 'a horse'. Evidently
Capilhors is corrupt, and the elements of the name *Capon(es)hors*
are *capon* and *horse*.
Cat and Fiddle was the name of a tenement in Cheap (St.
Benet Sherehog). This name is found in the early 16th century
(1542 LP), but in early records it appears as *le Catfethell*,
-fethele 1361, 1407 (1408) CW ii. 51, 380, 1367 LBG 217. A
fourth instance is very likely *le Catfithele* 1358 (1374) CW ii, 161,
but the situation is not indicated. As pointed out by Harben,

there was another Cat and Fiddle in St. Peter (Cheap): *The Catt and Fyddell* 1544 LP, and there was a *Katt and Fydyll* in Fleet Street (1552 HMC, Rutland MSS iv. 572). *Catfithele* must consist of the words *cat* and *fiddle* (ME *fithele*). The name is found a good deal later than Capon(es)hors and Coneyhope, but it may be equally old.

In these names we find formations consisting of two nouns combined into a compound instead of later groups of two nouns combined by means of a preposition or *and*. This may be an archaic way of forming names of houses (inns, taverns &c.). *Caponeshors* appears to mean 'the horse with a capon' and might designate a sign which showed a horse with a capon on its back. Such a sign might have been that of a hostelry, which drew attention to good cheer and accommodation for horses. *Catfithele* seems to mean 'cat-fiddle', 'the fiddle with a cat'. It is not easy to see what such a sign was meant to convey. The fiddle might indicate that there was music to listen to in the house (tavern), but the meaning of the cat remains to find out. *Conyhop* would be 'the hoop with a cony (rabbit) on (or in) it', a suitable sign for a place where rabbits were offered for sale.

Harbour Lane. See p. 57.

Haywharf Lane, now **Campion Lane** [Dowg; Thames Street–the Thames at the Haywharf, separating the parishes of All Hallows the Great and the Less]: *Heywharflane* 1328 CW i. 335 &c., *Haywharflane* 1384, 1422–3 Plea, *Hay wharfe lane* Stow, *Hay Lane* 1562–3 Machyn 302. Named from the Haywharf, clearly a wharf where hay was unloaded. An early form of the name is (All Saints *del*) *Heywarf* 1235 ADA 1791. The lane was successively called *Wancelineslane*, *Germayneslane*, *Batteslane*, Haywharf Lane, Campion Lane. The last name is explained by the fact that a brewery in the lane was

held in the late 16th century by Henry Campion, and after him
by his son Abraham (Stow i. 235). Master Campyon *berbruar*
is mentioned by Machyn as a resident in Haywharf Lane in
1562–3.

Pillory Lane [Ports; East Smithfield–Little Thames Street,
now built over]: *Pylorylane* alias *Weylandeslanende* 1421 Plea,
le Pillorye lane 1542 LP. Evidently named from a pillory.

Rood Lane [Bill, Langb; Fenchurch Street–Eastcheap]:
Rood Lane 1577 f. Arber, *Roode lane* Stow, according to Stow
named from a rood erected in the churchyard of St. Margaret
Pattens, while the church was rebuilt, and destroyed in 1538.
The rood seems to have been erected some time before 1538.
The lane was earlier called St. Margaret Pattens Lane.

Rother Lane, now **Pudding Lane** [Bill, Bridge]. There are
three types of the name: 1. (lane called) *Rederisgate* (*Rederesgate*) 1279–80, 1283 CW i. 44, 65, (venella vocata) *Retheresgate*
1343 LibCust 449; 2. *Retheresgate(s)lane* 1322–3 CW i. 299,
301, *Rotheresgateslane* 1325–6 ib. 317, *Retheresgatislane* alias
Podyng lane 1477 BM; 3. *Redereslane* 1301 CW i. 153, 1319
LBE 107, *Retherlane* alias *Puddynglane* 1372–3 CW ii. 153,
Rethereslane 1444–5 ADC 508, *Rother Lane* Stow (an old
name). Occasional *Retherhethe Lane* 1551–2 (1564–5) LIpm,
Raderiff Lane 1571 PaulsMSS 14 b is due to association with
the place-name Rotherhithe. In *Rede Rose Lane* 1318 CW i.
278, *Rederoslane* 1369 Pat, popular etymology has been at work,
the meaning having been taken to be 'Red rose lane'. Stow
says *Red Rose Lane* was so called 'of such a signe there.'

The lane was named from a watergate on the Thames called
Rederesgate 1108–48 ADA 7309, 1275 RH 415 &c. This name
means 'the cattle gate', the first element being *rother* (OE

hrȳðer) 'a horned beast'; this was suggested already by Sharpe (LBI 22). Presumably cattle for the butchers' market at East-cheap were unloaded there. The name of the watergate was sometimes transferred to the lane leading up from it, or a new name was formed by addition of *lane* (type 2). The third type is elliptical from type 2.

Sherborne Lane [Langb, Walbr; south from King William Street; formerly from St. Mary Woolnoth to St. Mary Abchurch]. The name shows a good deal of variation, but only a few forms are here given: *Shitteborwelane* 1272–3 CW i. 13, *Schiteburuelane* 1305 ib. 171, *Shiteburghlane* 1321 Pat, *Shiteburuelane* 1396–7 CW ii. 323; *Shitheburnlane* 1311 CW i. 220, *Shitebournelane* 1313 ib. 240 and often, *Shetebournelane* 1367 Pat; *Shirbouruelane* alias *Shetbouruelane* 1467 (1483–4) CW ii. 586, *Shirborne lane* 1540 LP, *Shirebourne Lane* 1550 Pat, *Sherborne lane* Stow. As pointed out by Kingsford, *Sherborne* cannot originally have denoted a stream, and its second element was ME *burgh, burwe* (OE *burg*), which began fairly early to be replaced by *burne* 'stream'. The reason may partly be that *-burue* was misread as *-burne*. A satisfactory explanation of the name has not been given. Harben's suggestion that *Shite-* is a personal name *Schet, Scheot, Scytta* cannot be accepted. The name must be explained in connexion with a name in Romford and probably another in Oxford. In Romford was formerly a lane called *Schiteburg-, Schyteburghlane* 1272, *Schit(e)burne Lane* 1366 (PNEss), and a lane in Oxford is referred to as *Schitebur' lan' c.* 1290 Fridesw i. 272 (an old name), as *Shitebourne, Schitebarnelane* 1362 Oriel Records. The former is certainly, the latter probably, identical in origin with Sherborne Lane. The common first element is an early name *Shiteburgh*, which evidently contains a derivative of OE *scītan* 'to void excrements', and which quite likely was a jocular name for a common privy.[1] Houses of public convenience are frequently mentioned in early London records, for instance in Plea Rolls of 1421 &c. Many streets were named from such houses in old Danish and German towns (Matthiessen 43 ff.). It is, of course, possible that *Shiteburgh* was an opprobrious name of an ordinary house, but if so the triple occurrence of the name would be remarkable. The change from *Shite-* to *Shirbournelane* is euphemistic.

Spittle Lane, now **Little Cheapside** [Vi]: *Spiteleslane* 1343 LibCust 450, *Spitellane* 1344 LBF 113, 1421 f. Plea, *Spittle lane* Stow (an old name). The lane was later called *Hardeleslane* and Stodies Lane. There must have been a hospital (spittle) in the lane, or a hospital had land there.

Stew Lane [Qu; south from Upper Thames Street]: *Stew lane* Stow. Named from a stew (hot baths), on which see *Parkerislane*, an earlier name. Synonymous names in Denmark are *Badstuestræde*, *Badstuegade* and the like (Matthiessen 41 ff.).

Turnbase Lane [Cordw, Vi; Tower Royal–Cordwainer Street, now merged in Cannon Street]: *Tornebaston(es)lane* 1328 f. CW i. 341, 352, *Turnebastonlane* 1335 (1337) ib. 421, *Turnebastlane* 1436 ib. ii. 481, *Turne(s)baslane* 1568 LIpm, *Turnebas(s)e lane* Stow. It is not certain that this name belongs in the present group. *Turnebaston* is identical with MF *tournebaston*, a noun of doubtful meaning recorded once in Godefroy. The word occurs in the following passage: 'Deux grosses

---

[1] Bonner gives no definite opinion on the etymology of the name. He mentions as a possible first element OE *scytta* 'archer' or some similar surname, but adds as a possible alternative that 'a different and unsavoury origin is indicated' without making a more definite suggestion. He seems to have considered connexion of the first element with the OE verb *scitan*.

pieces de bois de fraisne a faire le tournebaston' (15th century), which means 'two big pieces of ashwood to make the *tournebaston*'. The word contains the verb *tourner* 'to turn' and MF *baston*, which means among other things 'a stick', 'a weapon, especially a gun'. Possibly *tournebaston* had the meaning 'turnpike'. A lane in Walbrook later called Turnwheel Lane is referred to by Stow (i. 229) as 'a little lane with a turnepike in the middest therof'.

Names from inns or taverns

Some lanes were named from inns or taverns. But the latter generally had names derived from the inn sign, and the lanes may alternatively be said to have got their names from the sign, which would form a characteristic feature. Most of these names are late, and only a few examples are adduced here.

Anchor Lane, now **Anchor Alley** [Vi]: *Anckur Lane* 1557 Machyn 144, *Anchor lane* Stow. Doubtless named from an Anchor Inn. There was an inn so called in Aldersgate. Earlier names of the lane are *Palmereslane* and *Cressynghamlane*.

Beer Lane [Tower; Tower Street–Lower Thames Street]: *Berelane* 1422 Plea (LoEngl 129), 1539 LIpm, *Beare lane* Stow. Harben mentions among possible derivations that from an inn sign and adduces four examples of The Bear as a name of tenements. An interesting example is 'the tavern where *le Bere toumbeth*' in St. Pancras 1341 CW i. 445. This seems to be a case of an inn named from a dancing bear. Alternatively the name might contain the word *beer*, but the common early spelling *Beare* tells against this. Bonner wrongly identifies Beer Lane with Bereward's Lane in Tower.

Bush Lane [Dowg, Walbr; Upper Thames Street–Cannon

Street]: *Le Busshlane* 1445 Fine, *Busshlane* 1511 LP, *Le Busshe-lane* 1446 Fine, *Busshelane* 1486, 1550 Pat, *Bush lane* 1494 GtChron, Stow. In the lane was a tavern called *Le Bussh(e)tavern* 1445 f. Fine, and the probability is that the tavern was named from a sign in the form of a bush, not, as Bonner and Harben thought, from a man called *Bush*. The word *bush* is commonly used of a branch or bunch of ivy hung up as a vintner's sign (see OED). It even occurs in the sense 'tavern'.

Emperor's Head Lane, now **Bell Wharf Lane** [Vi; Upper Thames Street–Greenwich Street]: *le Emperours Headlane* 1550 Pat (St. Martin, Vi), *Emperors head lane* Stow ('of such a signe').

Friar Lane. See p. 138.

Harp Lane [Tower]: *Harpe Lane* 1543, *Harpelane* 1545 LP, *Hart lane* for *Harpe lane* Stow. Named from a messuage called *le Harpe* (anciently a brewhouse).

Hartshorn Lane [Dowg]: *Herteshornelane* 1421 Plea. *Harts-horn* was a common name of houses. The name is now obsolete.

Lily Pot Lane [Aldersg; Staining Lane–Noble Street]: *Lilipot lane* Stow. Named from a tenement called *Lyllye potte* 1540–1 LP. A lily-pot is a flower-pot with a lily growing in it, a symbolic accessory in pictures of the Annunciation (1540 &c. OED). A tenement in St. Andrew Undershaft is referred to as (the sign of) *le Lillypotte* 1500–1 Pat.

Names from Churches

Most of these names are self-explaining and of little interest; they are therefore dealt with briefly. Many churches have double names, consisting of the dedicatory saint's name and an earlier name (as St. Mary Abchurch) or an additional explanatory element (as St. Mary le Bow). The name of the lane is occasionally formed from this earlier name or additional element.

Abchurch Lane [Cand, Langb, Walbr; Cannon Street–Lombard Street] *c.* 1240–50 BM, *Abbechirchelane* 1291–2 Pat &c. St. Mary Abchurch was originally *Abbechirche* and the like, as *Habechirce c.* 1200 ADA 7821, *Abbechurche* 1211 ib. 1449, probably named from an early incumbent. OE *Abba* is a known name.

Bow Lane, earlier Cordwainer Street and Hosier Lane [Cordw, Cheap]: *Bowe lane* 1537 LP (alias *Hosyar lane*), *Bowe Lane* 1550 Pat. Named from Bow Church (St. Mary le Bow): *the Bowe* 1384 LoEngl 30, *Bowe* 1557 Machyn 131. *Bow*, in early records often *de Arcubus*, according to Stow, was 'builded on Arches of stone' (i. 253). Heavy Norman arches survive in the crypt of the church according to Kissan, LMAS, N.S. viii. 197.

Paternoster Lane, now **College Street** [Vi, Dowg]: *Paternosterlane* 1300–1 Cor 17, *Paternostercherchelane* (near *Walebrok*) 1313–14 CW i. 244, *Pater Noster Lane* 1544 LP, *Pater noster Lane* Stow. The name is probably elliptical for *Paternosterchirchelane*, *Paternosterchirche* being the old name of St. Michael Paternoster Royal; cf. Paternoster Street, p. 97. Harben suggests that the church was named from paternosterers living in Paternoster Lane. If the latter suggestion is correct, the lane may alternatively have been named from paternosterers, the name meaning 'lane of the paternosterers'.

Several lanes took their names from a church named after its dedicatory saint. Formally such names contain a personal

name, but a street-name such as St. Dunstan's Lane in reality
denoted a lane by the church of St. Dunstan or in St. Dunstan's
parish. In many cases the *St.* was dropped and it looks as if the
name contains an ordinary Christian name. A few of these
names offer real problems that are worth discussing. Only
genuine Latin or Middle English forms are as a rule quoted,
obvious renderings into Modern English being as far as possible avoided.

Bartholomew Lane [BroadSt; Lothbury–Threadneedle
Street past St. Bartholomew by the Exchange] : *Seint Bartilmew
lane* t. Edw 3 PaulsMSS 4 a, *saynt Bathellmuw lane* 1552–3
Machyn 32.

Botolph Lane [Bill; Lower Thames Street–Eastcheap] :
Seyntbotulfeslane 1348–9 CW i. 539, *Botulpheslane* 1432 (1433–
4) CW ii. 467, *Saint Botulpheʒ lane* 1477–9 StMary 76,
Botoulfslane 1493 LIpm, *Botulphe Lane* 1544 (1546) CW ii.
651, *Butholphelane* 1550 Pat. The modernized St. Botolph's
Lane is found t. Edw 1 ADB 2025. Named from St. Botolph
(Bill).

Bride Lane [FarrE; south from Fleet Street by the church of
St. Bride] : (Osbert de) *vico Sancte Brigide* 1205 Cur, *venella
Sancte Brigide* 1279 *RHT* m. 19, *Bridelane* 1349 CW i. 557,
1556 Pat, *Brideslane* 1374 Pat, *Seintebrideslane* 1379 CW ii.
209.

Clement's Lane [Cand, Langb; Cannon Street, now King
William Street–Lombard Street, past the church of St.
Clement Eastcheap] : *vicus sancti Clementis iuxta Kandel-
wiccestrate* 1241 PaulsCh 269, *Seint Clementeslane* 1348 CW i.
505, *saynt Clement lane* 1553 Machyn 34, *S. Clements lane*
Stow.

St. Dunstan's Lane, later **St. Dunstan's Hill** [by St. Dunstan East]: *Donstoneslane* 1329 CW i. 351, *Seint Dunstoneslone* 1363 Pat.

Foster Lane [FarrI, Aldersg; north from Cheapside past St. Vedast church]. The meaning of the name is clear; it means 'the lane of St. Vedast' (or by St. Vedast church). But the history of the name is complicated. St. Vedast (in the genuine French form *St. Vaast* or *Waast*) was Bishop of Arras and is stated to have died in 540. About a dozen places in France called Saint Vaast (Waast) testify to his popularity. Foster Lane is generally *venella Sancti Vedasti* in early Latin texts, e.g. 1275 RH 410, 1393 BM. But sometimes the genuine English form crops up, the earliest being *Seint uastes lane* 1271 *PaulsMSS* (Harben), where the initial *v* of French *Vaast* is retained. As a rule *Vast* became *Fast* owing to a change for which there are parallels elsewhere, and the name appears as *Seint Fastes lane* 1321 Misc, *Fasteslane* 1337 Cor 186. Next an intrusive *r* was added after *t*,[1] and a form *Fastre* or *Faster* arose, first found in the name of the parish or church, as (parish of) *S. Faster* 1315–16 CW i. 260, *S. Fastre* 1349 ib. 608. The lane is *Fasterslane* 1359 (1361) CW ii. 52, *Seynt Fastreslane* 1360 PaulsMSS 55 a, *fasterlane* 1422 Plea (LoEngl 123), *Vaster lane* 1477–9 StMary 76, *Faster Lane* 1524 ADA 2701, *Faster lane* Stow. The change from *Faster* to *Foster* is late; the earliest examples of the latter found are *Foster lane* 1428 (1486) StMary 13, *Fosterlane* 1547 LP, *Saynt Foster in*

---

[1] The intrusive *r* is due to an Anglo-French change, which is frequently to be noticed after dentals, especially *st*. Thus *provender* is ME, AF *provendre* from earlier *provende*. *Chorister*, ME *queristre*, comes from AF *cueristre*, *cueriste*, Lat *chorista*, *sophistre* from OF *sophistre*, Lat *sophista*, ME *arbalestre* 'cross-bow' from AF *alblastre*, Lat *arbalista*. Other instances occur in Anglo-French literary texts, as *celestre* from *celeste* 'celestial'. See Stimming, *Boeve*, p. 215.

Foster [*lane*] 1552 Machyn 16. Stow has *Foster* and *Fauster lane*, *S. Fosters* (*Fausters*) *church*. Apparently the meaningless name *Faster* was supposed to be an incorrect variant of *Foster* (from *Forster*); *Forster lane* actually occurs 1477–9 StMary 85, *Forsterlane* 1547–8 ff. Pat. The spelling *Foster* was introduced, and the pronunciation gradually followed the spelling.

Laurence Lane [Cheap; north from Cheapside by St. Lawrence Jewry church]: street of St. Laurence in the Jewry t. R 1 ADA 1787 f., *venella Sancti Laurencii de Judaismo, la venele seint lorenz* 1279 *RHT*, S. Laurence Lane in *la Giuwerie* 1299–1300 CW i. 144, *Seintlaurencelane* 1416 (1417) CW ii. 414, *seynt laurence lane* 1425–6 LoEngl 190, *saynt Laurans lane* 1552 Machyn 22, *S. Laurence lane* Stow.

Laurence Pountney Lane [Dowg, Cand, by St. Lawrence Pountney church]: St. Laurence's lane 1248 ADB 2105, *Seint Laurencelane* 1320 Pat, *Seint Laurenceslane* 1348 CW i. 507, *Seynt laurence lane* 1494 GtChron, *Poultney lane* Stow i. 238.

Martin's Lane [Cand, Bridge; south from Cannon Street, past St. Martin Orgar church]: *venella Sancti Martini* 1236–7 Clerkenwell 337, *vicus Sancti Martini Orgor'* 1275 RH 421, *Saint Martins Orgar lane* Stow.

Miles's Lane, olim **St. Michael's Lane** [Bridge, Cand; south to Upper Thames Street past St. Michael Crooked Lane church]: *Seint Micheleslane* 1303 LBC 192, *Saynte Mighelles Lane* 1548 Pat, *Saint Michaels lane* Stow. The form *Miles's* is not corrupt, as Harben thought; it represents a common early variant of the name *Michael*, ME *Mihael, Mihel. Michaelmas* is ME *Miȝheles-masse, Mighel-masse, Mielmasse* (see OED). St. Michael Crooked Lane is *sant Myghell in Crokyd lane*

1562 Machyn 285 and St. Michael Bas is *sant Myghelles in Bassynghall* 1556 ib. 116. See *Miell, Mihell, Myhill* in Bardsley. After all, *Miles's* is an incorrect form; *Miles Lane* would be better.

Nicholas Lane [Langb, Cand; Lombard Street–Cannon Street past St. Nicholas Acon]: S. Nicholas Lane 1258–9 CW i. 3, *Seint Nicholaslane* 1381 (1384–5) CW ii. 248, *S. Nicholas lane* Stow.

Pancras Lane [Cordw, Cheap; Queen Street–Queen Victoria Street]: *St. Pancresse Lane* 1548 Pat. For earlier names see Needlers Lane, *Panerichstrete*.

Peter Lane, now **St. Peter's Hill** [CastleB, Qu]: *Venella sancti Petri* 1263 Harben, the lane of St. Peter 1341 Cl, *Seint Petre-lane* 1378 Pat, *Peter Lane* 1564 LIpm.

Sise Lane [Cordw; Queen Victoria Street–Budge Row]: *Seint Sytheslane, Seintsitheslane, Seint Sydes lane* 1401, 1437 (1438), 1419 (1439) CW ii. 351, 484, 486, *Seynt Sythes Lane* 1550 Pat, *S. Sithes lane* Stow. Named from St. Sithe's church or chapel. The church of St. Benet Sherehog was also dedicated to St. Sithe and is called *St. Cite* 1355–6, *Sancte Cidis* 1358, (St. Benet Shorog and) *Seinte Site* 1363 Cl. St. Sithe's Chapel in St. Benet Sherehog is mentioned 1398–9 CW ii. 338. *Parochia Sanctæ Sithæ in Soperlane* is referred to t. Hy 8 Mon iv. 555. *Sithe* is generally derived from *Ositha* (OE *Osgȳð*, the name of a saint), but Kingsford, Add. Notes, 16, prefers Santa Zita of Lucca. The late appearance of the name St. Sithe for the church tells in favour of this suggestion. The worship of the saint may have been introduced by Lombard merchants in London.

St. Swithin's Lane [Walbr, Langb, named from St. Swithin's church in Cannon Street]: *vicus Sancti Swithuni* 1269–70 HMC, Middleton MSS 73, *venella Sancti Swithuni* 1279 *RHT* m. 24, *Seint Swithoneslane* 1410–11 CW ii. 387, *St. Swithens Lane* 1532 LP, *S. Swithens lane* Stow.

Trinity Lane [Qu, by Holy Trinity the Less]. There are now Great and Little Trinity Lanes, the former running east from Knightrider Street, the latter branching off south from Great Trinity Lane. Trinity Lane in early records generally refers to Little Trinity Lane: Trinity Lane 1271 ADC 1910, (*le*) *Trinite lane* 1332 ADA 2531, 1422 Plea (LoEngl 127), *Trinitie lane* Stow.

E. Lanes named from some activity carried on there.

Do Little Lane [CastleB; Knightrider Street–Carter Lane, now apparently Knightrider Court]: *Do lyttle lane, Do lite lane* 1281 ff. PaulsMSS 19 b, *Dolytelane* 1314–15 CW i. 252, *Dolitellane* 1373 Plea, 1398–9 CW ii. 338, *Do little lane* Stow, *Doo-little Lane* (a top o' the hill there) 1632 Ben Jonson, *Magnetic Lady*. Stow says the lane was not inhabited by artificers or open shop keepers, but serving as a near passage (from one street to another), apparently implying that the name meant 'lane where little business is done'. This is probably right. The surname *Dolittle* might be supposed to be a more probable source, but it has not been found early, and the fact that the first element never has the genitive form tells against this alternative.

Gropecuntelane is the lost name of a lane in St. Pancras and St. Mary Colechurch. As the two parishes are on opposite sides of Cheap, it is difficult to see how the lane can have touched both, unless one extended across Cheap. The probability seems to be that the lane was north of Cheap. The examples noticed are: *Gropecontelane* 1279 CW i. 42, *Groppecounte Lane* 1276 (1279) PaulsMSS 48 b, *Gropecuntelane* 1323 CW i. 302, *Gropecountelane* 1340 (1341), 1348 (1349) ib. 448, 581. The name is an indecent one; ME *cunte* means 'cunnus'.

The name is found in other towns, sometimes varying with the euphemism Grope Lane. In some towns it is recorded earlier than in London. Magpie Lane in Oxford is *Gropecuntelane c.* 1230 StJohn, *c.* 1230–40 Fridesw i. 392, *Groppecuntelane* 1260–1, *Gropelane* 1261 Oriel Records 75 f. A lane in Northampton is *Groppecuntelane* 1274 RH, one in Wells (Somerset) *Gropecuntelane* 1285–91, *Gropelane* 1312 HMC, Wells MSS, one in Peterborough *Gropelane* 1500. A *Gropecountelane* in Stebbing Ess is found *c.* 1325. Grope Lanes are recorded in Chipping Barnet Hrt, Bristol and Worcester. There is a Grape Lane in York (*Grapcunt lane* 1328–9 Cl, *Grapelane* 1370 PNER). See the volumes of the Place-name Society (passim).

Love Lane. There are or were four lanes with this name in the City. One in Aldermanbury [CripI; Wood Street–Aldermanbury] is *Lovelane* 1336 CW i. 412, *Love Lane* 1544 LP, 1582–3 CW ii. 706, *Louelane* Stow i. 290. Another in ColemSt [east from Coleman Street] is *Lovelane* 1339 CW i. 434, *Loue lane* Stow i. 284. A third in Bill [Eastcheap–Lower Thames Street] is *Lovelane* 1394, 1428 (1433) CW ii. 311, 464, *louelane* 1422 Plea (LoEngl 124), *Lovelane* (formerly *Roperelane*) 1455 (1458) CW ii. 536, *Loue Lane* (formerly *Roape Lane*, and *Lucas lane*; *Loue Lane* corruptly) Stow i. 210. A fourth in St. Christopher [BroadSt], now lost, appears as *Lovelane* 1343 LBF 85, *la Lovelane* 1357 CW i. 699. An earlier instance of the name than any of those mentioned is (Arnald de) *Lovelane*

1323 Cl. The same name occurs in Salisbury (*Lovelane* 1455); see PNW 21, where it is stated that the name is common in old towns. The name means literally 'love lane' and is generally held to refer to houses of ill fame; Stow says the lane in Crip was so called 'of wantons'. But the name may have a more innocent connotation, at least in some cases.[1] A name of the same meaning is found in Swedish towns under circumstances that exclude the coarser meaning. In these cases the name means 'lane where loving couples are wont to walk'. Harben's suggestion that *Love* is a personal name must be rejected.

Pissynglane 1425–6 LoEngl 190. The situation of the lane is doubtful; it might be the later Pissing Alley. The name is self-explaining and has an analogy in *Mihindelone* (venella) in Gloucester 1263–84 GloucesterCart ii. 243. Cf. OE *migan* 'to make water'.

Three names may be added here which possibly refer to an activity pursued in the lanes or were supposed to do so. They are Amen Lane, Ave Maria Lane and Creed Lane, which according to Stow took their names from textwriters living near St. Paul's.

Amen Lane, according to Stow added to Creed Lane, ran from Warwick Lane to Ave Maria Lane. Now Amen Corner (*Amen Corner* 1661 PaulsMSS 27 b), which runs west from Paternoster Row.

Ave Maria Lane [CastleB, FarrI; Ludgate Hill–Paternoster Row and Amen Corner]: *Ave-maria aly c.* 1510 Cocke Lorelles Bote (OED), *Aue Mary lane* Stow, *Ave Maria Lane* 1602–3 PaulsMSS 27 a.

---

[1] Miss Rawlings rightly remarks that 'many [Love Lanes], no doubt, were named from innocent everyday romances'.

Creed Lane [FarrI and CastleB; Ludgate Hill–Carter Lane]: *Crede Lane* 1548 Pat, *Creede lane* Stow.

The three lanes are near each other. Probably the names were given in imitation of that of the neighbouring Paternoster Row, which was supposed to contain the word *paternoster* in its original sense of the Lord's Prayer.

III. NAMES IN -*ROW*

These are few in number. The word *row* (*rew*) from OE *rāw* (*rǣw*) is used particularly in the senses 'a number of houses standing in a line; a street (esp. a narrow one) formed by two continuous lines of houses' (OED *row* sb. i. 4). According to OED the word is chiefly Northern English and Scotch; the earliest reference to the sense here in question given dates from *c.* 1450 (the Northern St. Cuthbert).

London names in -*row* are found from the 14th century, but they did not in all cases designate a street. Goldsmiths' Row was a line of houses along the south side of Cheapside. It is described by Stow (i. 345) as extending from Bread Street to the Cross in Cheap and containing 10 fair houses and 14 shops, 'all in one frame, vniformely builded foure stories high'. No earlier example of the name than in Stow is on record, but it is often mentioned later.

Names in -*row* as a rule have as first element an occupational term.

Bowyer Row [FarrI; an alternative name of Ludgate Street east of Ludgate]. The earliest reference (1359 PaulsMSS 49 b) is (*Ludgatstrete*, commonly called) *Bowiarresrowe*. Later references are: *Bowiersrowe* 1373 Plea, *Bowyerrowe* 1378 (1379), 1411–12 CW ii. 209, 392, *Bower Rowe* 1548 Pat, *Bowier row* (high street), *Bowyers row* Stow. Bowyers are often referred to in FarrI. In the Subsidy of 1319 are mentioned, for instance, Richard le Arblaster, Adam de Bramptone (alias A. le Boghiere), William de Cestre (alias W. Bouere), Aubin Larblaster, Richard Larblaster (nos. 53, 54, 56, 58, 59), some stated to be resident near Ludgate. They may well have been resident in Bowyer Row.

Budge Row [Cordw, Walbr; Watling Street–Cannon Street, a continuation of Watling Street and probably so called till *c.* 1350]: *Bogerowe* 1342 Bonner, 1356 (1361) CW ii. 35, 1555 Pat, *Bogerouwe* 1359 Cl, *Bugerowe* 1383–4 LBH, *Bowgerowe* 1549 Pat, *Bouge Rowe* 1553–4 Machyn 51, *Budgerowe* 1591 (1595) CW ii. 723, *Budge Row* Stow (who says the street was so called 'of Budge Furre, and of Skinners dwelling there'). *Budge*, ME *bugee*, *boge*, was a kind of fur consisting of lamb's skin with the wool dressed outwards (OED, first reference 1382). But budge was also fur of cony, as seen from an entry in LBA 220[1] (A.D. 1288). Kingsford, p. 327, draws attention to Ben Jonson's allusion, *Barth. Fair* i. 1, to 'the coneyskin woman of Budge Row'. *Budge* is doubtless a word of French origin, but etymologically disputed. A derivative *budger* 'a dealer in budge' is not known, but may well have existed; if it did, it is very likely the first element of the name Budge Row.

Curriers' Row [BroadSt], an earlier name of London Wall, is *Curriers row* Stow. The street in Stow's time was for the most part inhabited by curriers.

Paternoster Row [CastleB, FarrI; Warwick Lane–Cheapside] may be referred to as 'vicum qui extendit se ab ecclesia sancti Michaelis in foro ad bladum uersus occidentem' 1236–

---

[1] There is mention of a hood furred with budge, whether it be of lamb or of conies.

41 PaulsCh 271. It is called *Paternosterstrete* 1307 Mayors 256, *Paternostrestrete* 1312 CW i. 234, *Paternoster Lane* 1320–1 PaulsMSS 49 a, 1335 (1341) CW i. 451, *Paternosterlane* 1321 LibCust 344. The modern name appears as *Paternosterowe* 1334 CW i. 397, *Paternosterrowe* 1349 ib. 591, 1421 Plea, *Paternostererowe* 1374 CW ii. 160, *Paternosterrewe* 1417 Plea, *pater noster rewe* 1425–6 LoEngl 190, *Pater Noster Rewe* 1549 Pat, *Paternoster Rowe* (of Pater noster makers) Stow i. 81. The original form was evidently ME *Paternostrere-strete* 'the street of the paternosterers or makers of rosaries'. The middle *r* of *Paternostrere-* was lost early. In fact *paternoster* occurs for *paternostrer*, as Andrew Paternoster 1281 LBB 4. Three paternosterers are mentioned as sureties in St. Michael le Querne, which is by Paternoster Row, in a document of 1278 in LBB 278. It is not easy to explain why the name *Paternosterstrete* was replaced by Paternoster Row. The paternosterers had left the street in Stow's time.

Spurrier Row [FarrI, CastleB, an old name of Creed Lane]: *Sporenereslane* 1386 PaulsMSS 28 b, *Sporyer Rowe* t. Hy 6 ib. 16 a, *Spurrier Rowe* (now *Creede lane*) Stow ('of *Spurriers* dwelling there').

Stockfishmonger Row [Bridge, an alternative name of Thames Street in Bridge ward]: *Stokfisshmongerrowe, -rewe* 1373, 1379 (1380) CW ii. 154, 213, *Stokfisshmongerowe* 1428 Pat, *Stockefishmonger Row* Stow (formerly so named 'of the stockefishmongers dwelling there').

IV. NAMES IN -*ALLEY*

Middle English *aleye* (*aly*) meant 'a passage in or into a house' (1388 &c.), further 'a bordered walk or passage; an avenue'. This latter sense is not to be reckoned with in street-names. Later appears the sense 'a passage between buildings', whence 'a narrow street, a lane; usually only wide enough for foot-passengers' (*c.* 1510 &c. OED). In early London names we have to reckon with the senses 'a passage into a house, an entrance-way' and 'a narrow lane'. Harben, pp. 12 f., states that *alley* was in use in its modern signification in Stow's time, but the alleys in an earlier period were in no sense streets as they are now, being passages which appertained to the owners or occupiers of the respective houses. It is doubtful if this is altogether true. Some early alleys were doubtless lanes in the modern sense. But it is a striking fact that alleys are often referred to as tenements. Lands, tenements, shops, &c., called *le Newe Aley* are referred to 1405–6 CW ii. 363. Cf. *Langhornesaley* (infra). Later New Alley ran from Cornhill to Threadneedle Street. For similar instances see Kings Alley and *Leggesaleye* infra. Here we may have to do with groups of tenements with a common alley or entrance-way. In the following example an alley is evidently thought of as belonging to one messuage: (the) capital messuage called *the horsehed* with alley called *the horsehead Alleye* 1582–3 CW ii. 706 (1557 ib. 664: messuage called *the signe of the horsehed* . . . together with the alley called *the horsehedd alley*).

Most names in -*alley* are found after the year 1500.[1] In the following survey only a number of names, most of them found before 1500, are discussed. Late names are often difficult to explain, and they generally offer little interest. The majority are probably derived from houses, and this group is therefore placed first. The house itself, in most cases an inn, a tavern,

---

[1] In some cases an earlier name in -*lane* was replaced by one in -*alley*. See for instance Anchor Lane, p. 157, Goose Lane, p. 106, Shoe Lane, p. 110, Windgoose Lane, p. 144, also Mede Lane, p. 108, Stephen Lane, p. 131.

or a brewery, was generally named from a sign. Here belong common names such as Ball Alley, Bell Alley, Chequer Alley, Cock Alley, Swan Alley, named from houses called The Bell, &c.

Names in -alley from houses or localities

Christopher Alley [FarrE]: (lands &c. called) *Christofer Alley* in *Secolelane* 1559 (1579) CW ii. 696. **Christopher Alley** [St. Martin le Grand; Aldersg, FarrI]: *Christopher Aley* 1540–1 LP. The latter was named from a house: (John Asshe) *atte Cristophore* (ny seynt Martyns þe graund) 1425–6 LoEngl 190. (Breweries called) *le Cristofre* (*Christofre*) *on the hoop* (*hope*) in St. Dionis (Langb) and in St. Botolph Aldersgate are mentioned 1405 (1406–7) and 1425 (1433) CW ii. 369, 465. That in St. Dionis is called *le Christopher* t. Edw 3 PaulsMSS 7 b.

Hercules' Pillars Alley [FarrE; south out of Fleet Street]: *Hercules-pillars Ally* 1667–8 Pepys vii. 297. Named from a tavern, called *Hercules Pillars* 1668 Pepys vii. 405.

Panyer Alley [FarrI; Paternoster Row–Newgate Street]: *ye Panyer Ale* 1442 Harben, *Paniar* (*Panier*) *Alley* Stow, *Pannyer Alley* 1666 Pepys v. 271. A brewhouse called *the Panyer* is mentioned 1425–6 LoEngl 190: John Brewester, '*atte panyer* yn pater noster rewe' (an ale-house-keeper). *Panyer* means 'basket'.

Three Legs Alley [St. Mary le Bow]: an alley called *The Three Legges* 1535–6 LP. Evidently named from the shop called *le Threlegges* in St. Mary le Bow referred to 1410 ADA 2509. Three legs was a common sign.

Three Nuns Alley [St. Christopher Broad Street, now lost]:
Three Nunnys Alley 1523 LP. A brewery called *lez thre Nonnes*
in St. Christopher is mentioned 1388 (1391–2) CW ii. 293.

Some names in -alley were named from a house or locality
with a different kind of name. Here belong the common names
Church Alley and Churchyard Alley; cf. pp. 27, 131.

Compter Alley, now Chapel Place [Poultry]: *le counter* and
le Counter Aley in le Pultree 1475 (1477) CW ii. 575. Named
from the prison called the Poultry Compter.

Mill Alley, now **Great Bell Alley** [ColemSt]: *Mille Aley*
1417 (1419–20) CW ii. 419, *Mill Alley* 1539 LP, *Mille Alley*
1550 Pat. Harben thinks the name was derived from a certain
William Mills, who lived here in the 16th century. But the
name is much older. The alley was presumably named from a
mill.

Names in -alley from early owners

Several names in -*alley* contain the name of an early owner.
Names such as Christopher Alley, George Alley, in which the
first element is the name of an inn or the like, do not belong
here.

Culver Alley, now **Fishmonger Alley,** runs from Lime
Street to Fenchurch street, dividing the wards of Langbourn
and Lime Street. It is *Culuer Alley* in Stow. Harben points
out that the name *Col(u)vere* is mentioned in the bounds of the
soke of the Knights' Guild (Portsoken) in LBC; on this name
(from OE *Culfre*, a woman's name) see ELPN 24. The heirs
of C. (*heredes Colu(v)ere*) owned a house on the boundary of
the soke, but that house cannot well have been in Culver Alley,

which was a long way west of Portsoken. The house was held before Coluvere by one Geoffrey the Tanner, who is mentioned as an earlier tenant about 1150 (1148–67 ADA 7279). Coluvere will have been in possession in the later 12th century or so. It is extremely unlikely that Culver Alley can have been named from the said lady, but the possibility that *Culver* in the name of the alley is a personal name is not to be rejected altogether. More likely, however, *Culver* is ME *culver* (OE *culfre*) 'a pigeon' or still better the name of a house. A tenement formerly called *le Culver on the hope* in St. Dunstan East is mentioned 1380–1 CW ii. 219.

Fastolf Aley [St. Stephen Coleman Street] 1417 (1419–20) CW ii. 419 (will of Johanna Fastolf, widow). The alley was named from Hugh Fastolf, grocer, a sheriff 1387–8, alderman of Tower 1381–2, of Bridge 1386–9. The surname is OE *Fastulf* from ON *Fastulfr*, ODan *Fastolf*. One Fastolf was a landholder in Lincs in 1066 (DB), and *Fastolf* was a known surname in Norfolk. There were several tenements in Fastolf Alley.

Fridaysaley (alias *Lyon Alley*) 1421 Plea (St. Andrew Under-shaft, Aldg). *Friday* may well be a surname here. William Friday was a surety in London in 1281 (LBB 5), and Bardsley has examples of the surname from various counties. Cf. *Sondayes Aley* infra.

Kings Alley [St. Stephen Coleman Street]: (tenements of William Kyng called) *le Kyngesaleye* 1393 (1394) CW ii. 312, *Kings alley* Stow. Named from William Kyng, draper, who mentions John his father and William his grandfather. Another *Kyngesaleye* in St. Vedast in Gutter Lane is referred to 1410–11 CW ii. 389 f., but it is not clear if *Kyng* is here a family name.

Langhornesaley 1421 Plea [Cornhill]. Cf. Longhorne's Alley in Harben. The alley was named from John Langhorne, *brasier*, of St. Michael Cornhill, whose will was enrolled in 1405–6. He had lands in *le Newe Aley*, evidently identical with *Langhornesaley*. Cf. also supra p. 170. The surname Langhorne is no doubt an old nickname.

Leggesaleye (tenements called) 1388 (1391–2) CW ii. 292 f., *Legges aleye* 1421 Plea (St. Bartholomew, Broad Street), *Logges Alley* (a former alley) 1548 Pat. The alley was named from Thomas Leggy (or Legge), skinner, whose will was enrolled in 1357, and who was of St. Christopher. The tenements were held in 1391–2 by William Power, skinner, of St. Christopher. Thomas Leggy was mayor 1347–8, 1354–5. It is stated, curiously enough, in the Calendar of Wills (ii. 184, footnote), that he was beheaded in 1381. In reality his will was enrolled in 1357, and Simon, his son, who expressly calls himself son of Thomas Leggy, late mayor of London, and whose will was enrolled in 1375, stipulated that he was to be buried in the church of St. Christopher near the tomb of his father.

Lennesaleye (tenements in an alley called) 1424–5 CW ii. 436 (will of J. Elyngham, stockfishmonger, of St. Michael Crooked Lane). Doubtless named from Ralph de Lenne, stockfishmonger of St. Michael Crooked Lane, who was a sheriff 1349–50, alderman of Billingsgate 1350–8, and (or) Andrew de Lynne, stockfishmonger of St. Michael, whose will was enrolled in 1362. The family will have come from Lynn Nf.

Moundevyle Aley, late **Middelton Aley** 1505 (1520–1) CW ii. 628 (St. Michael, Bas), *Moundevile Aley* 1518 (1527–8) LIpm. John de Middelton in his will of 1382 left his tenements in London to Isabella his wife. In her will, enrolled in 1410, she left tenements in St. Michael (Bas) to Thomas Mundeville, husband of Matilda her daughter. This explains the two names of the alley.

Popesaley (messuage and alley called) 1474 ADB 2029 (St. Christopher, Broad Street). Cf. Pope Lane, p. 140.

Puppesaley 1447–8 PaulsMSS 16 b [St. Martin Orgar, Cand], *Popys Allye* 1542 ib. Geoffrey Puppe, stockfishmonger, is mentioned in the will of Idonea Salesbury (dated 1386, enrolled 1389) as her late husband, evidently dead shortly before 1386. Idonea had property in St. Martin Orgar and elsewhere in the ward. No doubt the alley was named from Geoffrey Puppe or someone connected with him.

Sondayes Aley 1539 LP [Abchurch Lane, Langb]. *Sonday* may be a surname derived from *Sunday*. As an example of the surname may be adduced John Sonday of Hatfield Regis, rector of St. Mary Woolchurch, whose will was enrolled in 1349.

Tristram's Alley [ColemSt]: *Trestremesaley* 1421 Plea (stated to have been a common way from Coleman Street to *Bassyngeshawe*), *Trystrams Alley* 1548 LIpm. A William Tristram, glover or brace-girdler, is mentioned 1349–50 LBF 205, and Tristram was a not uncommon surname in medieval England.

Wringesaley (a lane in ColemSt) 1363 ADA 2056, *Wryngeresaley* (in St. Stephen Coleman Street) 1438 (1453) CW ii. 523. Perhaps named from William le Wrenghere 1319 Subs (a taxpayer in ColemSt). But *wringere* may be an occupational word, though of doubtful meaning.

Names in -alley after occupations

A few names in -*alley* have a first element indicating an activity carried on in the alley.

Pissinge Alley, leadinge from *Paules Church* into *Pater Noster Rowe* 1574 PaulsMSS 27 b. Two other alleys with this name are mentioned by Harben. Cf. *Pissynglane* p. 166, possibly identical with one of the Pissing Alleys.

Scalding Alley [St. Mildred Poultry]: *þe Skaldynge aley yn þe pulterie* 1424 LoEngl 184, *le Scaldynglane* 1435 (1436) CW ii. 479, *Scalding Alley* Stow. The alley was near the scalding house (*Scaldynghous* 1361 CW ii. 33), where poulterers scalded their poultry (cf. Stow, i. 186).

Scalding Alleye in St. George in *Podynglane* [Bill] 1550 Pat. There was a scalding house here also (*la Scholdynghous* 1349 CW i. 579), though it will have been one for scalding hogs. It is possible that in both cases Scalding Alley is elliptical from Scalding-house Alley.

V. NAMES IN -*HILL*

The word *hill* in these names, which are mostly late, has the special signification 'steep or sloping road (street)', a sense not recognized in OED, but at any rate common in occasional use nowadays. In modern Swedish the word *backe*, which originally meant and still sometimes means 'hill, mound', is mostly used in the special sense 'road on an incline, steep road' and the like. Another word for 'steep hill', *brink*, is used in names of short steep lanes in the medieval part of Stockholm, as *Storkyrkobrinken* ('Great Church Hill').

The most important London street with a name in -*hill*,

Cornhill, does not belong in this section; the name did not originally denote a street. It is doubtful if the names Lambeth Hill and Snow Hill are cases in point either, but they are dealt with here. A lost name, **Oyster Hill**, now apparently Water Lane in St. Magnus (Bridge), is one of the earliest instances of *hill* in the sense 'steep street', being recorded as *Oystrehull* 1305–6 CW i. 174, *Oysterhull* 1389 ADC 6990. *Oyster Hill* is probably elliptical for *Oystergate Hill* (cf. p. 192).

Most of the streets with names in -*hill* run or used to run from Thames Street north to Knightrider Street (Queen Victoria Street), Cannon Street or Tower Street. Some ran up from the Fleet (Holborn): Holborn Hill, Ludgate Hill, Snow Hill. The following list is not quite complete. Streets leading up from Thames Street are taken first and are dealt with in the order from west to east.

Addle Hill, formerly **Addle Street** [CastleB]. Addle Hill is the name of the street from Knightrider Street to Carter Lane, but Addle Street denoted this street and its continuation to Upper Thames Street, which is now merged in Queen Victoria Street. Very likely it was the southernmost part that was first distinguished as Addle Hill. The modern name is first recorded as *Adling Hill* 1596 ff. Arber, and on the title-page of Dekker's *Shoemakers Holiday*, ed. 1600, which was printed by Valentine Sims 'dwelling at the foote of Adling hill, neere Bainards Castle, at the signe of the White Swanne'.[1] *Addle Hill* is elliptical for *Addle Street Hill*.

Bennet's Hill [CastleB, Qu; by St. Benet Paul's Wharf]: common lane of St. Benet 1341 Cl, *Pawles wharfes hill* 1588 LIpm, *St. Benet's Hill* 1666 Harben. Cf. p. 122.

[1] V. Sims is described as of the White Swan in *Adling street* 1594 f. Arber.

St. Peter's Hill [CastleB, Qu; by St. Peter Paul's Wharf]:
St. Peter's Hill 1588 LIpm, *Saint Peters Hill, Peter hill lane*
Stow. Cf. Peter Lane, p. 163.

Lambeth Hill [CastleB, Qu] leads from Upper Thames
Street to Queen Victoria Street, originally to Old Fish Street;
this latter part is now **Old Change Hill.** (Cf. **Old Change,**
p. 197.) The earliest reference is (house at) *Lamberdeshelle*
1281 CW i. 54, but here the street is hardly meant. The street
is referred to as a lane at one end of *Lamberdeshill* 1306 ADA
2362, the highway on *Lambardeshill* 1448 Pat, where the name
is not that of the street. But it is (the street called) *Lamberdeshul*
(*Lambardeshull*) 1283 PaulsMSS 19 a, 1324 CW i. 308, (regia
strata) *Lombardehulle* 1400 EpHeref, *Lambert-Hill* 1645
Character-Books 101. Stow calls it *Lambart* (*Lambard*) *hill
lane, Lambard hill.* The modern name-form, first noted 1659–
60 Pepys i. 20, must be due to popular etymology (association
with the place-name Lambeth). The hill was named from a
person with the name *Lambert* (*Lamberd*), quite likely Lam-
bertus wodemangere, who was a tenant in St. Peter Paul's
Wharf *c.* 1200 (PaulsCh 170). Lambeth Hill runs near St.
Peter's church.

Old Fish Street Hill [Qu] ran from Upper Thames Street
to Old Fish Street. It is *Old Fishstreete hill* in Stow.

Bread Street Hill [Qu] : (the Star on) *Bread street Hill* 1589 f.
Arber, *Bredstreete hill* Stow. It is a continuation of Bread
Street and was doubtless formerly called Bread Street. In
Stow's time it apparently ran down to the Thames.

Garlick Hill [Vi; Upper Thames Street–Cannon Street]
was formerly Cordwainer Street. The new name is first
instanced by Harben from Arnold's Chronicle (1500–21) as

Garlyk hill. An alternative name was Garlickhithe: *Garlickhith* (alias *Cordwalstrete*) 1550 Pat (St. James'). Stow has *Garlicke hill* or *hith*. The street was named from St. James' Garlickhithe, which is on its east side, not, as Harben suggests, direct from Garlickhithe, which was on the Thames.

College Hill [Vi, Cordw], formerly Royal Street or Tower Royal (cf. p. 198), also Paternoster Street (cf. p. 97), was re-named from Whittington College (cf. p. 95). The new name is first recorded by Bonner from 1648.

Dowgate Hill, formerly **Dowgate** [Dowg]. Harben records the longer name first from 1666.

Fish Street Hill [Bridge], formerly (New) Fish Street and still earlier Bridge Street: *Fysshstretehyll* 1568 LIpm, (on) *newe fishestreete hill* 1584 ADA 12959, (St. Leonard on) *Fishestreete Hill* 1632–3 CW ii. 754. St. Leonard is at the northern end of the present Fish Street Hill, which extends from Lower Thames Street to Eastcheap. The name Fish Street Hill seems sometimes to be restricted to the northern part. Stow (i. 216) says *Fishstreet hill* is at the upper end of *new fishstreete*. Pepys mentions both Fish Street and Fish Street Hill (see Diary viii. 86, i. 88).

St. Dunstan's Hill [Tower; Lower Thames Street–Tower Street] is first mentioned in a map of *c.* 1570 (Harben). It was formerly St. Dunstan's Lane (cf. p. 161). Stow (i. 135) restricts the name *Saint Dunstans hill* to the southern part of the street.

Holborn Hill [FarrE; west from Holborn Bridge] will have been steep, since the name *Holborn* indicates a stream in a deep valley. The name is first recorded in 1587 (Harben). Stow has the form *Oldboorne hill*.

Ludgate Hill, formerly **Ludgate Street** and Fleet Street
[Farr; St. Paul's–Ludgate Circus]: *Ludgate Hill* 1548 Pat,
1662–3 Pepys iii. 36, *Lugate Hill* 1559 LIpm. Stow speaks of
'the high streete called Ludgate hill downe to Fleete lane.'

Snow Hill [FarrE; Holborn Viaduct–Farringdon Street]:
Snore Hylle t. Hy 3 PNSr 284, *Snowr' Hill, Snowrehille* 1504,
1507 Pat, *Snowre-Hill* 1509, *Snourehilstrete, Snourehyll* 1544
LP, *Snower-, Snowrehilstrete* 1563 LIpm, *Snor(e) hill, Snore
lane* Stow. The street formerly ran differently from now and
was narrow, steep, and circuitous (Harben). The name is
identical with the Surrey names Snower Hill, found in Betch-
worth (*Snorehill* t. Hy 8) and Chipstead, Snow Hill in Horne
(*Snower Hill* 1789), and the lost *Snorhull* in Farnham (found
in 1308). The editors of PNSr suggest that these names have
a first element identical with that of Snore (or Snower) Hall
in Norfolk (*Snora* DB) and Snoreham in Essex (*Snorham* 1238,
&c. PNEss), namely a lost OE word *snār-*, corresponding to
Norw *snaar*, Swed *snår* 'brushwood, thicket'. But the base
must have been OE *snor-* or *snōr-*,[1] probably the latter in view

---

[1] The only known word with which a stem *snōr-* can be compared is
OScand *snōr*, OHG *snuor*, MLG *snōr*, Du *snoer* 'string, cord, twine'.
The word is not found in Old English, but a derivative is OE *snēr*
'string of a harp', formally identical with Gothic *snōrjō* 'basket'. The
probability is that the element *snōr-* is identical with the Scand and
German *snōr*, though it was used in a different, perhaps transferred
sense. The fact that *snor* is five times combined with the word *hill* may
be explained either so that its meaning rendered it liable to be used in
that way, or so that *snōr* itself denoted a hill and that *hill* is an explanatory addition. A meaning 'hill' would suit the first element of Snore
Hall and Snoreham. Snore Hall is in a low situation on the north bank
of the Wissey, it is true, but immediately north of the place the ground
rises from about 15 to 85 feet at Ryston. Hill Farm is on the hill.
Snoreham is on the slope of a marked long ridge, which rises from
about 15 to about 140 feet. In this case a meaning 'long ridge' would
be a very suitable meaning of *snōr-* and would have easily developed
from that of 'string'. It is doubtful if such a meaning would suit Snore

of early spellings with *ou*, *ow*. The change from *Snor-* to *Snow-* may be due to popular etymology (association with the word *snow*).

It will have been seen from the examples given that names in *-hill* are often preceded by the preposition *on*, even when denoting a street. Some further late examples are: (S. Stafford dwelling on) *Adling Hill* 1596 ff. Arber; (R. Ward dwelling upon) *Lambert Hill* 1589 ib., (the Dragon on) *Lambeth Hill* 1659–60 Pepys; (the Holy Lamb on) *Ludgate Hill* 1597 f. Arber, (on) *Ludgate Hill* 1659–60 Pepys; (The Monument on) *Fish Street Hill* Dickens, *Our Mutual Friend*, II. iii.

VI. STREET-NAMES FORMED WITHOUT A DESIGNATION FOR 'STREET' OR THE LIKE

There are a good many such names on the modern map, but several of them in early records show forms containing a word for street, and the present name is elliptical. The names to be discussed here belong to very different types. Certain groups can be distinguished, but it is not always easy to assign the individual names to each.

A. Streets originally market-places

Some streets were at the same time market-places ('market-streets'), and their name was or contained a word for 'market'. The old English word for market-street, *cēapstrǣt*, found in glossaries rendering Lat *forum*, is not met with in London records. To this group first belongs medieval London's chief street, Cheap.

Hall and Snow Hill, &c. But *snōr-* comes from the base *snō-* 'to twist' or 'to plait' and a derivative of that base may have had other meanings than 'string', for instance 'knot' or 'ball of string' or the like, whence a transferred sense such as 'hillock'. It need hardly be said that this is only a suggestion given with all reserve.

Cheap or **Westcheap,** later **Cheapside,** now running from St. Paul's Cathedral to Poultry. Cheap was the chief market-place of London, but also a main thoroughfare. The name, which represents OE *cēap*[1] in the sense 'market, market-place', is recorded in the form *Westceap* in a spurious charter of 1067 (1335 Ch), which is held to have been written in the time of Henry I (1100–35). The charter contains very good Old English forms, and *Westceap* was very likely taken from a genuine Old English document. In the Latin translation *forum* the name occurs in the list of manors of St. Paul's of *c.* 1130 (PaulsMSS 66 b; also *uicus fori, Warda Fori*). The usual medieval form is *Chepe*, found also in Chaucer and Langland. Exceptional is *the Chepe* in Lydgate's *London Lickpenny*. *Chepe* is often referred to as a street. In the early Romance *King Alisaunder* the streets (*hyghe stretis*) of Thebes are said to be 'Al so noble of riche mounde, So is Chepe in this londe'. One MS has the variant reading 'þat is in londe', where *londe* must be London. The highway of *Chepe* is mentioned 1304 ADA 7373, *stratum nobilem vocatum le Chepe* 1377 LibCust 476, the great street called *Westchepe* 1249 PaulsMSS 25 a, *vicus de Westchep* 1275 RH 408, the king's high road of *Westchep* 1286 Pat. *Westcheap* was used for distinction from *Eastcheap*. It is found occasionally quite late, e.g. 1633 CW ii. 754 f. A rare variant is *Westchepinge* 1104 (13th) Colchester Cart 3, which contains OE *cēapung* 'market'. Stow (i. 258) gives *West Cheping* as the name of the market from which Cheap ward was named, and (i. 264) refers to Cheap as *the large streete of West Cheaping*. With this name may be com-

---

[1] Early instances of OE *cēap* in place-names are *Riðerescæp* 605 (*c.* 1400) BCS 5 and Wincheap Street (*Wenchep(e)* 1226 &c.), both in Canterbury (Wallenberg, *Kentish Place-names* 5). The first name means 'cattle-market', the other apparently 'cart-market' (*Wen-* from OE *wægn* 'wain'). A market where goods were sold in carts will be meant.

pared *Cornechepinge*, an old name of the corn market at St. Michael le Querne mentioned in a document of 1320–1 (Pauls MSS 49 a). *Cheping* is common in names of market-places in other towns, as Coventry, St. Albans, Worcester.

The name Cheap lived on into early Modern English time, but was gradually superseded, except as the name of the ward, by the extended form *Cheapside*, which is now alone used of the street. But the street is both shorter and narrower than old Cheap was. The name Cheapside is first recorded by Harben from 1510, but is a good deal older. There is an example already in 1436 Pat[1] (messuages in St. Vedast in *Chapeside*) and one in 1479 Paston iii. 244 (a goldsmith dwelling in *the Chepe Side*). Other early instances are: (the Bowe chyrch in) *chep syde* 1496 HMC, Var. Coll. ii. 49, (the church of St. Thomas . . . sett in) *the Chepe Syde of the Citee of London* 1511 ADA 7409, (in) *Cheppes syed* 1527 LP, (Seint Myghell atte Querne . . . in) *Chepesyde* 1534 ADA 13611, *Chepissyde* 1542 Acts Privy Council, (the Key in St. Pancras in) *Cheapeside* 1590 (1597) CW ii. 723. An early Germanized form is (in) *Schiepsijden* 1469 Hansisches Urkundenbuch ix. Even West Cheapside has been found: (a messuage in) *West(e)chepe syde* 1558 Pat. Stow does not use the name, the nearest to it being *the Southside of west Cheape* (i. 81), *that North side of Chepe* (i. 259) and the like.

A satisfactory explanation of the name *Cheapside* has not, so far as I know, been given. In OED, under *cheap* sb., it is stated that this word in the sense 'market' is found in *Cheapside*, and that is true, but only in a way. In various topographical handbooks, as Clunn's *Face of London*, the name is said to be derived from OE *ceapian* 'to sell or bargain'. Harben does not discuss the name, possibly because he did not think it offered

---

[1] *Cheppesyde* 1400 Grey Friars is not a trustworthy example, since the Chronicle was compiled in the 16th century.

any difficulty. *Cheapside* comes from *Chepes side*, lit. 'the side of Cheap', but the exact implication of that designation when it first arose is by no means clear. It may at first have referred to the houses facing the market-place, inclusive of the road-ways along them. But it is also possible that the name originally was restricted to the roadway and the houses on the south side, for in the earliest instances it is apparently houses or places south of Cheap that are stated to be in Cheapside. The goldsmith mentioned in the example of 1479 may be supposed to have been of Goldsmiths' Row. St. Vedast (see the example of 1436) extended south of Cheap. It is worthy of notice that Cheapside seems to have been a street-name already in the earliest instances, since it is regularly preceded by the pre-position *in*. But whatever the original meaning of *Chepes side* was, it soon became synonymous with *Cheap*, as seen from such examples as 'the king's highway (*via regia*) of *Westchepe* alias *Chepeside*' 1549 Pat and the usage in Machyn's diary (1551–63). The houses will be referred to there in a passage on p. 263, where it is stated that 'Chepe-syd [was] hangyd with cloth of gold and cloth of sylver', but in other places *Chepe* and *Chepesyd* are used interchangeably. There is mention of pillories in *Chepe* and in *Chepesyd* and hanging in *Chepesyd*, the Standard in *Chepe* and in *Chepsyd*. In Shakespeare's *2 Henry VI*, iv. 2, 74, Jack Cade says: 'In Cheapside shall my palfrey go to grass', which must refer to the market-place. Cheapside in Birmingham (1786 &c.) and in Nottingham (1826 &c.) were evidently named from the London street.[1]

After the above was already written I find that Bonner has collected several forms of Cheapside older than those in Harben, the earliest being that of 1436 given supra, and he has

---

[1] A similar case is **Bankside**, the name of a district in Southwark on the bank of the Thames: *the Banke* 1519, 1524–5 LP, *the Banke syde* 1554 Machyn 78, *Banckes syde* 1593 Norden's Map, *the bank side* Stow.

rightly seen that the name means 'the side of Cheap', but he makes no attempt at explaining the name further.

Little Cheapside, formerly **Spittle** and **Stodies Lane** [Vi; Vintners' Hall–the Thames] is first recorded in a map of 1667 (Harben). It was doubtless named from Cheapside, but for what reason is unknown.

Eastcheap [Bill, Bridge, Cand; Gracechurch Street–Tower Street]: (land in) *eastceape c.* 1100 LMAS, N.S. viii. 58, (Reinerus de) *Hestchepe* 1185 Templars, (St. George's in) *Eastcheap* t. Hy 2 ADA 1686, *Eastcheap c.* 1200 ib. 1687, *Estchep* 1213 ib. 6884. Eastcheap market is referred to 1189–99 ib. 2124. It was from an early date a butchers' market; *Macellum* (the shambles) *de Estchepe* is mentioned 1211 P. The street called *Estchepe* occurs 1246 Ch, the highway called *Estchep* 1348 ADA 11610. In the earliest instances the name probably referred to the market-place. The name no doubt goes back to the Old English period. A distinction was formerly made between Great Eastcheap, the western part, and Little Eastcheap, the eastern part. Examples are: *Great Eastcheap* 1569 (1574–5) CW ii. 691, *great Eastcheape* Stow i. 216; *Lytyll Estchepe* 1560–1 Machyn 249, *little East Cheape* Stow i. 212.

Poultry [Cheap ; Cheapside–Mansion House] in early times was the name of that part of Cheap where poultry was sold, as *Poletria* 1301 StAug 346, 1303 LibCust 229, (þe Market of) *Pulterye* 1422 Plea (LoEngl 126), *þe pultrie* 1424 LoEngl 184. The usual form in editions of records is *the Poultry* (e.g. 1299 LBC 55), a translation of Lat *Poletria* or the like. The earliest instance of *Poultry* in Harben (*Polettar'* 1275 RH 403) is due to a mistake. *Polettar'* is short for *Polettarii*. The street of the Poultry (*Puletrie*) is referred to 1315 ADA 11941 (here also St. Mildred in *Pulletria*), the high streete, called *the Poultrie* in Stow. Other late examples are *le Pultrye* 1547 LP, *le Pultre*, *le Poultre* 1550 Pat. Poultry is ME *pultrie* 'a place where fowls are sold for food; a poultry-market', from OF *pouletrie*, a derivative of OF *pouletier* 'poulterer, dealer in poultry'. Poultry is now used only of the street, which is doubtless much narrower than the old market-place.

Cornhill [Cornh], east from Mansion House, formerly as far as Lime Street, but the eastern part, from Gracechurch Street, is now Leadenhall Street. Cornhill is one of the most important streets of London, but the name was not originally that of a street. It is possible that the street-name developed out of that of a market-place. *Cornhill* means 'corn hill', and Stow says (i. 187) the ward was so called of a corn market, time out of mind there holden. This is possibly right, but no reference to a corn market at Cornhill has been met with in early sources, and it may be doubted if Stow's statement is correct. If so, the name does not belong in this section. A market was held on Cornhill about 1300 and probably earlier, but it was apparently something like the Caledonian Market of our days, being frequented chiefly by dealers in old clothes and furniture. Cornhill is a very old name, doubtless an Old English one, and the name may have arisen at a time when corn was still grown to some extent inside the City wall. The meaning may conceivably be 'hill where corn was grown'.

Cornhill in the earliest examples doubtless refers to the hill itself or the district (soke or ward). The earliest example found, according to Harben and Kingsford, is (ecclesia b. Michaelis in) *Cornehulle* 1055 Chronicle of Evesham, p. 75, where it is stated that the church was given to Evesham by Alnod sacerdos. But there is no reason to assign so early a date to the donation.[1] Other early references are (terra apud) *Cornhillam* 1115 Pauls MSS 61 b, (Edward de) *Cornhilla* a 1116 ib. 31 b, (*Edward*) *Upcornhill* 1125 (*c.* 1425) LBC 219. It is significant that in early records *Cornhill* is generally preceded by the preposition *on*, sometimes *at*, not by *in*, as (house on) *Cornhell* 1259–60 CW i. 5, (houses upon) *Cornhull* 1274–5 ib. 22, (the tun upon) *Cornhulle* 1324 Cor 85. (Land in) *Cornhill* is exceptionally found *c.* 1250 ADA 2126, but the ward may be meant. In the 14th century *in* grows more common, e.g. (a tenement in) *Cornhull* 1375 CW ii. 179, (*le Tonne* in) *Cornhull* 1419 (1427) ib. 444.

Cornhill, the street, is called the high road from Cornhill towards Alegate late 13th ADA 2434, *vicus de Cornhelle* 1193–1211 Clerkenwell 251, the street of *Cornhulle* (*Cornhell*) 1283, 1293 CW i. 66, 110 &c. *Cornhill* alone was doubtless often used to denote the street about the same time, but it is impossible in many cases to be sure if the street or the market-place or the ward is meant. The ward of Cornhill was hardly named from the street, more likely from the hill itself or the district.

Newgate Market, formerly a widened part of Newgate Street opposite to Christchurch (Christ's Hospital) and referred to 1574 ff. Arber, is sometimes called a street: a street called *Newgate Markett* 1566 LIpm.

The Shambles or **Fleshshambles** was formerly sometimes used as a name of Newgate Street. See p. 30.

1 The note on Alnod's gift is found in a list of donations to Evesham Abbey headed by that of Edward the Confessor, dated 1055. Most of the following donations were evidently of post-Conquest date, and there is no reason to suppose that Alnod's gift, which comes after those of Warin Bussel and Milo Crispin, was a pre-Conquest one. According to Stow (i. 195) the church was granted by the Abbot of Evesham to Sparling (Sperling) the priest, apparently in 1133. Alnod's donation thus antedates the year 1133 and may have been made about 1100.

B. Streets named from fortifications

Some free space would be left on the inside of a wall or line of fortification for the purpose of communication, and this space might become a street. In an early period there was in various places a street inside and along the City wall, which in certain cases was later blocked up. An example will be found referred to at p. 29. A street might also run on the top of an old line of fortification, like the Paris boulevards. Only one street was named from the city wall, the present London Wall.

London Wall [BroadSt, Bas, ColemSt, CripI; Old Broad Street–Cripplegate]: (a tenement at) *London Walle* (in All Hallows London Wall) 1547 LP, *London wall* Stow i. 81, 291, *London Wall* 1665 Pepys v. 7 (probably the street). The street is referred to in early times variously as the highway near London Wall (All Hallows London Wall) 1388 CW ii. 269, *le Brodestrete* within the parish of All Hallows at the Walls of London 1550 Pat, Curriers' Row (q.v.). An interesting old name is also *Babeloyne* 1385–6, 1386 CW ii. 252, 256, described as a street in St. Alphage (CripI) along the city wall (*per murum civitatis London*). This is the medieval English form of the name *Babylon* (*Babiloyne* Alliterative Poems B 1373, Chaucer, Langland &c.) applied to the London street. The reason for the name is obscure. Possibly the city wall was compared to the Tower of Babel.

The Bailey, later **Old Bailey** [FarrE; from Ludgate to Newgate]. A street branching off from the Old Bailey was formerly known as Little Old Bailey. The Bailey is referred to early. Terra de *Bali* was demised *c.* 1166 to one Richard Parmentarius (PaulsCh 179), who is called Richard de Baillio 1198–1211 ib. 266. It is doubtful if William de Balio (1130 P) was named from the Bailey. In the 13th century it is referred to as (in) *ballio*

c. 1245 ADA 7499, the bailey (*ballio*) opposite the city wall
1260 ib. 2336, *le Bail* 1298 CW i. 138, later as the *Baily* (without Newegate) 1307 ib. 193, *le Baille* (without Ludegate) 1311
ib. 221. It is not always clear if the street is meant or the bailey
itself. The street along the Bailey is named the highway called
la Ballie 1287 ADA 2568, the street called *Le Bayl* between
Newgate and Ludgate 1290 Ch, the high street of *la Baillye*
1431–2 LBK 140. *The grete bayli* 1423 LoEngl 135 will be an
alternative name of the Bailey. The name *Old Baily* is first
instanced by Harben in 1444–5 (ADB 2176, not in the printed
edition). An early instance is *the Old bailly* 1481 Stonor ii. 119.
Other examples are *tholde Baylye* 1549 Pat, *Old Balee* (*Bayle*)
1556 Machyn 120. Stow mentions the street called *the Old
Bayly* and *the little Bayly*. Possibly *Old* was added for distinction from the Little Bailey. Stow (ii. 37) suggests that the
name was given to the Bailey because the court of the Chamber-
lain seems to have been held there, and Harben is inclined to
adopt this explanation. But the Bailey was clearly an outwork
in front of the city wall. ME *bail* (*bailey*) meant 'the wall of the
outer court of a feudal castle; also any of the circuits of walls
or defences which surrounded the keep'. Possibly the bailey
itself is referred to in 1423 (LoEngl 135) as 'the mud wall in the
grete bayli', which was defective and in want of repair. Identical in origin is The Bailey (Worcester): *la Baillie* 13th (PNWo
21). There was formerly a Great Bayley Street in Oxford near
the Castle.—The court of justice named from the Old Bailey
is *le Justice Hall in le Olde Bailie* 1554–5 Pat.

Barbican [Aldersg, CripE; Aldersgate Street–Red Cross
Street]. A garden outside (*extra*) *Barbecanam de Aldresgate* is
mentioned 1279 *RHT* m. 2, a tenement without *Barbekan* (in
Aldersg) 1294–5 CW i. 119, tenements outside *le Barbecan*
1307 ib. 192, shops at *la Barbican* 1315 ib. 257. We find

Barbecanstret 1348–9 CW i. 525, *la Barbycanstret* 1377 (1378) ib. ii. 201, the street called (*le*) *Barbican* 1385–6, 1408 ib. 252, 379 (St. Giles'), *the Barbican* 1421 Plea (the street), 1508 LIpm, *Barbican* 1535, *le Barbycane* 1547 LP. *Barbican* as a street-name appears to be elliptical for *Barbican street*, and early examples of *Barbican* probably do not refer to the street. A barbican was an outer fortification or defence to a city or castle, especially a double tower erected over a gate or bridge (OED). It is from F *barbacane*, OF *barbaquenne* (12th cent.). Stow and Harben take the name to have been originally that of a tower in Cripplegate Without, but in the earliest instances Barbican is mentioned in connexion with Aldersgate ward, and the probability is that it was a line of fortification, which may well have included a watch-tower. There is a Barbecan Road in Barnstaple D (*Barbigan Lane* 1610), and *Barbican* was formerly a street-name in Exeter (PND 21, 26).

Houndsditch [Ports, BishE; Aldgate High Street–Bishopsgate Street]: *Hundesdich* 1502 LIpm, (highway called) *Hownsdych* 1534 LP, (lane called) *Houndesdyche* 1550 Pat, (a messuage and garden, 9 cottages each with a garden, 11 gardens, all in) *Hownsediche* 1557 Pat (St. Botolph Bishopsgate), *Houndes ditch* Stow. The street was named from Houndsditch (the City ditch): *Hondesdich* (p) 1275 RH 424. The street developed along the ditch, which was eventually filled in. *Houndsditch* probably has as first element OE *hund* 'hound'; Stow suggests that the name was derived from filth and dead dogs thrown into the ditch. Since the ditch seems to date from the time of John, the name cannot well contain the Old English personal name *Hund*.

C. Streets with names originally signifying a gate

The gate was mostly a watergate on the Thames, whose

name was transferred to the lane or street leading up from it. Cf. also Desborne Lane.

Aldgate [Aldg], a short street leading west from the old gate of Aldgate. It was Aldgate Street till about 100 years ago. See p. 90.

Dowgate, now **Dowgate Hill** [Dowg, Walbr; Cannon Street– Upper Thames Street]: *vicus Regius de Douegat* 1244 Harben, *regius vicus de Douegate* 1275 RH 429, the high street of *Douegate* 1324 Cor 84, which may mean 'the main street of Dowgate ward'; (street called) *Duuegate* 1300 Pat, *the high street called Dowgate* Stow. Dowgate was a watergate and wharf: *Duuegate* 1067 (1335) Ch (forgery of t. Hy 1), 1150–1 Fr &c., (Robertus medicus de) *Duuegate c.* 1200 PaulsCh 251, *Duuesgate* 1189–90 (13th) Clerkenwell 269. The first element is probably OE *dūfe* 'dove, pigeon'. A side-form of the name is *Dounegate*, e.g. 1275 RH 430, 1298 Mayors 5 (*Downgate* Stow). If genuine, *Doune-* might represent OE *dūfena* gen. plur.

Ebbgate, now **Swan Lane,** on the boundary between Bridge and Dowgate, and running from Upper Thames Street to the Thames. Ebbgate (*Ebbegate c.* 1190, early 13th Colchester Cart, 1246 Ch) was a watergate. The lane leading from it is often *Ebbegate* also, e.g. t. Edw 3 PaulsMSS 14 a, 1421 f. Plea. Stow calls it *Ebgate lane*, now *the olde swan*, which is a common stayre on the Thames (i. 213). *Ebb-* will be the word *ebb*, though it is not apparent why this particular gate should have had such a name.

Kingesgate [CastleB; now apparently St. Peter's Hill, which runs from Thames Street to Knightrider Street]: *Kingesgate* (venella) 1275 RH 433, *Kinggesgate* (venella communis) 1279 *RHT* m. 1, *porta regis* (in St. Peter Paul's Wharf) ib. m. 18;

probably *Lekynggeslane* 1343 LibCust 452, *Kyngeslane* 1430 (1449) CW ii. 517 (alias *Arouneslane*, an otherwise unrecorded name). The meaning is 'the King's gate and lane'.

Oyster Gate [Bridge; Lower Thames Street–the Thames]: (the corner of) *Oystregate* 1259 CW i. 4, (venella vocata) *Oystergate* 1343 LibCust 448. Oyster Gate was a watergate opposite to St. Magnus, probably so called because oysters were landed there (LMAS, N.S. ii. 198). Stow says oysters were sold there. The lane was sometimes called *Watergate* or Water Lane.

Rothergate. See p. 154.

Suthgate (lane so called) 1320–1 PaulsMSS 49 a (near St. Paul's). Complaints were made against the Dean and Chapter that they had placed wooden posts at the corner of the lane and iron chains across it. This suggests that the lane is identical with the later Paul's Chain, which runs (or ran) south from St. Paul's Churchyard. *Suthgate* will have been the name of a gate leading to the Churchyard. It is *porta australis Sancti Pauli* 1279 *RHT* m. 18.

Watergate [Tower]. See Water Lane, p. 148.

Here may be mentioned a name containing the word *stair* in the sense 'a landing-stage'.

Faukesteire (venella in Vinetria) 1279 *RHT* m. 12. The name has not been found elsewhere. It must mean 'the stair belonging to Faukes'. *Fauke* or *Faukes* was a common Norman font-name.

D. Street-names originally river-names

Holborn [FarrE], west from Holborn Circus, continued as

High Holborn outside the City boundary. Holborn was origi-
nally the name of a stream which formed the upper part of Fleet
river. It is recorded in Old English as *Holeburne* (959 BCS
1351, copy); the name means 'stream in a hollow bed'. From
the stream was named a manor, mentioned in DB as (ii cotarios)
Ad Holeburne, which may, however, mean 'on the river
Holborn'. The manor developed into the Borough of Holborn.
The street leading west from the stream is generally called
Holeburnestrete or the like till the 14th century, thus (St.
Andrew) *Holeburnestrate* late 12th ADB 2197, *Holeburnstrete*
1249 MxFF 32, *Holeburnestrete* 1295-6 CW i. 124. Early
instances of the name as that of the street are (the street called)
Holebourne 1322 (1331) CW i. 366, (yn) *Holbourne* (*Hobourne*)
1423 LoEngl 149. This is a shortening of *Holeburnstrete*, which
may mean 'the street leading to Holborn stream' or 'the street
of the Holborn district.'

Redye, Rydye, an old name of Rose Street [FarrI], which
leads from Newgate Street to Paternoster Square. The name
appears as (Dycy lane, otherwise) *la Rydye* t. R 2 PaulsMSS
23 a, (Diceres Lane, otherwise) *le Redye* 1423 ib. 48 a, 1423-4
CW ii. 435. The last two references are from the same document, the will of one John Westyerd. An earlier instance is
seen in the surname (Nicholas) *atte Rydye* 1319 Subs (CripE).
Rydy, *Redy* is OE *rīþig* 'stream', cognate with old Frankish
rīth 'stream, ditch', OFrisian *rīth* 'brook'. There must have
been a brook or ditch by the street. *Dicereslane* is found a good
deal earlier than *Rydy*.

Walbrook [Walbr] runs from Mansion House to Cannon
Street a little to the east of the course of the Walbrook, a stream
that fell into the Thames at Dowgate. The stream is *Walebroch*
1104 (13th) Colchester Cart, *Walebroc* 1114-30 (copy) Ramsey

O

Chron, and the name means 'the stream of the Britons' (OE *Wealas*[1]). From the stream were named the street and the soke and ward of Walbrook. The surname *de Walebroc* is common from an early period, as Michael de Walebroc, merchant 1223 Pat, Warner de Walebrok' 1253 ExchJews 16, Richard de Walebroc, sheriff 1261–2 BM. The street is *vicus de Walebroke* 1236 LibAlb 97, *Walbrokstrate* 1291–2 LBA 190, *Walebrok-stret* 1297–8 CW i. 131. This may mean 'the street running along the Walbrook' or 'the street of Walbrook ward'. Later appears *Walbrok* as the name of the street: (the highway called) *Walbrok* 1343 Cl. *Walebrok* Street seems to be used of the present Budge Row 1312–13 CW i. 236, where land in St. Antholin is stated to be in a street of this name. The king's highway leading to *Walebrok* 1280 Cl may refer to the same or some other street.

E. Streets with names originally denoting a group of tenements or a tenement

Here may first be discussed three names ending in *-bury*; Aldermanbury, Bucklersbury and Lothbury. The element *-bury* is OE *burg* 'fort', later, in forms like *bury*, *biry*, *borough*, 'a court, manor-house', also 'a large farm'. The London names in *-bury* doubtless denoted large houses or groups of houses, manors and heads of sokes, residences of wealthy people. A fourth name of this type may be added here, though it has disappeared and did not give rise to a street-name, *Sabelines-bury* (in St. Laurence Jewry) 1258–9 (1380–1) Plea ii. 286. The manor was named from Sabeline, wife of Laurence Buccuinte, who is mentioned *c*. 1140 &c. PaulsMSS 66 b, PaulsCh 219.

---

[1] This is the only London name that points to a British element in the early London population. The identification of *Wal-* with the word *wall* (referring to the City Wall) suggested by Stow (i. 118) and accepted by Bonner is ruled out by the earliest forms.

Sabeline will have been in possession about 1150. See on the family Page, *London*, 238 f.

Aldermanbury [CripI; Gresham Street–London Wall] is not with certainty found with this name till about the middle of the 14th century (lane called *Aldermannebury* 1336 Cl). The street is referred to as *via regia, vicus Regis, vicus publicus* 1275 RH 407, 415, 430, *vicus Regius de Aldermannebur'* 1279 *RHT* m. 20. In early records the name is used of a manor or group of tenements or a district. Early references are *Aldresmanesberi c.* 1130 PaulsMSS 66 b, *Aldremanesburi* 1111–38 PaulsCh 218, *Aldermannesberi* 1108–48 ADA 7309, *-buria* 1178–87 Oxf, *Aldermanesbury* 1189–99 ADA 1952. See also p. 13. The name is frequently found as a surname, as Simon de Aldermanneberi 1190 P, Gervase de Aldermannesbir' 1198 P. The name means 'the manor of the alderman', as proposed by Kingsford (Add. Notes 19) and by Bonner, but there is nothing to indicate who the alderman may have been. It has been suggested that Aldermanbury was the king's residence in London till the time of Edward the Confessor (Page, *London*, p. 140) and later became that of an alderman, possibly the alderman of the Frith Guild. The evidence for this is not satisfactory. If the name Aldermanbury is old, it is possible that the alderman was Æthelred, son-in-law of Alfred and alderman of Mercia, who for some time was Governor of London. Professor Stenton takes the name to represent OE *ealdormanna burh* 'fortified enclosure of the aldermen' (*Norman London*, p. 12).

Cripplegate ward is called (*balliva*) *Aldermanesgarde* 1268 ExchJews 46. This name is probably an elliptical shortening of an early appellation of Cripplegate ward meaning Aldermanbury ward. This would imply that the ward at an early date was named from Aldermanbury.

Bucklersbury [Cheap, Walbr; Cheapside–Walbrook]: (the

street or high way of) *Bokerellesbury* 1343 Bonner, *Bokereles-bury* Street 1350 Cl, (street called) *Bokelersbury* 1477 (1489) CW ii. 590, *Buckles Bury* (a street) Stow. Bucklersbury was originally a manor or tenement. A tenement called *Bokerelesberi* is mentioned 1277–8 CW i. 29, *Bukerelesbyr'* 1279 *RHT* m. 21, houses near *Bokerelesbury* 1275 CW i. 26. The wealthy and influential Bukerel family is recorded in London from about 1100, e.g. Warin Bucherel 1104 PaulsMSS 61 b, Geoffrey and William Bucherell' 1130 P. Kingsford, p. 318, adduces a statement of 1270, according to which Thomas Buckerel had lately held property in *Bukerelesbury*, but Bonner shows (p. 296) that the property had descended to him from Thomas Bukerell, senior, his father, who probably died *c.* 1240.

Lothbury [BroadSt, ColemSt; Throgmorton Street–Coleman Street]: (the highway of) *Lothebury* 1348–9 CW i. 539, 1411 ADA 7825, where *Lothebury* itself need not be a street-name, (the King's high street called) *Lothebury* 1532 LP. In earlier sources the name no doubt refers to a manor or neighbourhood or to a ward. Broad Street ward was formerly Lothbury ward: *Lodingeberi* (ward) 1285–6 LBA 209 f., *Lotheberi* (ward) 1293 LBC 12. The name is mostly found in the parish name St. Margaret Lothbury, as (St. Margaret de) *Lodebure* 1181–1204 PaulsMSS 15 a, *Lohdeber'*, *Lothebery* 1222–48 ADA 10391 f., (upon) *Lodingeberi* 1286 CW i. 78. Other early instances are *Lothebiri* 1232 Ch, (a house in) *Lothyngebire* 1275 CW i. 20, (a house at) *Lothebery* 1285 ib. 74, (a house upon) *Lodingeberi* 1293–4 ib. 113. Lothbury was also a fairly common surname in London from about 1250 on.

The name has been a good deal discussed. It is clear that the manor was not named from Albertus Loteringus, whose land in Warda Haconis is referred to *c.* 1130 PaulsMSS 66 b. The first element varies between *Lothe-* and *Lothinge-*, a fact which suggests that the name is old, probably an Old English formation. *Lothebury* represents an Old English *Loþan* or *Hloþan burg*, while *Lothingebury* presupposes an OE *(H)loþinga burg*, the two name forms meaning respectively 'the manor of Loþa' and 'the manor of Loþa's people or descendants'. *Hloþa* would be a normal short-form of OE *Hlophere*, found as the name of an early king of Kent and very likely in the lost place-name *Lopereslége* 959 BCS 1050, *Lohðeres leage, Loðeres leaga* 972 ib. 1290 (in or near Edgware, Mx). The modern pronunciation of *Loth-* in *Lothbury* with the vowel of *loth* is no doubt due to influence from the latter word. Derivation of *Loth-* from an OE name containing the name-stem *Hloth* is suggested already by Gover and by Stenton, *Norman London*, p. 16.

Old Change [CastleB, BreadSt, FarrI; Cheapside–Knight-rider Street]: (street called) *la Chaunge* 1297–8 CW i. 132, Old Change (probably for *Vetus Escambium* or the like) 1293–4, 1297–8 CW i. 111, 131 (St. Vedast), *le (la) Eldechaunge* 1316–17, 1329 ib. 271, 354, *Oldechaunge* 1373 Plea, *le Oldechaunge* 1396 ADC 3055, *the Oldechonge* 1422 Plea, *Vetus Escambium* 1447 ADA 10355, *the Olde Chaunge* 1555 Pat, *the old Exchange* Stow, *the Old-Change* Dekker, *Shoemakers Holiday* iii. 3, 51. The name seems to be recorded only as that of the street, which was called *the Change* or *the Old Change* from the change or royal mint situated there. Stow says the Change was about the middle of the street. It is rather remarkable that the name (Old) Change seems to have been transferred at an early date from the houses of the Change to the street without an inter-mediate *Change-strete* or the like. The Change must have been removed to some other place before the end of the 13th century, since the name Old Change was in use as early as 1293–4. It is noteworthy that this name in the earliest reference is applied to the northernmost part (at Cheap). Old Change is quite a long street, and the new name must have been given to the whole length of it at an early date.

Tower Royal or **Royal Street,** now **College Hill** [Vi, Cordw] was called *Paternosterstrete* or *Paternosterchurchstrete* in the 13th century (cf. p. 97). The old name agreed with that of Paternoster Row, and this may partly be the reason why a new name, taken from *the Riole*, a house or group of houses, was given to the street in Vi and Cordw. Houses in *Paternosterstret* called *la Ryoll* are mentioned 1265 Pat, the tenement called *La Ryole* 1276 Ch, a messuage called *La Ryole* 1280 Cl. The house was so named from La Réole, a town near Bordeaux, from which wine was imported. It must have been a big house. The street is referred to as the street of *la Ryole* 1303–4 CW i. 161, which will mean 'the street by the Ryole', but soon afterwards as (the street called) *la Ryole (Riole)* 1331, 1349 CW i. 368, 590, (the highway called) *la Reole* 1365 ADA 2387, *þe Riall* 1423 LoEngl 168, (the street called) *le Royall* 1455–6 ADA 9048, (the tower or great messuage called *le Riall* alias *le toure in le Rioll* in the street called) *le Riall* 1528–9 LP. Stow calls the street *Royall streete*, while the house is *Tower Royall*. The latter name was later applied to the street also, but was replaced in the 17th century by College Hill. The late form *Royal*, which is preserved to this day in the parish name St. Michael Paternoster Royal, is due to association with the ME adjective *rial* 'royal'. When this form of the adjective was replaced by the side-form *royal* the names of Tower Royal and the street followed suit.

On the early street-name *la Ryole* in Kingston-on-Thames see p. 128. The same name occurs also in Salisbury (1356 PNW). It was no doubt transferred from London.

The following street-names may be placed in this group. Two of them were originally names of London monasteries.

Crutched Friars [Aldg; Jewry Street–Hart Street]: *le Crouchedfrerestrete* 1405 (1408) CW ii. 381, *the Cruchydffrers* 1550–1 Machyn 3, *Crouched Friars, Crutched Friars* 1666, 1668 f. Pepys v. 314, viii. 6, 293. The street was named from a house of the Crutched Friars or Friars of the Holy Cross. It is not always clear if the name refers to the old Friary or to the street, as (John Aleyn, Brewer, atte Cok ny) *crouched Freres* 1424–5 LoEngl 185, (St. Olyfe beside) *the Crossed Friars* 1533 LP. *Crutched* is derived from ME *crouch* 'cross'.

Minories [Ports; Aldgate High Street–Tower Hill] was named from the Abbey of the Minoresses, founded in 1294. Here again it is often difficult to say if the name refers to the Abbey or the street, as when letters are dated *From the Mynerz, at Meners, From the Meners* 1537 LP, or when a certain Richard Moore is described as *of the Mynorisse without Algate* 1567–8 ADA 12986. A probable example of the street-name is *le Menoryse* (*extra Algate*), the *Menorise* (without Algate) 1554 Pat.

Bevis Marks [Aldg; St. Mary Axe–Duke Street]: *Bewesmarkes* 1405 (1407), *Bevys Marke* 1450 CW ii. 372, 518, *Bevysmark* 1421 Plea, *Burysmarkys* c. 1460 MemStEdmund iii. 299, (messuage called) *Bevesmarkes* 1513 LIpm, *Bevys Markys* (messuage), *Bevyse Markes* 1540–1 LP, *Buries markes*, corruptly *Beuis markes* (a great house pertaining to the Abbots of Bury) Stow i. 146. The examples given may in all cases refer to the house, a hostel of the Abbot of Bury, very likely that mentioned as situated near Holy Trinity Church *c.* 1150 Bury Charters 157 f. *Bevis* is corrupt for *Beris*, the genitival form of *Bury* (*Bery*). Probably *Beris* was simply misread as *Bevis*, because in some medieval English handwritings an *r* is very much like a *v*. An example is offered by the hand that wrote the return for Queenhithe in the London Subsidy Roll of 1319, where a final -r sometimes looks like a v. The misreading *Bevis* became traditional. It is not quite easy to explain the second element *Marks*, but it seems to be the plural of ME *mark* in the sense 'pillar, post, stone, fence, &c., placed to indicate the position of a boundary'. Marks would then mean 'boundary', later 'territory' and Bevis Marks 'the territory belonging to Bury (Abbey)'.

F. Street-names originally names of parishes or churches

In three cases a street is called by the name of a parish or church. The street-name is an elliptical shortening of a fuller name containing an element *street* or *lane*.

St. Martin le Grand [Aldersgate; Cheapside–Aldersgate, according to Stow the main street of Aldersgate ward]: the street of St. Martin le Grand 1265 Pat, *Seint Martynslane* 1414 LBI 128, *Seint Martyn lane* (vicus) 1415 EpCant, *S. Martins lane* Stow. The street is named from the collegiate church of St. Martin le Grand.

St. Mary Axe [LimeSt, Aldg; Leadenhall Street–Houndsditch]: *strata Sancte Marie atte Ax, via regia Sancte Marie atte Nax, vicus Sancte Marie Attenaxe* 1275 RH 420, 426, 431, *vicus qui ducit uersus ecclesiam Sancte Marie del Ax* 1279 *RHT* m. 8, *Sainte Marie Strate* 1260 ADA 2663, (street called) *St. Marie at Axe* 1595 LIpm, *S. Marie streete* Stow, *St. Mary Axe* 1675 Character Books 147. Named from the church of St. Mary Axe.

St. Mary at Hill [Bill; Eastcheap–Lower Thames Street]: *venella Sancte Marie de la Hulle* 1275 RH 406, *seint mary hill* *lane* 1520–1 StMary 308, *saint Marie Hill lane* Stow, *St. Mary Hill* 1666 (Harben). Named from the church of St. Mary at Hill.

G. Street-names originally names of districts or neighbourhoods

Old Jewry, formerly Colechurch Lane [Cheap, ColemSt; Poultry–Gresham Street]: (St. Olave in) *la Oldeiuwerie* 1327–8 CW i. 329, (street called) *la Elde Jurie* 1336 ib. 412, *Juwerielane* 1348 (1351) ib. 653, *þe olde Jurye* 1425–6 LoEngl 190, *the Olde Jury* 1552–3 Machyn 29, *the Jure* (*Jurye*) *lane* 1559 LIpm. The Jewry was a large district in Cheap and Coleman Street wards and embraced also St. Lawrence parish and Laurence Lane a good way west of Old Jewry. It is generally referred to in Latin documents as (*vetus*) *Judaismus*, which is translated by editors as (*Old*) *Jewry*, e.g. (St. Olave) *in iudaismo* 1181–3 PaulsCh 233, 239, (St. Lawrence) *in* (*veteri*) *Iudaismo* 1218–28 ib. 311, 1291 Orig, 1434 EpCant, (St. Olave in) the Jewry 1181 PaulsMSS 68 b. *Vicus judeorum c.* 1130 PaulsMSS 66 b may, but need not, be Old Jewry. The name Old Jewry arose after the expulsion of the Jews in 1290 and means 'the district formerly held by Jews'. *Jewry*, AF, ME *giwerie, juerie*, OF *juierie*, means 'the land of the Jews', 'the Jews' quarter'.

Jewry or **Jewry Street,** formerly **Poor Jewry** [Aldg; Aldgate High Street–Crutched Friars]: (tenement *apud*) *pauperum Judaismum* (St. Olave Hart Street) 1349 CW i. 553, *la Porejewerie* (lane so called in Holy Trinity by Aldgate) 1366 ADA 2047, Little Jewry (in *Algatestrete*) 1390–1 Pat, *the poore Iurie* Stow. According to Harben named from Jews returning to England after the expulsion in 1290, but this is doubtful and the name may be older. The later shortening of Poor Jewry to Jewry is no doubt due to a conscious change.

Petty Wales [Tower; Lower Thames Street–Tower Street, really a continuation of Lower Thames Street]: *petit Walles* 1298–9 CW i. 140, *Petit Wales* 1334 (1336–7) ib. 418, (the street called) *Pety Wales* (*Petiwales*) 1349 ib. 615, 1396 (1410–11) ib. ii. 387, *pety wales* 1423 LoEngl 149, *Pyttywales* 1550 Pat, *Petywalys lane* 1392 Plea. The name means 'little Wales', but the reason for it is unknown; a number of Welsh people may have settled there. *Petywales* (1548) in Kingston-on-Thames was no doubt named from the London street. *Petywales* also occurs as the name of some tenements in St. Bartholomew the Great (West Smithfield) 1543 LP, 1563 (1566) LIpm. It is not clear if the name in this case was transferred from Petty Wales in Tower or is an independent formation.[1]

H. Various

Adrenwell' (venella in Billingesgate) 1279 *RHT* m. 30. Not found elsewhere. Etymology obscure; -*well* probably means 'a well, spring'.

Outwich [BroadSt]. In my edition of Two Early London Subsidy Rolls, p. 223 (BroadSt no. 8, footnote) I suggest that the surname *Oteswich* may possibly be an old street-name. The surname appears about 1200. Martin de Ottewich was dead about 1230; his widow Matilda, wife of one Fribern, granted land opposite the church of St. Martin Ottewich, and Agnes his daughter, wife of Pain Tabur, confirmed the grant about that year (ADA 2681, 2683). Later we find Edmund le Taillur

---

[1] A similar name may be mentioned here: *Pety Cales lane* 1574–5 LIpm (in St. Mary Aldermanbury, CripI). This must mean 'Little Calais Lane', the lane having been named from Calais, which in early records is often *Cales* or the like: *Cales* 1391 CW ii. 291, *Cales, Calles* 1557–8 Machyn 162 f. Little Britain is a different kind of formation. See p. 85.

de Otteswich 1293 LBC 18, Master William de Oteswyche, surgeon 1300 ADA 2667 (a tenant in St. Martin de Oteswyche), 1319 Subs (BroadSt), John de Oteswich, son of William 1332 Subs (BroadSt). There is no reason to suppose that the late bearers of the surname Oteswich were descendants of Martin of *c.* 1200. Apparently all got the surname from a locality called *Ote(s)wich.* A place so called has not been found outside London, and the surname must be connected with the name of the parish and church of St. Martin Outwich.

The parish or church is frequently referred to from the late 12th century on. Alfwin Finke, on whom see under Finch Lane, p. 136, had a grant of land in St. Martin Otteswich, probably about 1180 (ADA 2658). There are references to the parish in the early part of the 13th century, e.g. ADA 2258, 2683, 2698, 2665, 2668. The form is variously *Otheswych, Ottheswich, Oteswich, Ottewich* and the like. St. Martin (in) *Owt(e)-wiche* is found 1545 MxFF, 1550, 1556 Pat. There is no reason to suppose that the parish was named from a person with the surname Oteswich, especially as such a surname is difficult to explain. The probability is that *Ote(s)wich* was the name of a locality in the neighbourhood of St. Martin, and since the church of St. Martin stands on the south side of Threadneedle Street, where it joins Bishopsgate Street, the conjecture is permissible that the short street from Broad Street to Bishopsgate Street (the east part of the present Threadneedle Street), was formerly known as *Oteswich.* No early name of this bit of street is known; it is called *vicus regius* 1378 Pat. If this is right, *wich* must mean 'street'. OE *wīc* has that sense among others. The first element will be the Norman font-name *Ote* (*Otho, Oto*) from OG *Otto,* a name well evidenced in London in the 12th century and later. A similar derivation is suggested by Loftie,[1] who, however, takes *wich* to mean 'dwelling'.

[1] *A History of London,* i. 369.

Paul's Chain [CastleB; Carter Lane–St. Paul's Church-yard]: *Poules cheyne* 1423–4 LoEngl 106, *Poulescheyne* 1442 (1444) CW ii. 503, *Poulls Chayne* 1500–1 HMC 9th Rep 147 b, *Powles chaine* Stow ii. 13, *Paules Chaine* 1666 Evelyn's Diary. According to Harben the street was so called from a chain drawn across the carriage-way of the Churchyard during public worship. The name is now lost. Cf. also *Suthgate*, p. 192. The street from about 1700 was called Godliman (or Godalmin) Street, whose first element is derived from the place-name Godalming in Surrey (*Godalmin vulgo Godliman* 1675 PNSr). Possibly *Godliman* is here a surname. See further Bonner and Harben.

Pye Corner [FarrE; Giltspur Street–West Smithfield; formerly *Rennerstrete*]: (besyd) *Pye Corner* 1559–60 Machyn 225, (place called) *the Pye Cornner* 1564 LIpm, *Pie corner*, *Py-Corner* 1599 Shakespeare, *2 Hy 4*, ii. 1, 29 (where Sir John Falstaff had gone to buy a saddle), (*le*) *Pye Corner* 1597 LIpm, *Pie* (*Pye*) *Corner* Stow ii. 21 f. ('a place so called of such a signe'), *Pycorner* 1618 Acts Privy Council, *Pye-corner* 1666 Pepys v. 425. Pye Corner originally referred to a street corner, at which was a tenement called *le Pye* (mentioned 1456 CW ii. 530; the street being *Rennerstrete*), and was later transferred to the street. The earlier meaning seems to be preserved in most of the examples supra. The inn of the Pye was doubtless named from a sign with a pie, i.e. a magpie (OF, ME *pie*) on it.

INDEX

PRINTED IN
GREAT BRITAIN
AT THE
UNIVERSITY PRESS
OXFORD
BY
CHARLES BATEY
PRINTER
TO THE
UNIVERSITY